IMAGES of America

# LACONIA

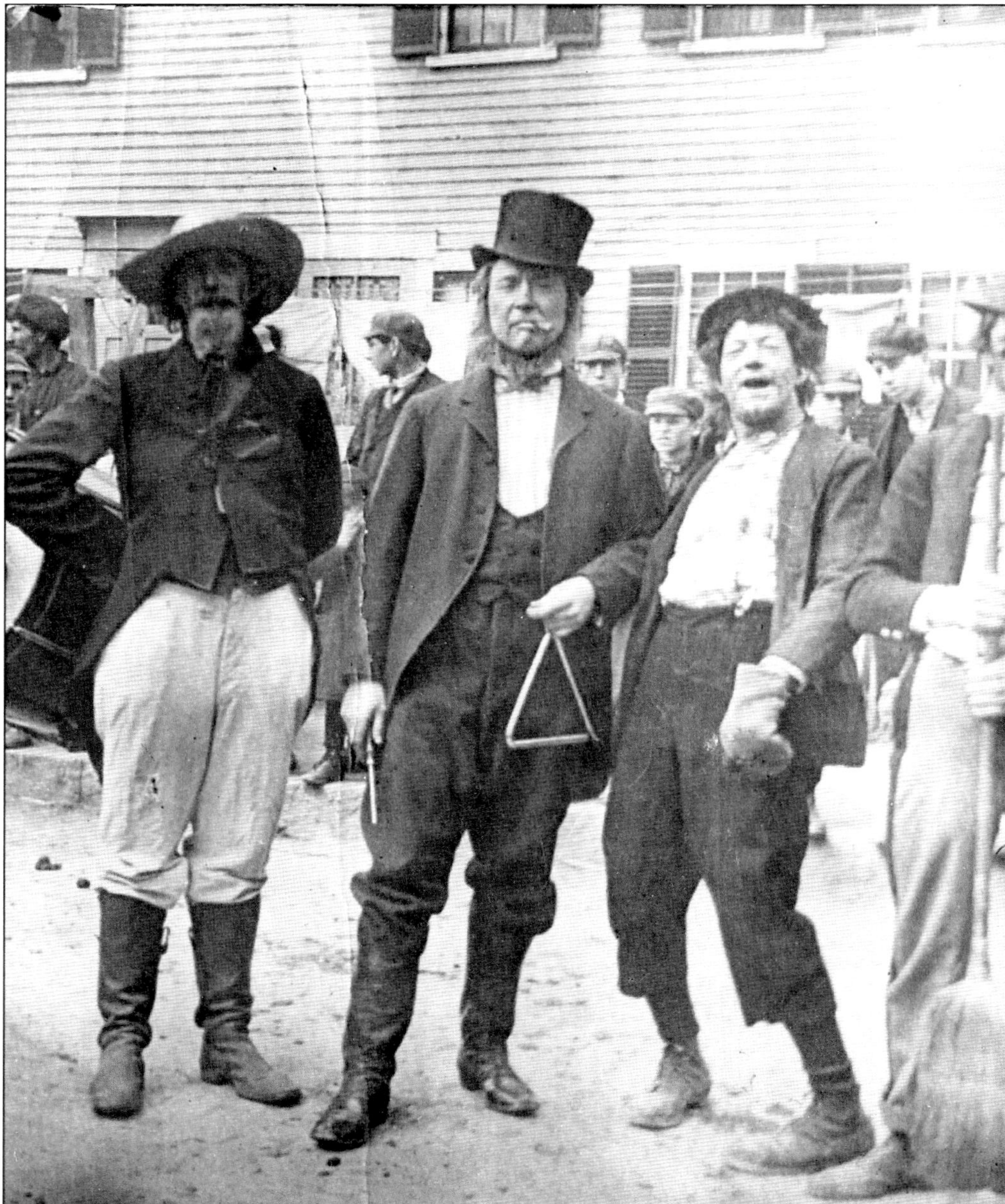

"Town Gathering." The Knights of Columbus staged this observance each year on Easter Monday from about 1908 to 1914. There was a big parade, most of it provided by the farmers—including all kinds of cattle, several hayracks carrying band members to provide music, and "a rube dressed to please the crowd." Each year people lined the streets looking forward to this event. In the evening, there were plays and dances. According to a notation on the back of the photograph, here are Michael J. Carroll, John M. Guay, James J. McCarthy, and Henry Johnson.

IMAGES
*of America*

# LACONIA

*By*
Warren D. Huse

ARCADIA
PUBLISHING

ISBN 978-0-7385-8988-6

Published by Arcadia Publishing
Charleston, South Carolina

Printed in the United States of America

For all general information contact Arcadia Publishing at:
Telephone 843-853-2070
Fax 843-853-0044
E-mail sales@arcadiapublishing.com
For customer service and orders:
Toll-Free 1-888-313-2665

Visit us on the Internet at www.arcadiapublishing.com

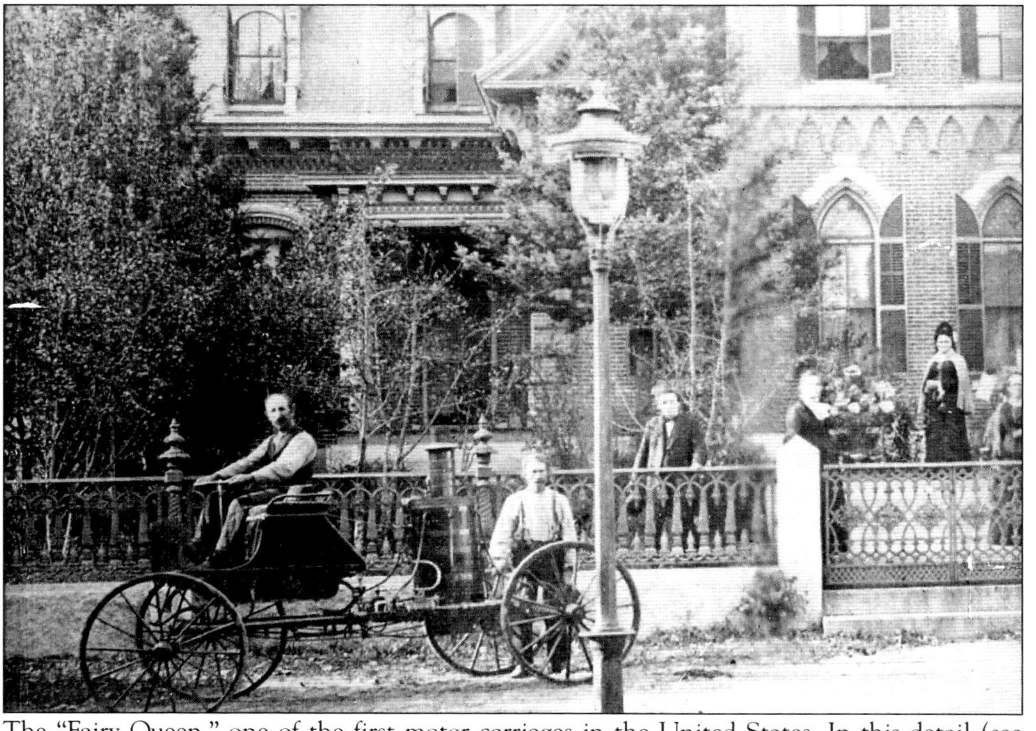

The "Fairy Queen," one of the first motor carriages in the United States. In this detail (see p. 16), the steam-powered vehicle is displayed in front of the mansion of Richard Gove on Orange Court. Constructed in 1873 by Enos M. Clough, an expert mechanic in the shops of the Boston, Concord & Montreal Railroad at Lakeport, the carriage was later purchased by Gove; and after Gove's death, by Lewis F. Busiel. (It was eventually destroyed in a fire.) Though moderately successful, the vehicle was "merely a matter of amusement" to its inventor and was abandoned "because it frightened horses."

Cover photograph: Main Street looking north, c. 1885.

# Contents

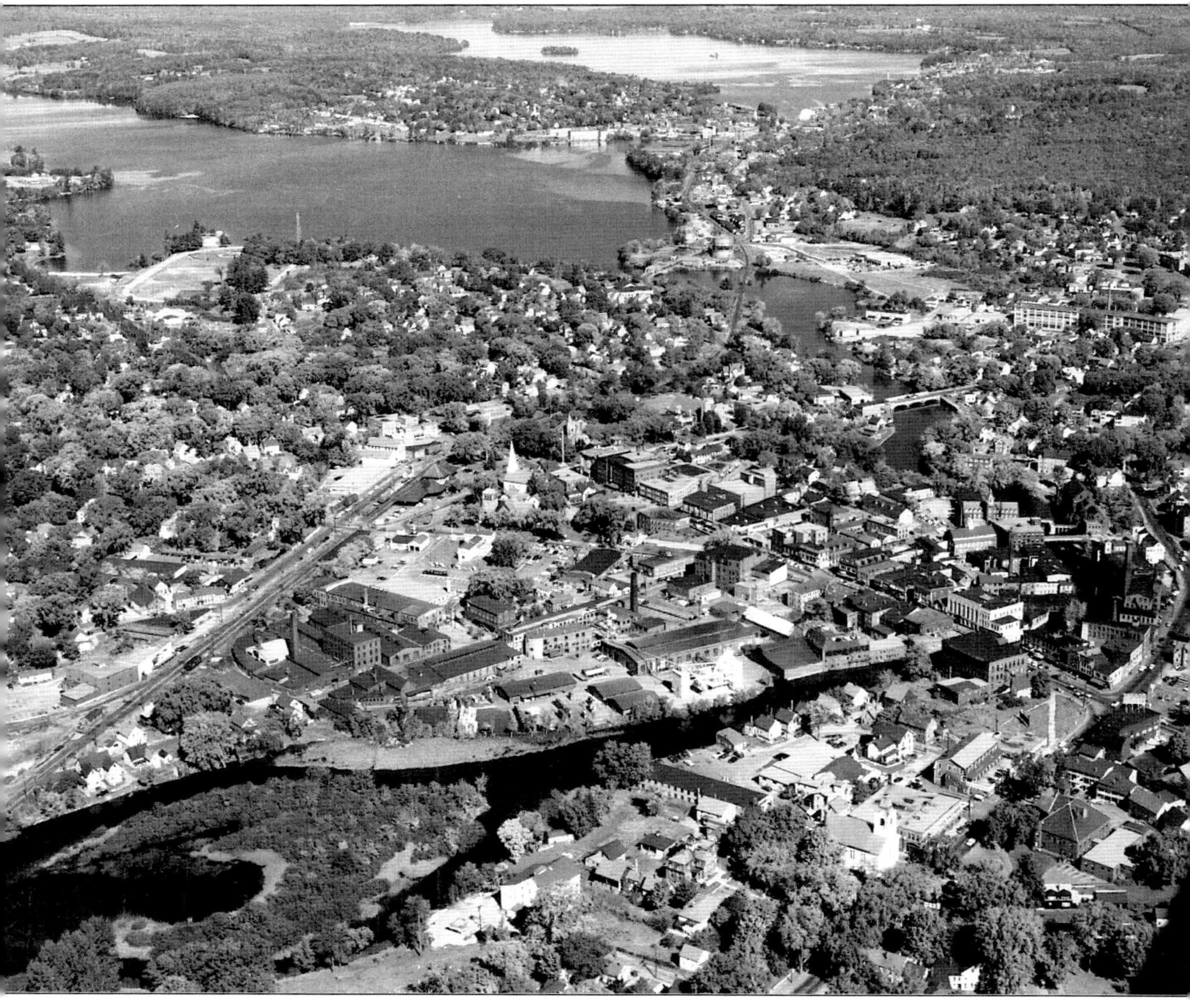

Aerial photograph, 1950s. Lake Paugus appears at the top, Lakeport at the top right, and Lake Opechee at the top left. The Boston & Maine Railroad tracks (lower left) cut past former Laconia Car Co. buildings and the 1892 passenger station. Mills still lined the Winnipesaukee River (right), along with the Scott & Williams plant and Laconia High School (both visible at the upper right).

# Introduction

Laconia, New Hampshire, is the seat of Belknap County. Located near the geographic center of the state, the "City on the Lakes" (Winnipesaukee, Paugus, Opechee, and Winnisquam) was incorporated as a town in 1855 and as a city in 1893. When the first settlement occurred here in the 1760s, part of the community was in Meredith and part in Gilmanton (Gilford after 1812). The early hamlet on the Winnipesaukee River, on the site of today's Downtown area, was known as "Meredith Bridge."

Initially, of course, agriculture was a major economic factor here. A trading center from the beginning and court site since 1820, the village soon developed industries, taking advantage of the abundant waterpower. In addition to hosiery, textiles, lumber, and shoes, the machine shops and foundries later expanded into the manufacture of knitting machinery and needles for knitting machines. With the coming of the railroad in 1848, the Ranlet Car Co. began manufacturing railroad cars, and eventually became the city's largest employer, making trolley and subway cars as well. The car shops went out of business in the early 1930s, but the manufacture of hosiery, shoes, knitting machinery, and needles continued to be principal industries here until the 1960s. Today, heavy industry has largely moved elsewhere, and the region's economy is comprised of light and high-tech manufacturing; commercial, professional, and service occupations; and a four-seasons tourist industry. The face of the Downtown area was changed drastically during an urban renewal program in the late 1960s–early 1970s.

The purpose of this volume is two-fold: to depict the landscape of the city of Laconia from the earliest available photographic evidence through the early years of the twentieth century; and to make available for wider viewing the most significant images in the collections from that period. The vast majority of the photographs presented here have been selected from the historical collections of the Laconia Public Library, with some additions from the Laconia Historical Society and a few from private collectors.

Because of the large number of photographs available—several thousand have been accessioned and organized—it was obvious at the beginning of the project that this first volume should be limited to the "lower end of the city," leaving Lakeport and The Weirs for subsequent efforts. (In fact, it was originally intended to carry the story of Downtown up through the transformation of the area during the Urban Renewal project, but it quickly became evident that such a comprehensive treatment would result in having to omit too many significant views from the earlier era; therefore, the continuation of the story of this part of the city will also have to await a future effort.) Selection of photographs was based on the goal of depicting as completely as possible the Downtown and the several geographic areas adjoining it, while being sure to include certain uniquely evocative pictures—"classics"—from the collection. The concluding "Neighborhood Potpourri" alludes to other parts of this end of the city. Because of space constraints, further exploration of these areas must be deferred to a future time. Included with most of the sections are aerial photographs from the mid-1950s which should be of assistance in locating various features before Urban Renewal.

In conclusion, much of what is presented here is reminiscent of a vanished time: the day of the ox and the horse, the streetcar, the mills, and much of Main Street itself. For some, these photographs will bring back memories; for others, they will provide a glimpse into a very different world from what we know today.

Acknowledgments pertaining to photographs contained in this volume appear on p. 128. It is appropriate here, however, to recognize the contributions of a number of individuals and organizations whose efforts have made this and subsequent volumes of photographs possible. Among the early local photographers whose work is represented are Elsam, T.C. Moon and George H. Tebbetts. Many, many residents and former residents of Laconia have donated pictures and other memorabilia to the library and historical society over the years. Their generosity is greatly appreciated. Two names in particular must be mentioned: Andrew L. Childs and Theo S. Jewett, who collected, annotated, and preserved a very large number of the images contained in this volume. In addition, a number of the views contained here were taken by Judge Jewett himself. Several years ago, moreover, the Laconia Rotary Club made a significant financial contribution to pay for copying and making slides of a portion of the library's collection. The work of former Librarian Barbara B. Cotton and local historian Gilbert S. Center, as well as members of the library staff past and present, in the early organization of the collection made subsequent efforts possible; and the dedicated service of a group of Laconia Historical Society members who contributed well over five hundred volunteer hours in 1990–1991 in sorting, organizing, accessioning, and filing the library's photographic holdings has greatly facilitated retrieval and research. A subsequent effort in 1994 by members of the Key Club, Boy Scouts of America, and other students at Laconia High School continued the work. Over the years, a great many other men and women have contributed to our knowledge of Laconia history. To all of them, a great debt is owed.

In the preparation of this book, the inspiration, input, and assistance of Gilbert S. Center and Julie Upham are gratefully acknowledged, along with the many contributions of Michael Joseph Guillory, editor, and Aaron Faulkner, who processed the photographs. Kirsty Sutton, senior editor, was a bedrock of strength throughout the preparation of this work. The encouragement and support of Carol Sykes, director of the Laconia Public Library, and JoAnne Whitticom, chairman of the trustees of the Laconia Public Library, and of the officers and directors of the Laconia Historical Society, have also been crucial to this effort.

Finally, tribute must be paid to the enthusiasm and unremitting efforts of Winnifred Norma Althea Hackett (1926–1994), founding president of the Laconia Historical Society when it was reactivated in 1980. For close to fifteen years, Winnie served as an inspiration to all who are interested in the history of Laconia. To her memory, this volume is affectionately dedicated.

Warren D. Huse

*One*

# The South End

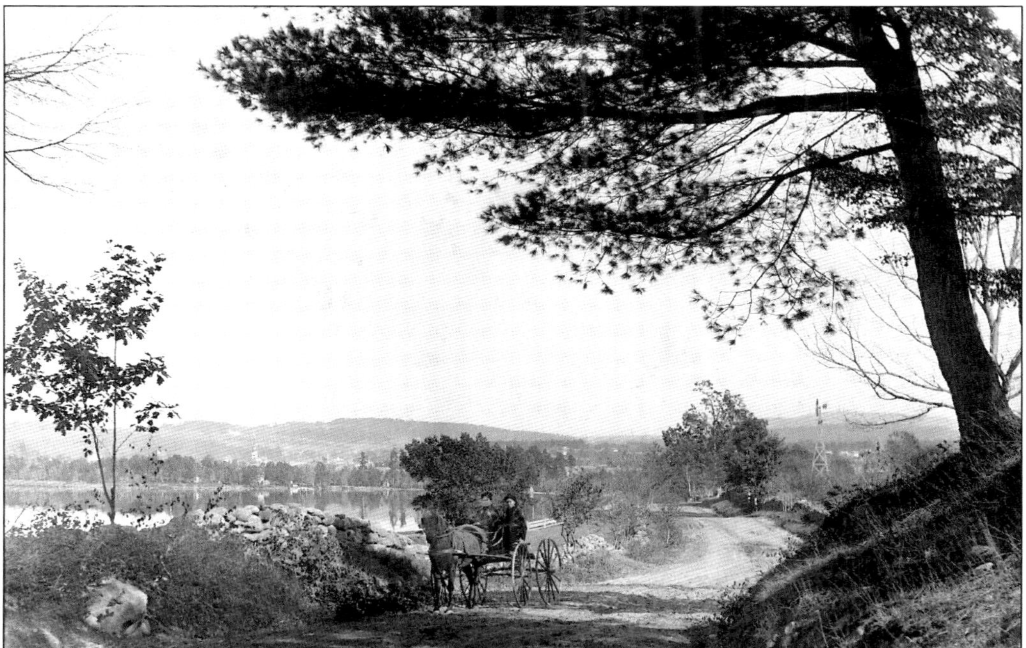

Route 3 South. Here is the entrance to the city, around 1883. Lake Winnisquam is on the left; today's St. Francis Home would eventually be located at the center right.

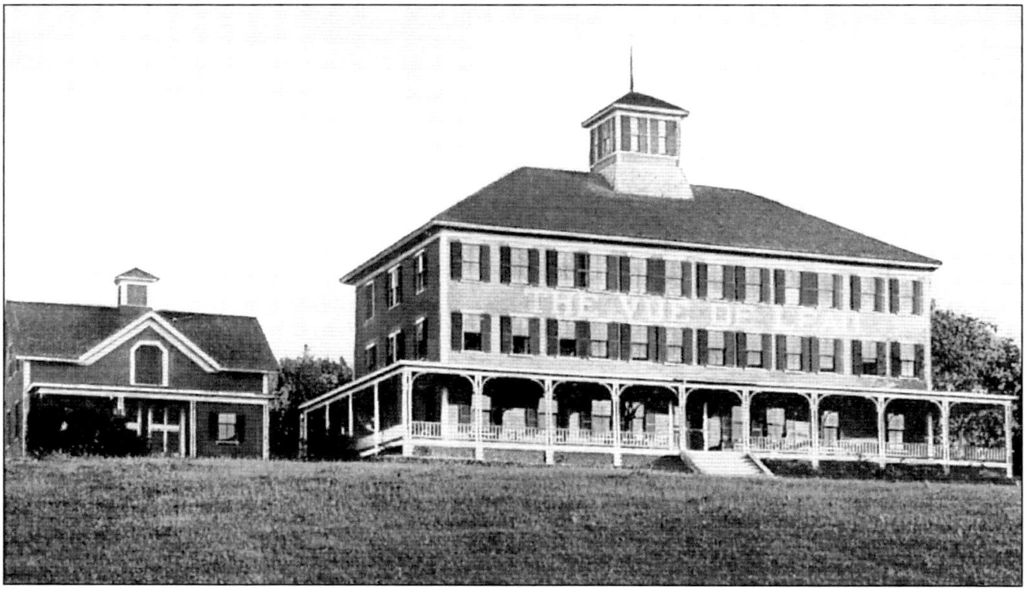

The Vue De L'Eau Hotel, Route 3 South, the modern site of the St. Francis Home.

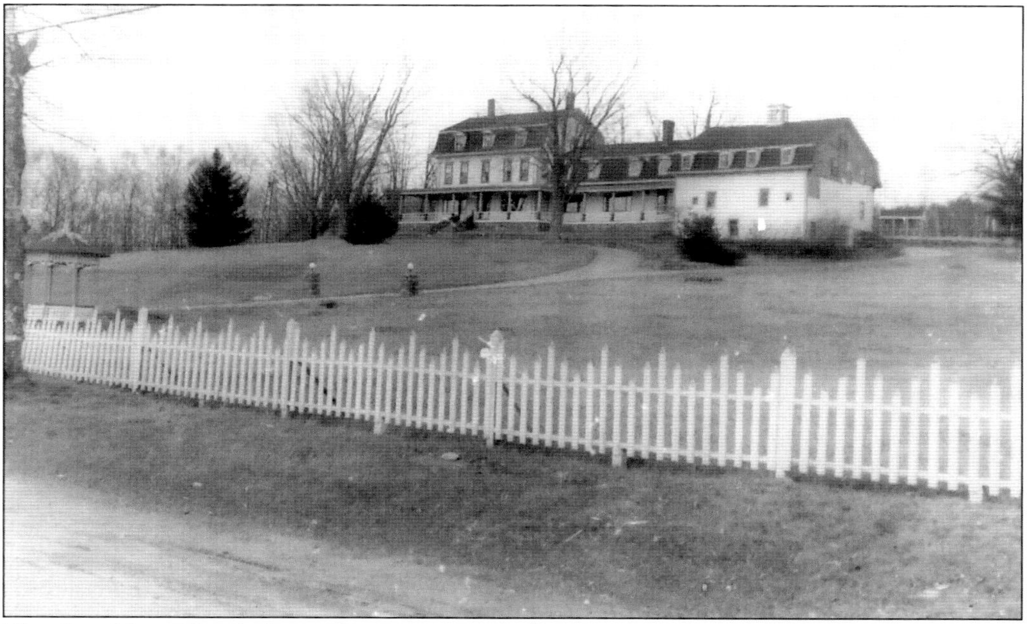

The Bay View Hotel (later the Terrace Hotel), Route 3 South. Originally the home of Mr. and Mrs. Stephen L. Taylor, the parents of Edward E. Taylor, benefactor of the Laconia Home for the Aged (now the Taylor Home), these buildings were later occupied by a succession of summer hotels.

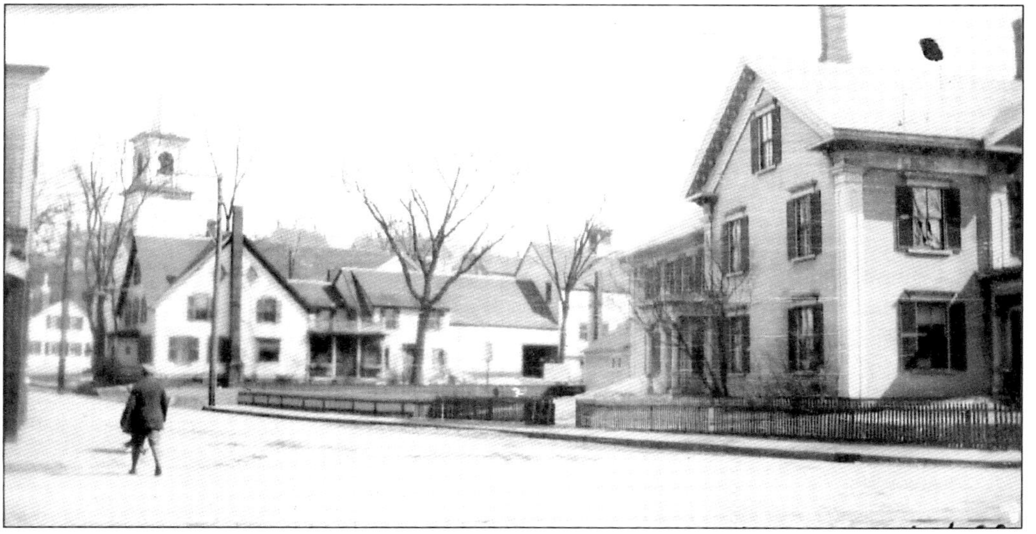

The corner of Union Avenue and South Main Streets, c. 1919. The Woodbury Melcher House (later the Bessie Clow House) was later moved to the rear of the lot when a diner (which eventually became Earl's and Dearborn's) and a gasoline station were built there. In the distance on the right, the Methodist Church occupies the modern site of Sunrise Towers. The church was enlarged and renovated between 1919–1924, considerably changing its appearance.

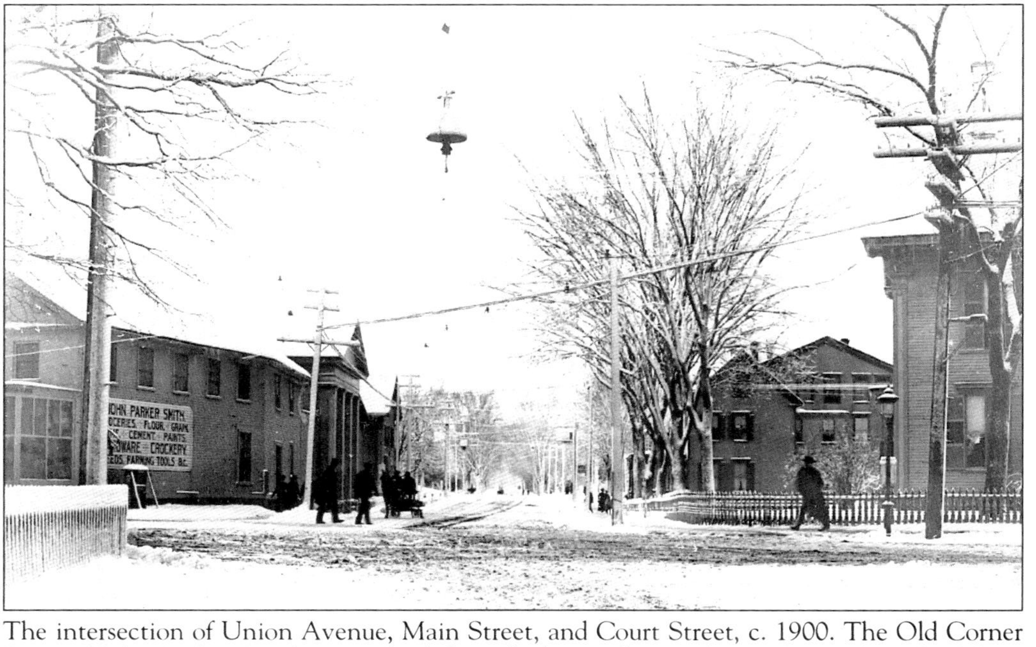


The intersection of Union Avenue, Main Street, and Court Street, c. 1900. The Old Corner Store of John Parker Smith is on the left, with the residence of Daniel A. Tilton (and later William F. Knight) on the right. The substantial buildings at the center right were torn down in the early 1940s for the construction of the South Main Market (more recently Rogers Stationery).

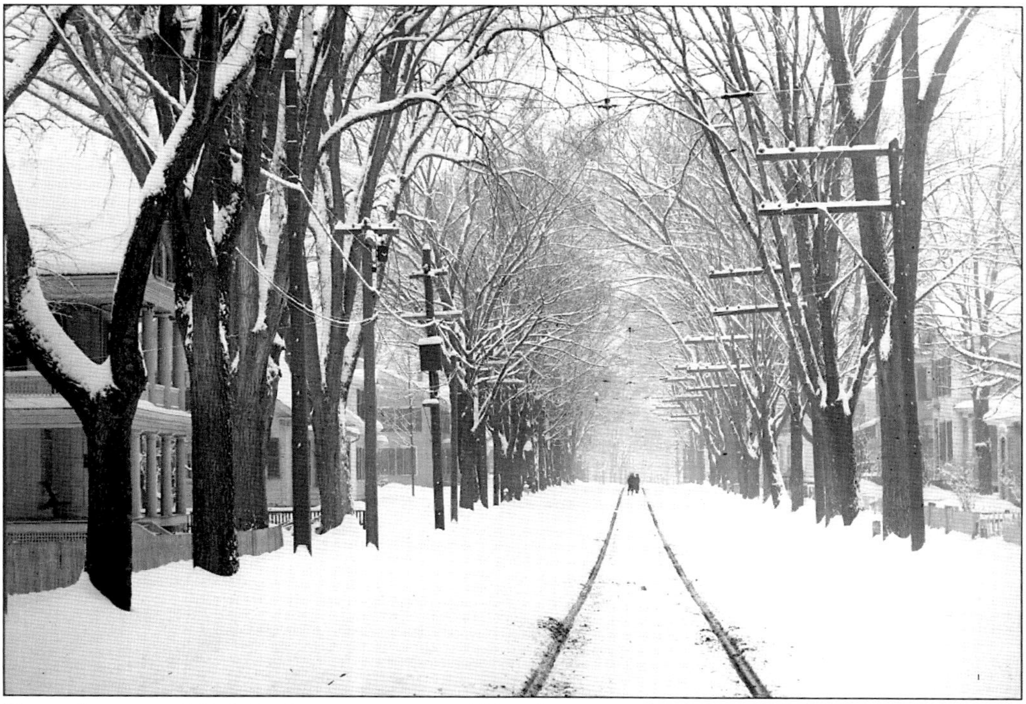

Court Street, c. 1916, looking west toward Fair Street, with the tracks of the Laconia Street Railway dominating this winter scene.

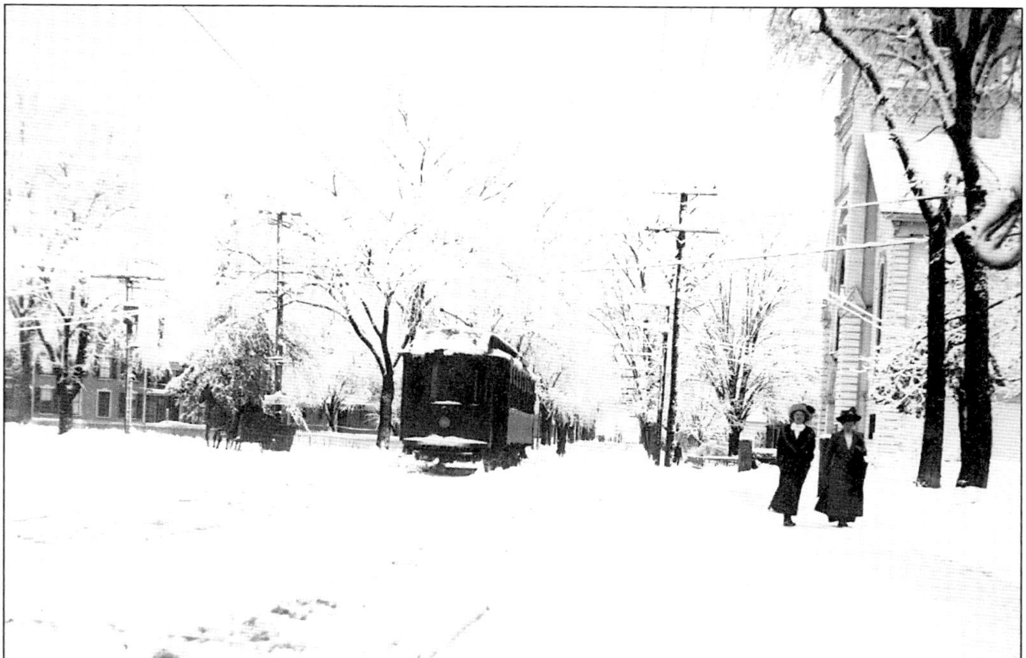

Court Street, c. 1912. This trolley heads east toward Main Street through the Academy Street intersection past the First Free Baptist Church (now the South Baptist Church).

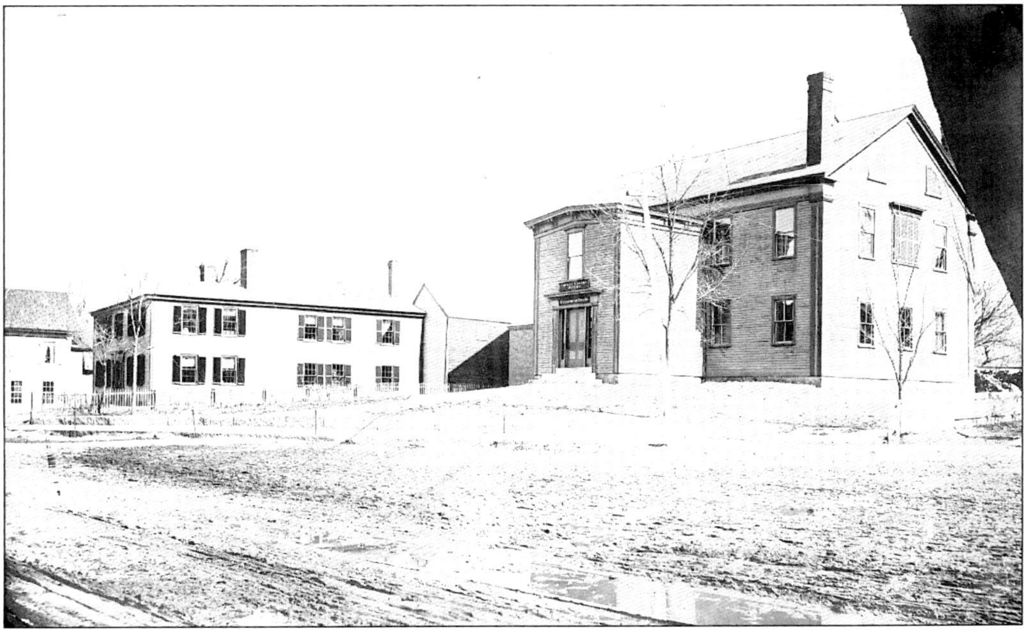

The original Court House, built c. 1822 and designated as the county court house when Belknap County was split off from Strafford County in 1841. When the new brick Court House was built on the site in 1893, this building was moved across the street, where it became the Peoples Church, then an armory, and eventually the Riverside Arena, before it burned in 1950.

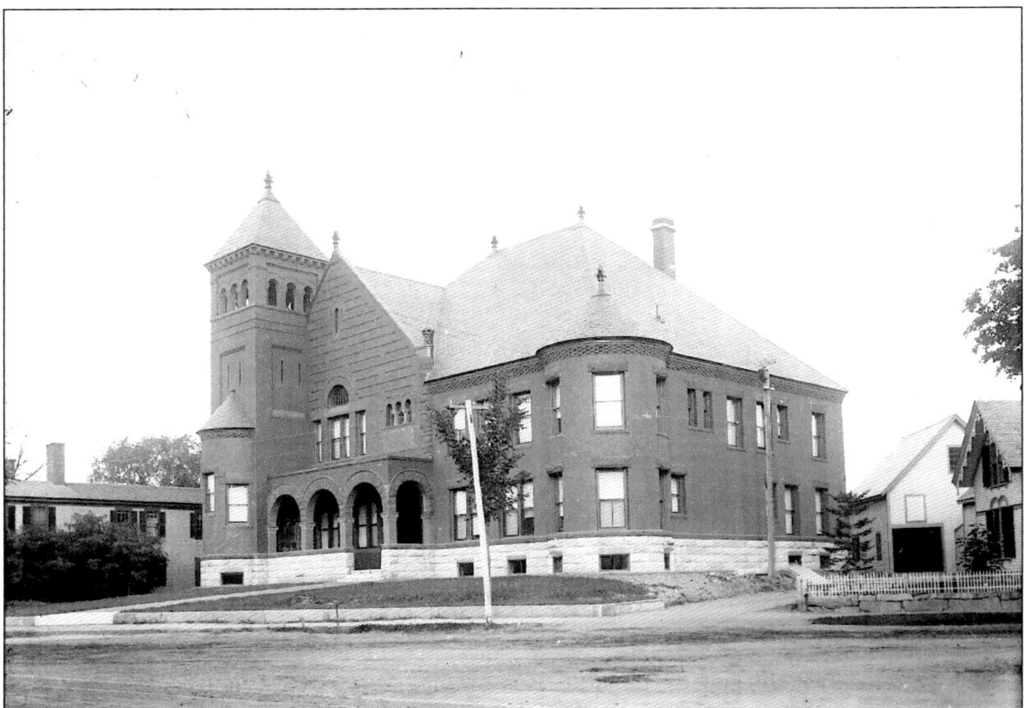

The new Belknap County Court House, dedicated March 28, 1894.

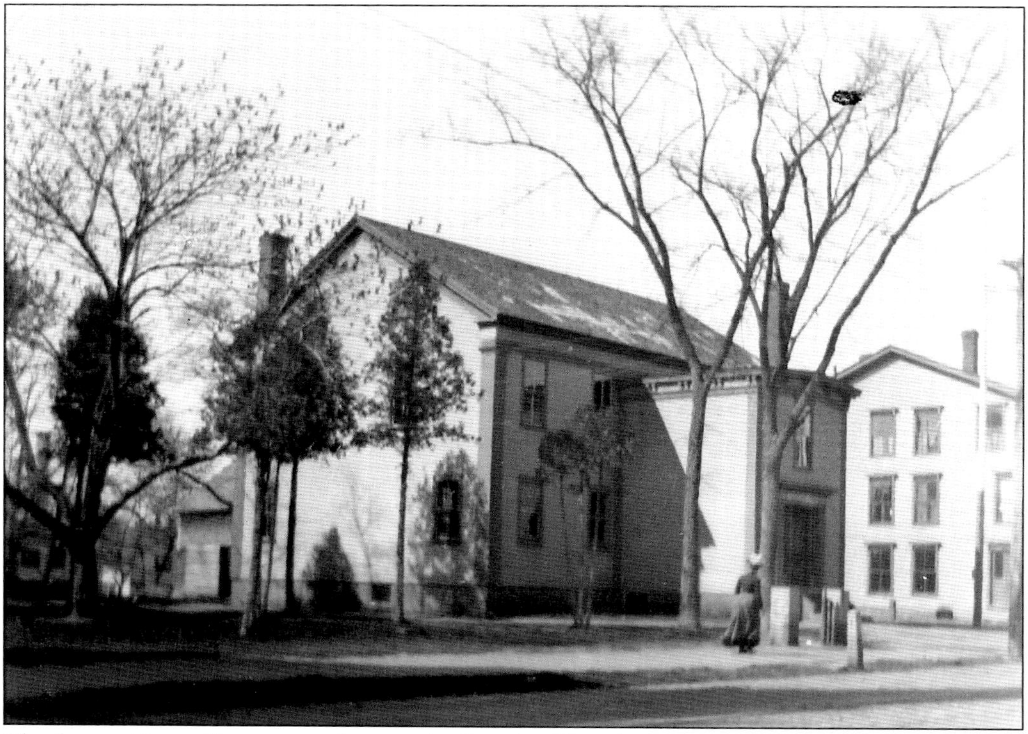

The former Court House, seen here as the Peoples Church, on Court Street in the late 1890s.

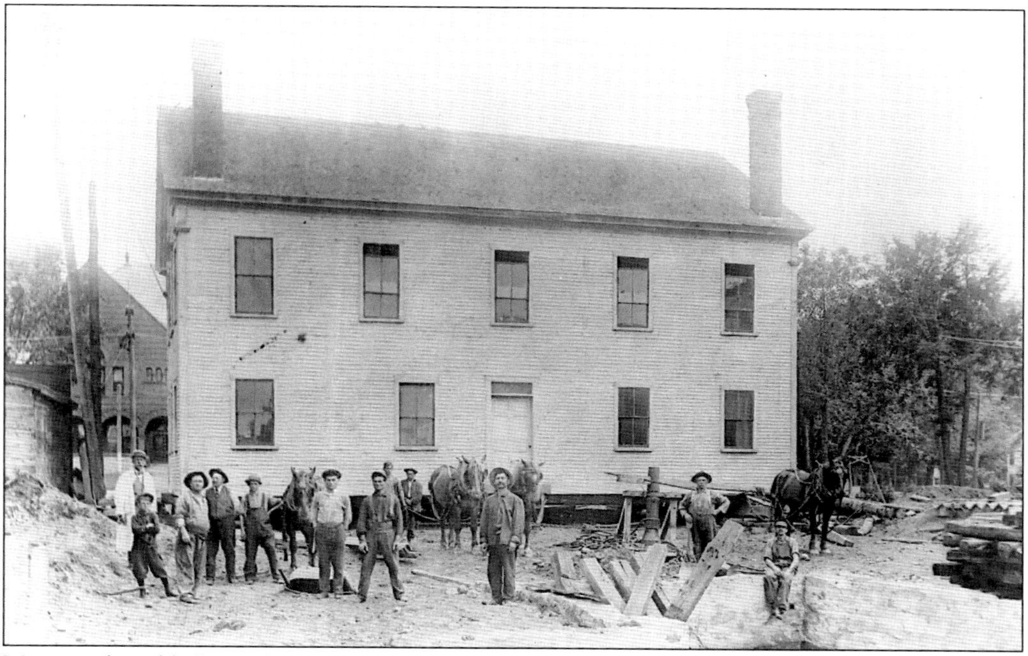

Moving the old Court House, 1914. After the Peoples Christian Church relocated in 1903 to the former Old North Church (Congregational) and moved it across Veterans Square (see pp. 100-101), the old Court House was moved closer to the river and redesignated as an armory.

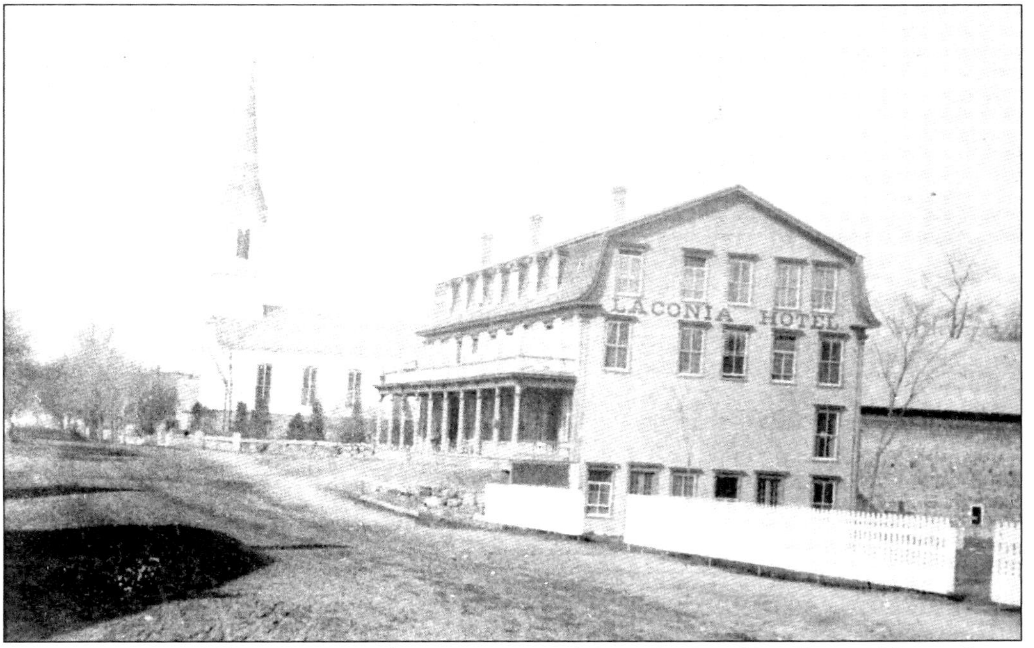


The Laconia Hotel (later the Wonalancet House, and then the City Hotel), c. 1870s, on Court Street. This was one of a number of hotels built in the 1830s to serve those attending sessions of court here, as well as commercial travelers. The First Free Baptist Church appears in the distance before the 1876 fire.

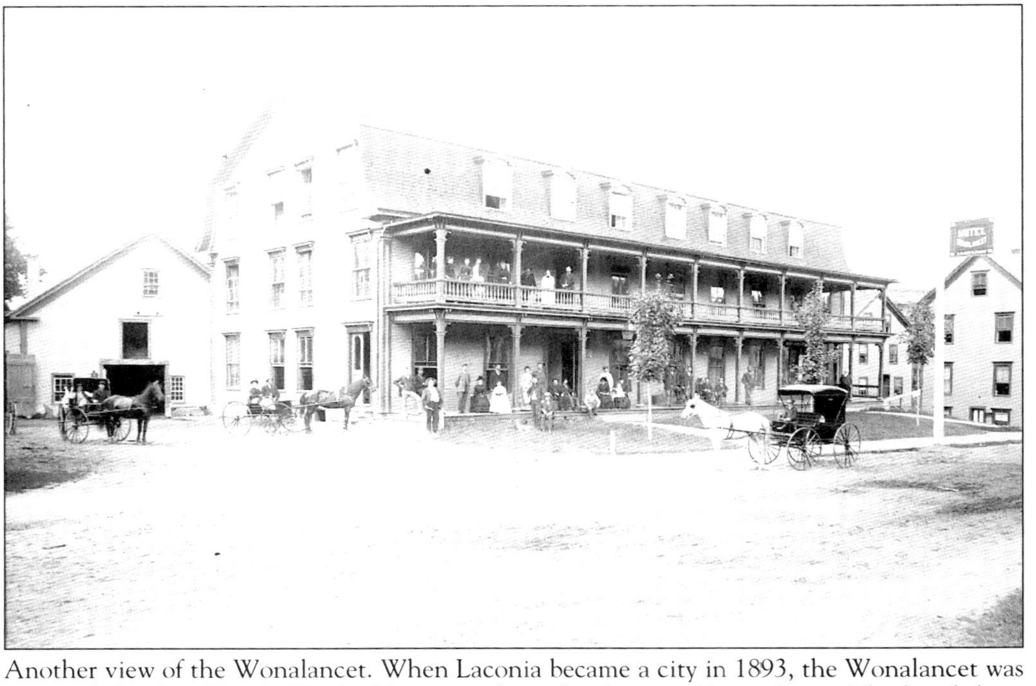

Another view of the Wonalancet. When Laconia became a city in 1893, the Wonalancet was renamed the City Hotel. The buildings, on the right, front on Rowe Court. The hotel, later remodeled into Chertok's Laconia Furniture Store, burned in 1961.

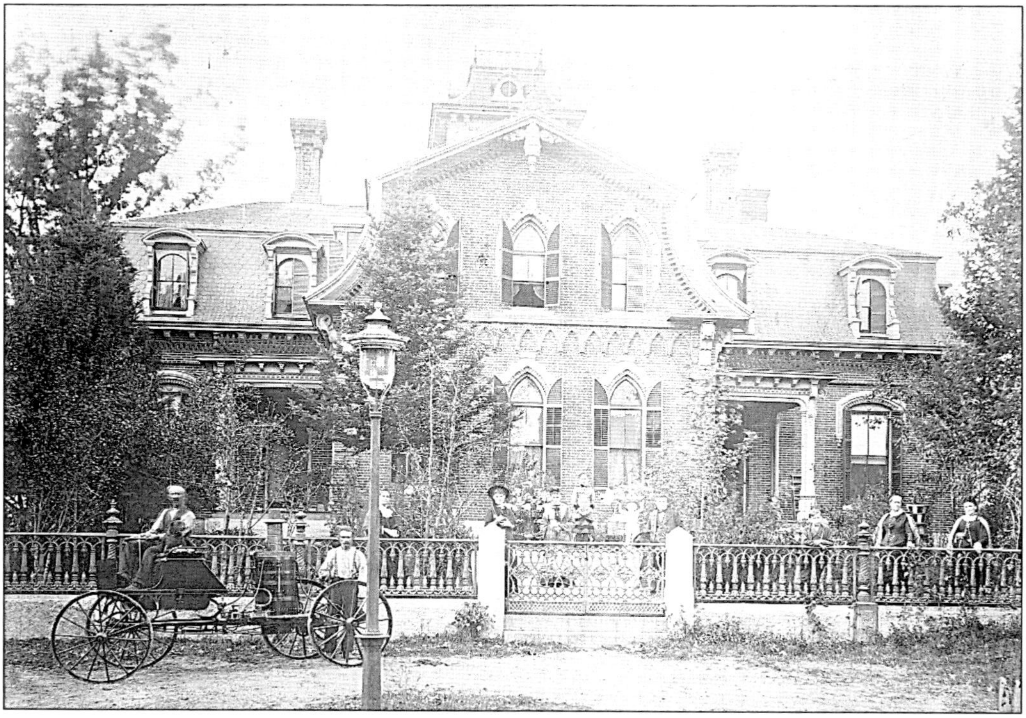

The Gove Mansion, c. 1890. Richard Gove, an early and very wealthy jeweler at Meredith Bridge from 1833–1883, built this brick mansion between the Winnipesaukee River and Orange Court. Later, it was home to merchant Frank H. Lougee. Today, hidden behind other buildings, the structure still survives. The early automobile (at the lower left) was called the "Fairy Queen" (see p. 4).

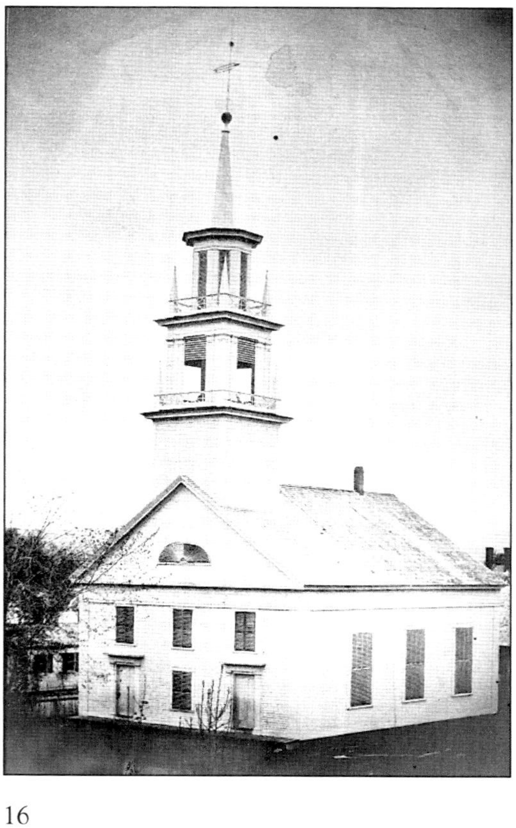

The First Free Baptist Church (later to become the South Baptist Church) building on Court Street. Dedicated in 1841, it was renovated and enlarged in 1873. It burned in 1876 (see next page).

The First Free Baptist Church building, as expanded, 1873. It was destroyed by an arsonist three years later.

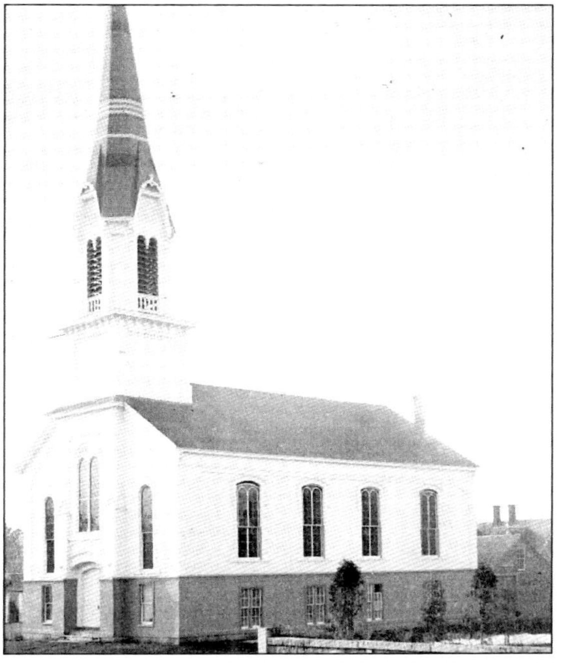

Today's South Baptist Church building as rebuilt after the fire of 1876.

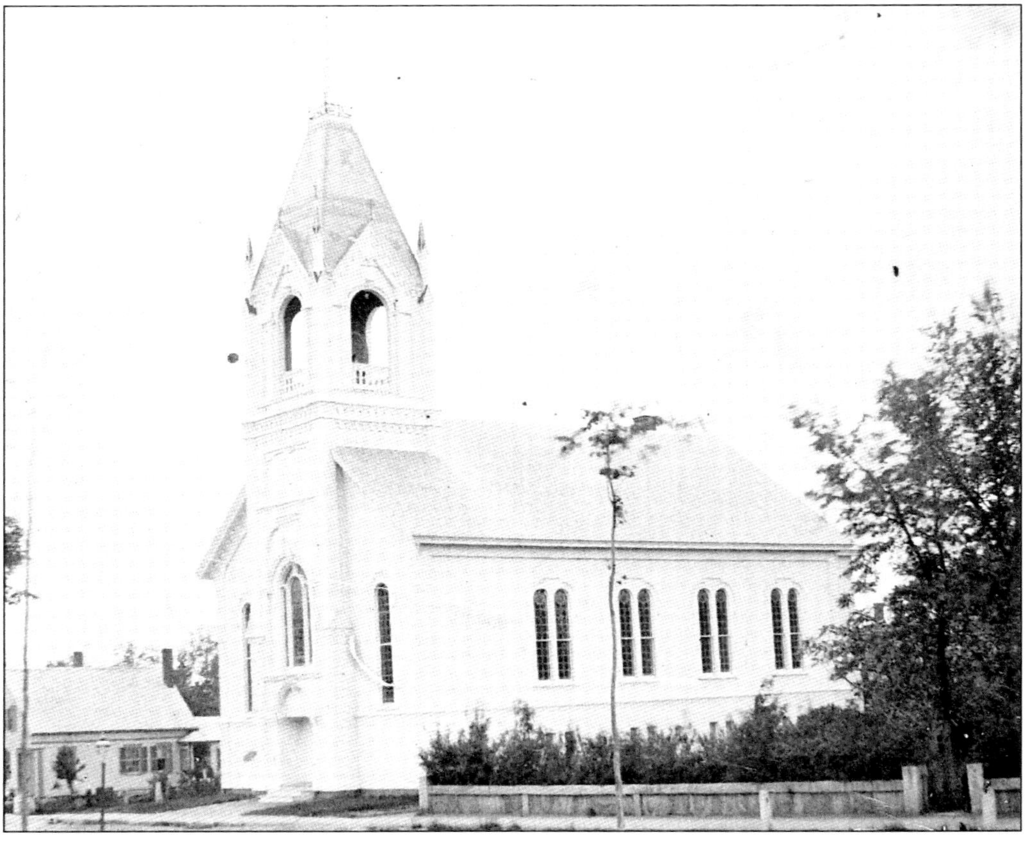

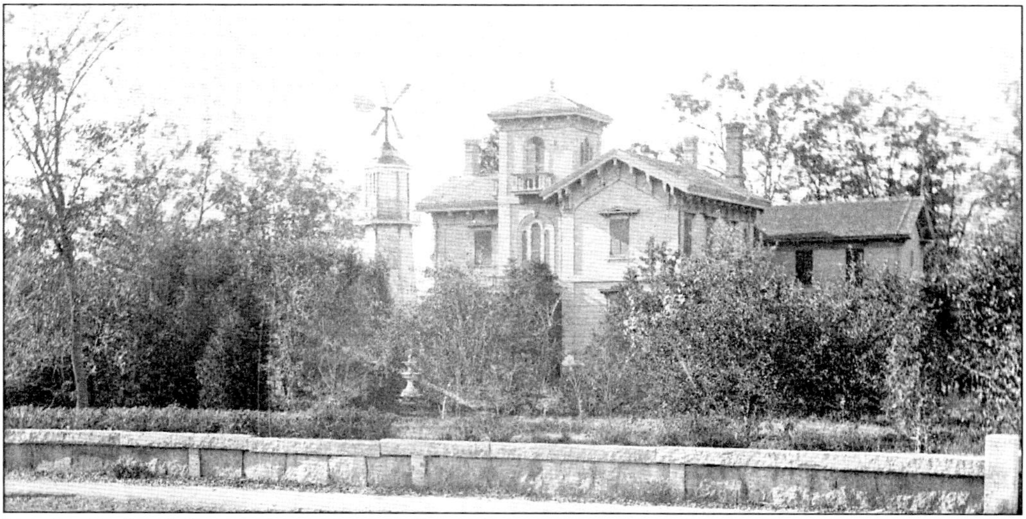

Jeweler Richard Gove's first mansion (later the residence of Alburtis S. Gordon) at 75A Court Street still stands at the rear of the large commercial building recently occupied by Groleau Millworks. Gordon was a senior member of Gordon & Booth Jewelry, having acquired the business established here in 1833 by his uncle, Richard Gove.

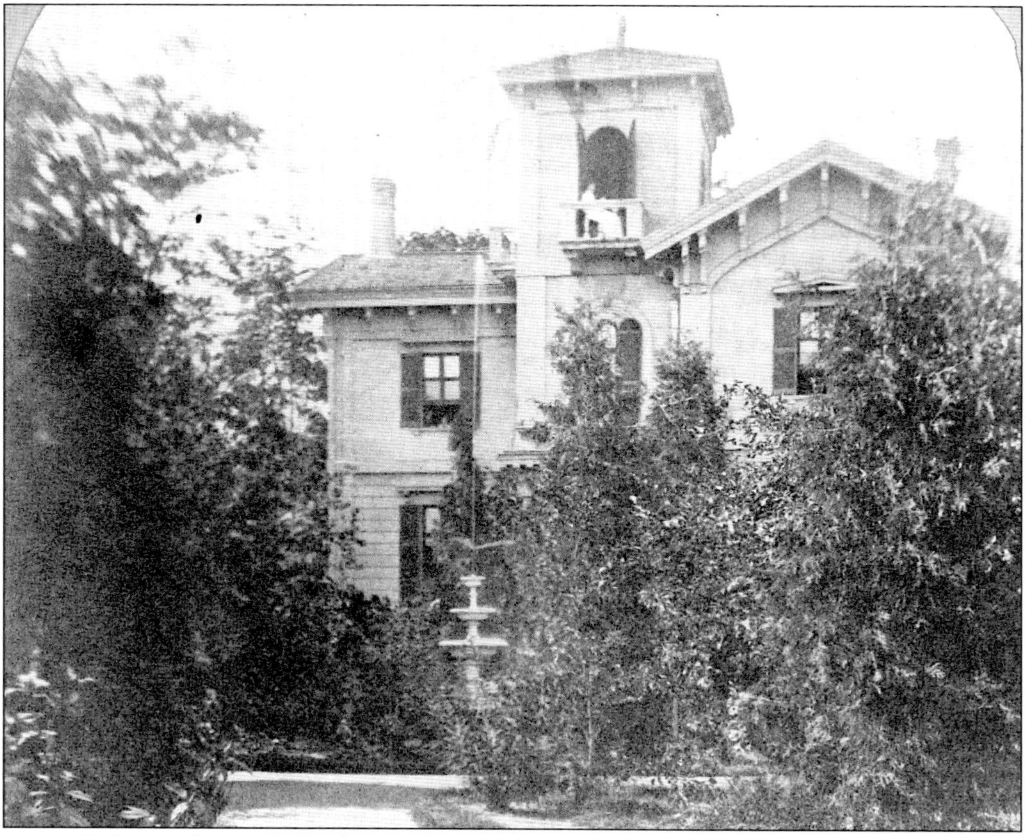

A detail of the Alburtis S. Gordon residence.

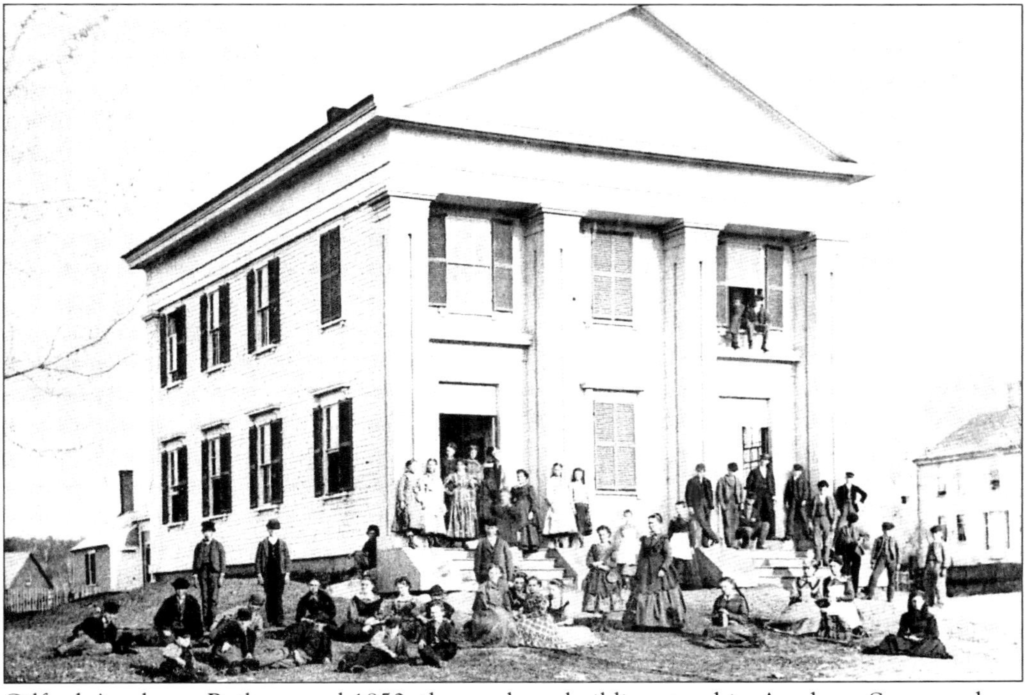

Gilford Academy. Built around 1850, the academy building stood in Academy Square, where it was displaced when the first Laconia High School (today's district court building) was built in 1886. Beginning around 1820, the academy held classes in private homes and in the old wooden Court House until the construction of this classical structure. In 1850, this part of modern Laconia was still part of Gilford; hence, the name.

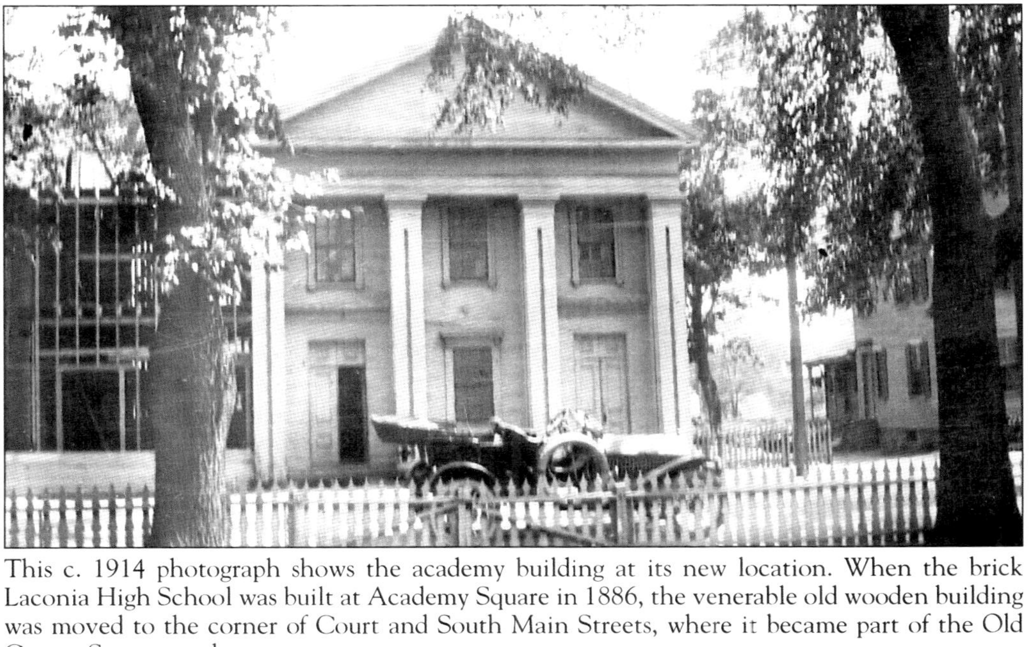

This c. 1914 photograph shows the academy building at its new location. When the brick Laconia High School was built at Academy Square in 1886, the venerable old wooden building was moved to the corner of Court and South Main Streets, where it became part of the Old Corner Store complex.

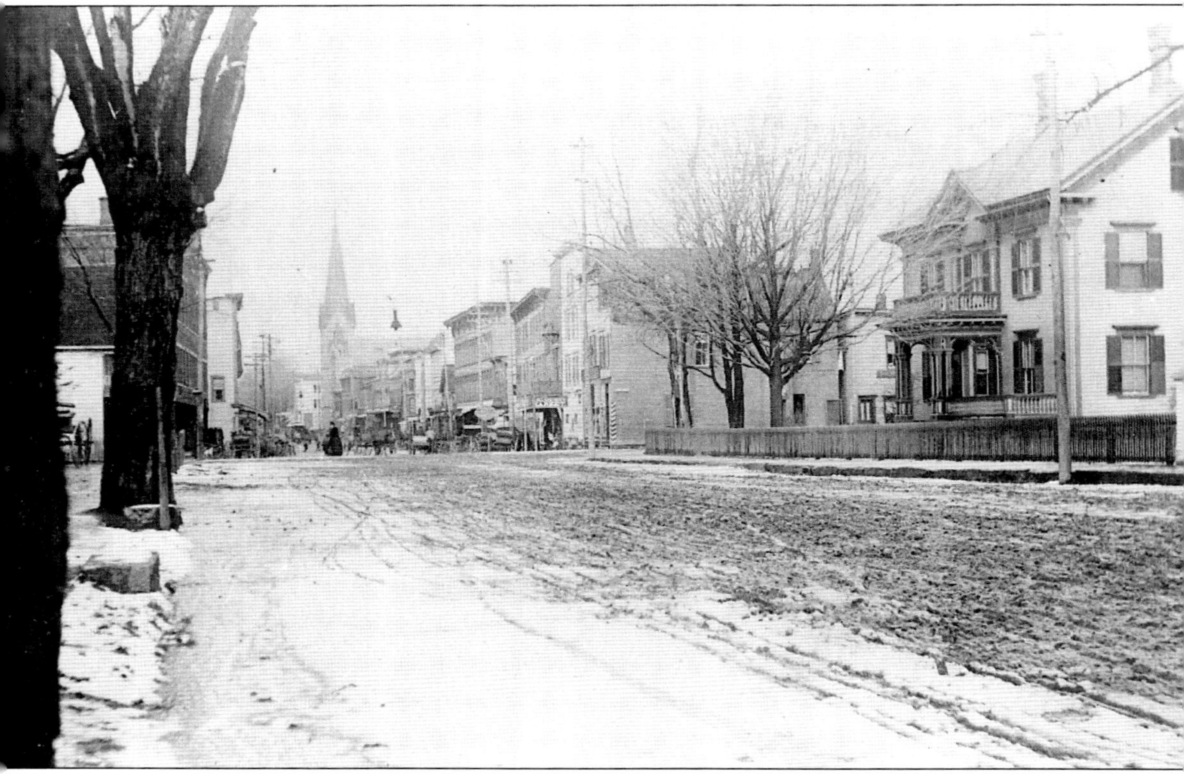

South Main Street, c. 1890s. The Woodbury Melcher House (on the right), was later owned by Bessie Clow. Much later, it was moved back to allow the construction of a series of diners (including Earl's and Dearborn's) and a gasoline station (long operated by Harold T. "Pappy" Whittum). Union Avenue begins on the right, just beyond the Woodbury Melcher House.

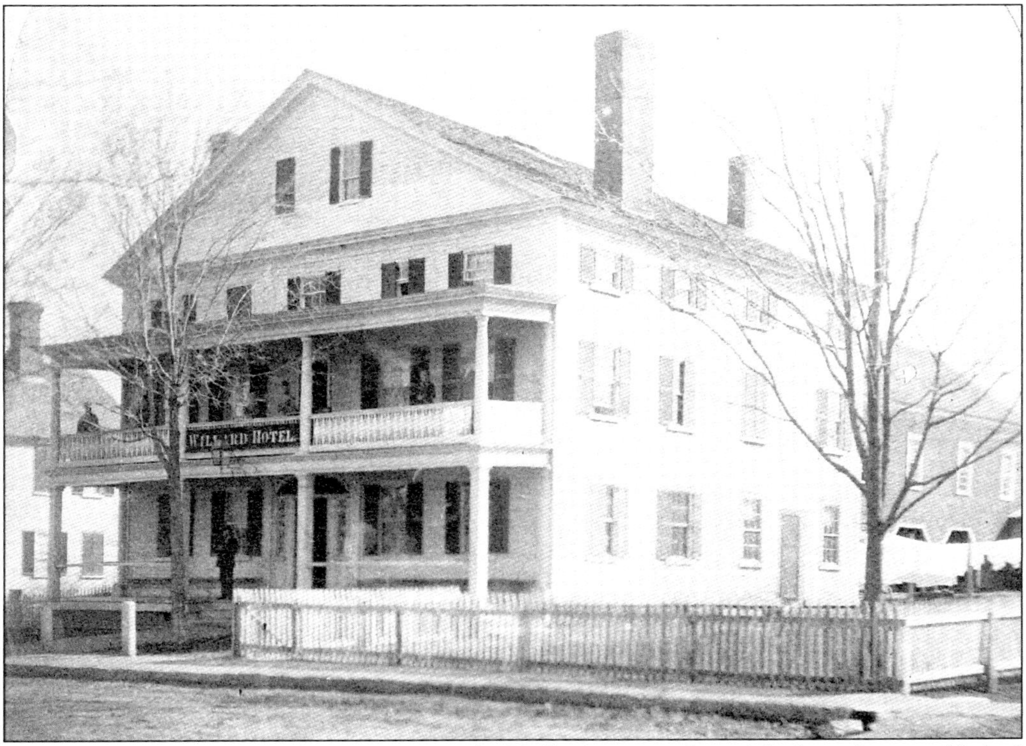

The Willard Hotel on South Main Street. The Willard was another of the hostelries established to serve the court and an increasing number of commercial travelers in the 1830s. Located approximately on the current site of the parking lot of the Melcher & Prescott building, the old Willard was torn down in 1939.

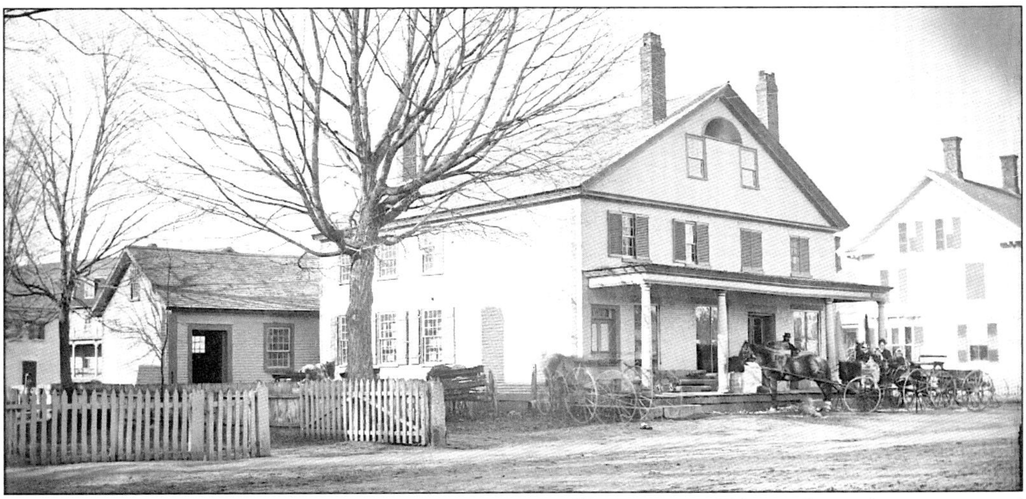

An 1870s photograph of the Old Corner Store, owned by James H. Tilton. Stores have occupied this site at the corner of South Main and Court Streets since at least 1812. The front part of this structure was built about 1834. On the right is the Daniel A. Tilton House (later, owned by William F. Knight), built in 1866 on land originally owned by Dr. Zadock Bowman, an early physician.

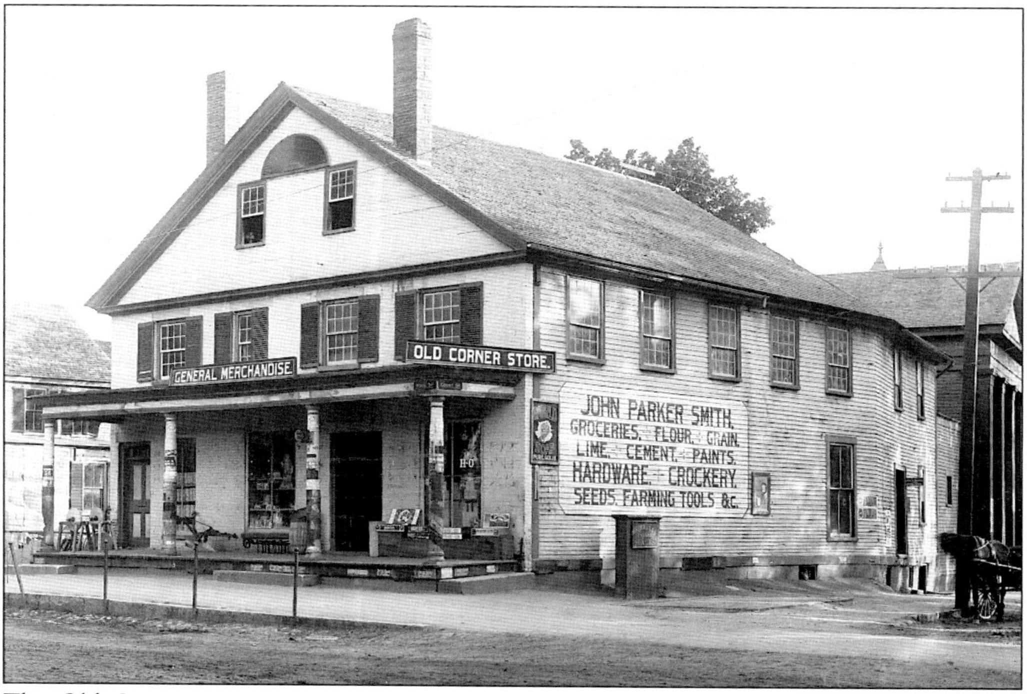


The Old Corner Store in the 1890s, operated by John Parker Smith. The former Gilford Academy building can be seen on the right.

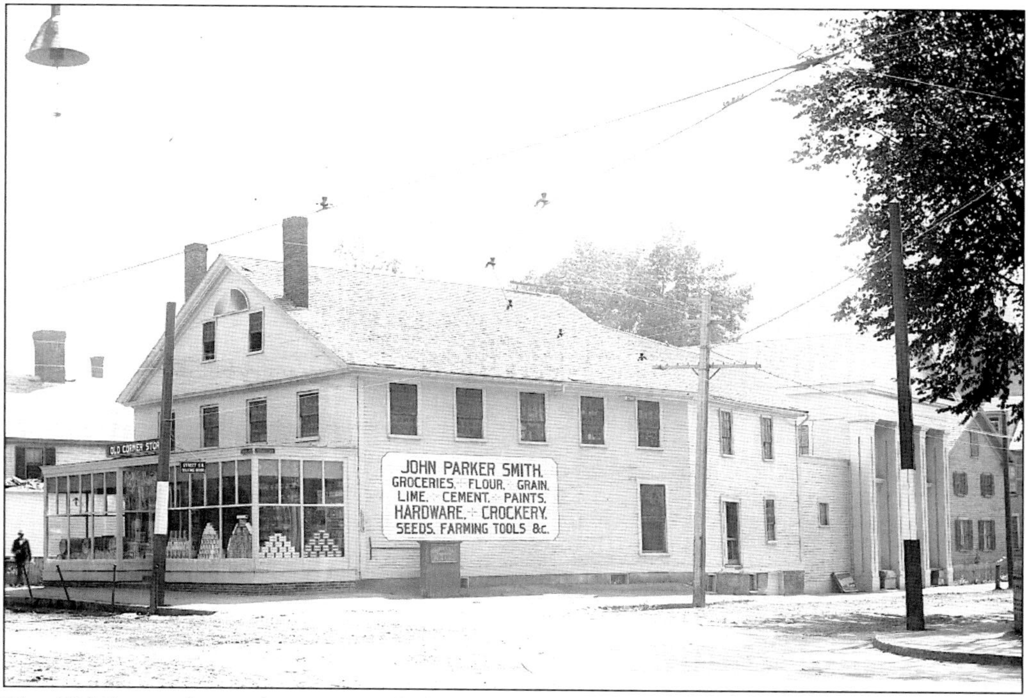


The Old Corner Store after 1898, with the overhead wires of the Laconia Street Railway visible.

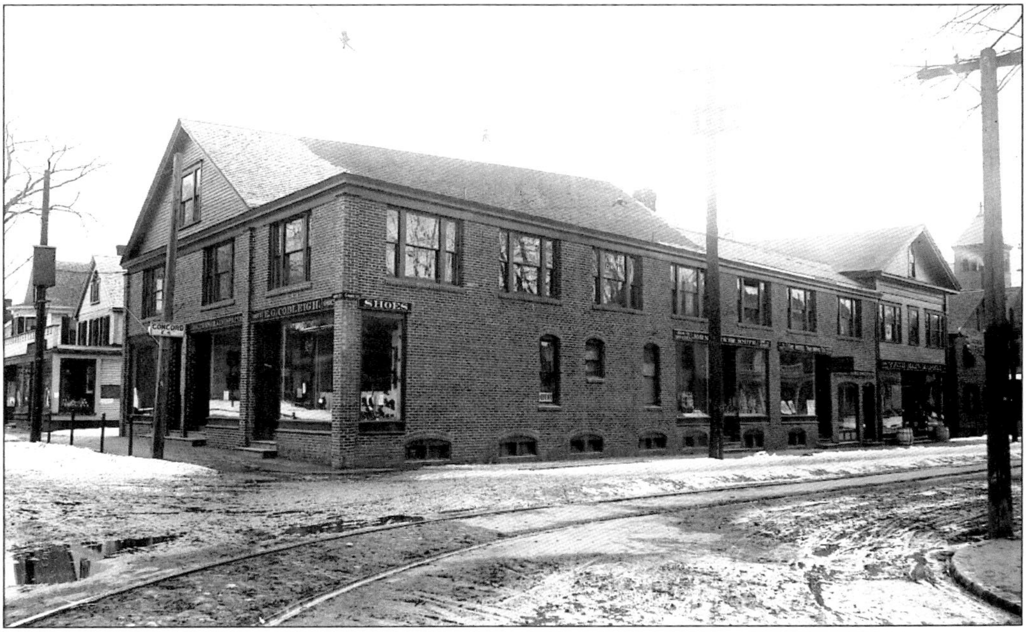


The Old Corner Store in the early years of this century. The tower of the Court House is just visible at the far right.

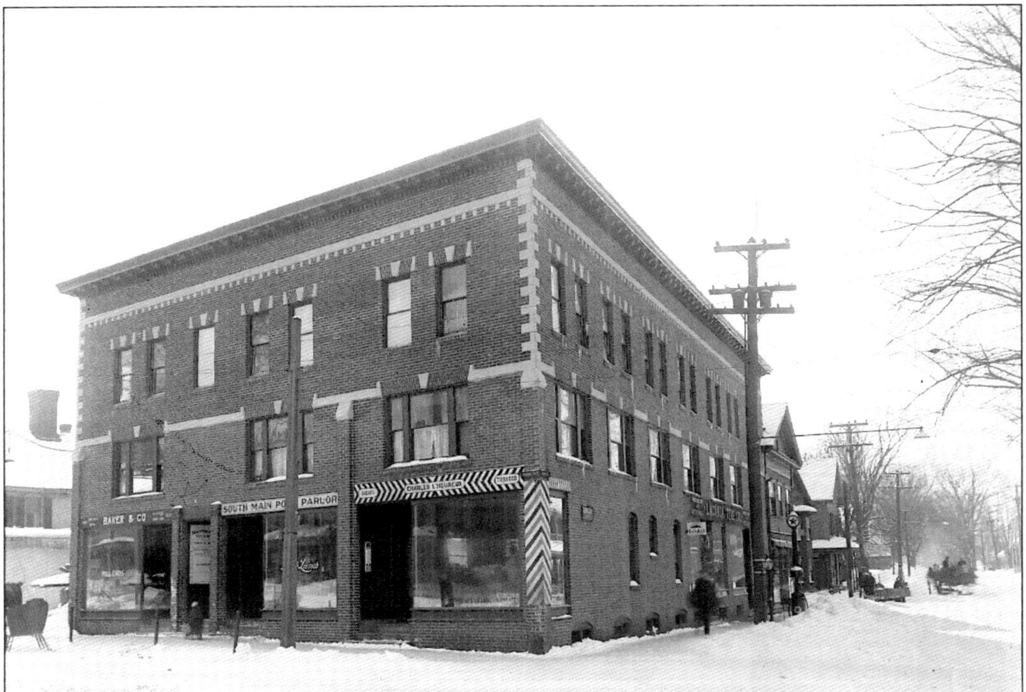


The Harriman Block in the early 1920s. The building maintained this appearance until its demolition in the late 1960s–early 1970s under the city's Urban Renewal program. A New England Telephone (NYNEX) business office currently occupies the site.

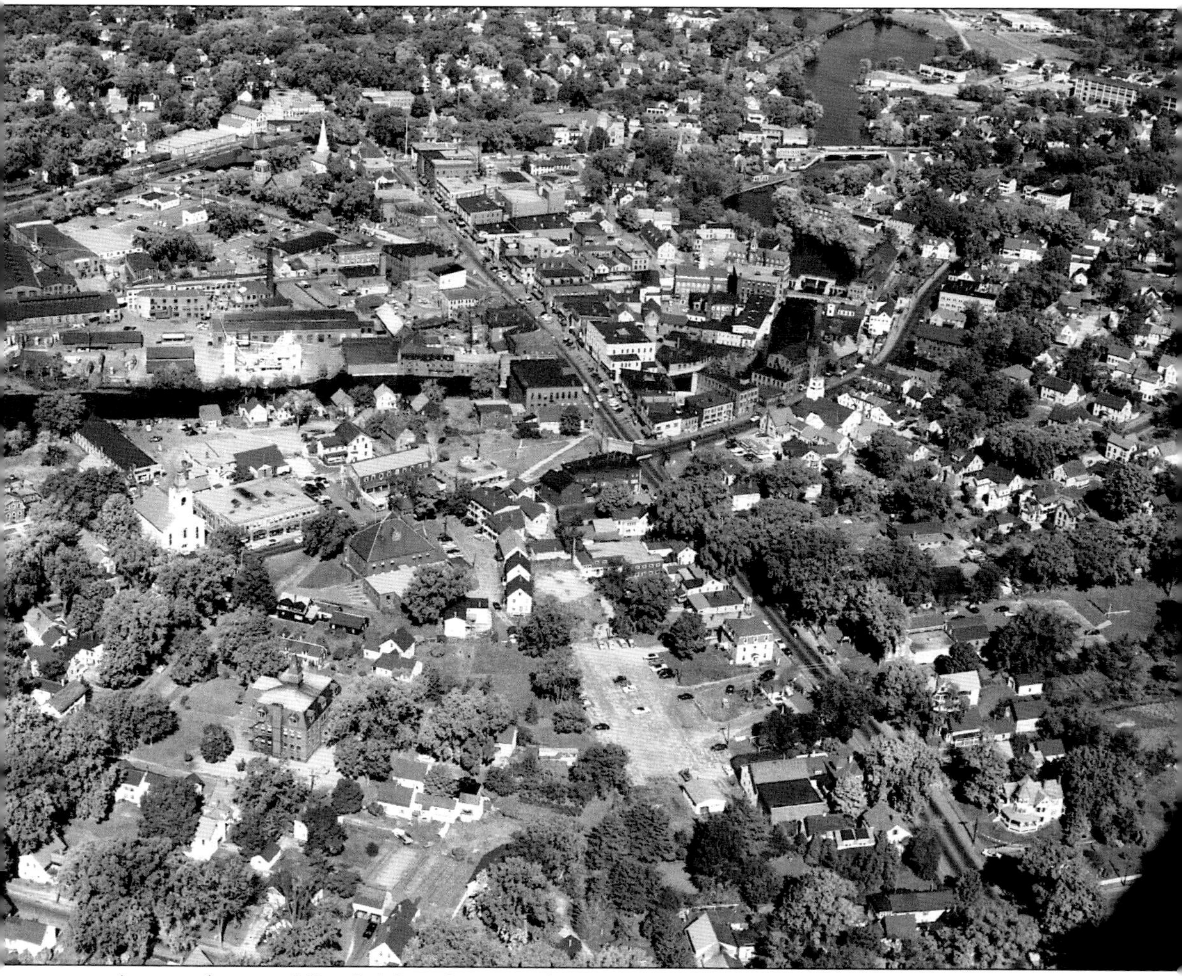

An aerial view of South Main Street and Downtown in the mid-1950s. The large open area in the center foreground is now occupied by Butson's Supermarket (formerly IGA and FarmFare).

## *Two*

# Main Street Before 1860

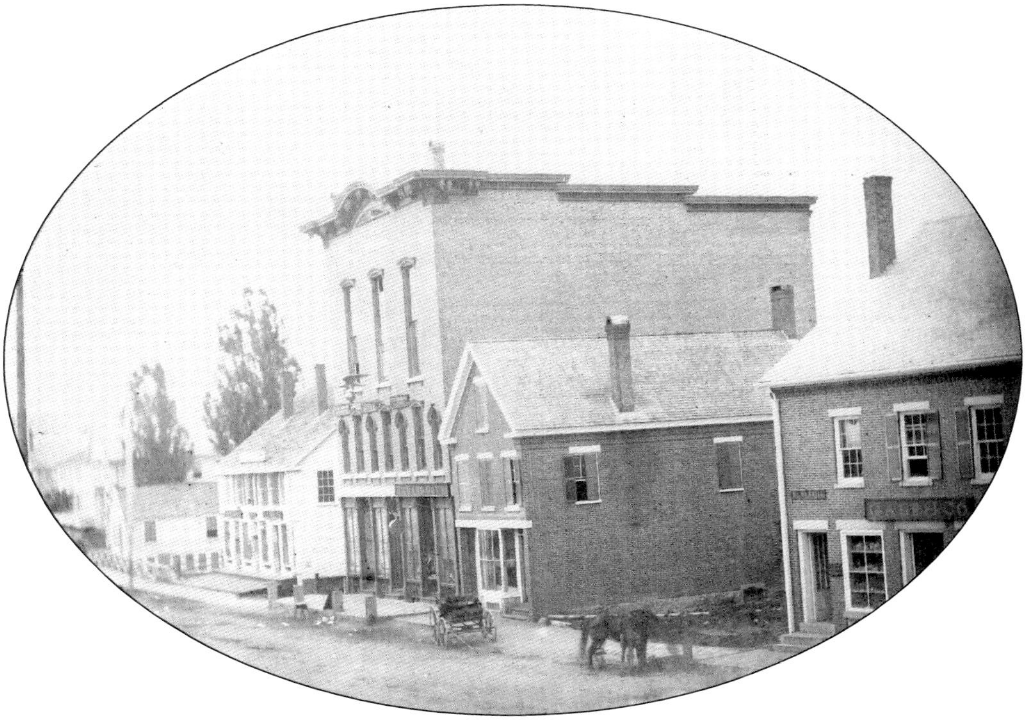

The west side of Main Street before the Great Fire of 1860. From the near end of the Main Street Bridge are the stationery store of John C. Moulton, the jewelry store of Richard Gove, Odlin's Drug Store, and Gale's Hardware Store. This area is today occupied by the former Story Drug Store, former Rosen's (more recently, Madhouse Music) and Sawyer's Jewelry.

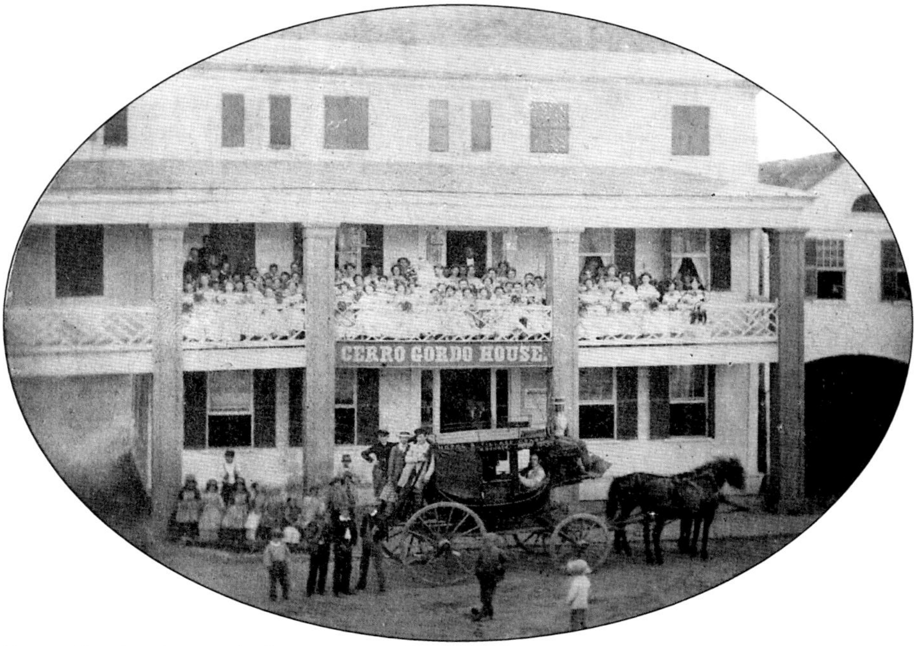


The Cerro Gordo House, before 1860. This hotel was located approximately on the site of today's Melnick's Shoe Store. On November 21, 1860, fire started in the stables of the hotel, ultimately laying waste to most of Main Street, from Mill and Water Streets to the river.

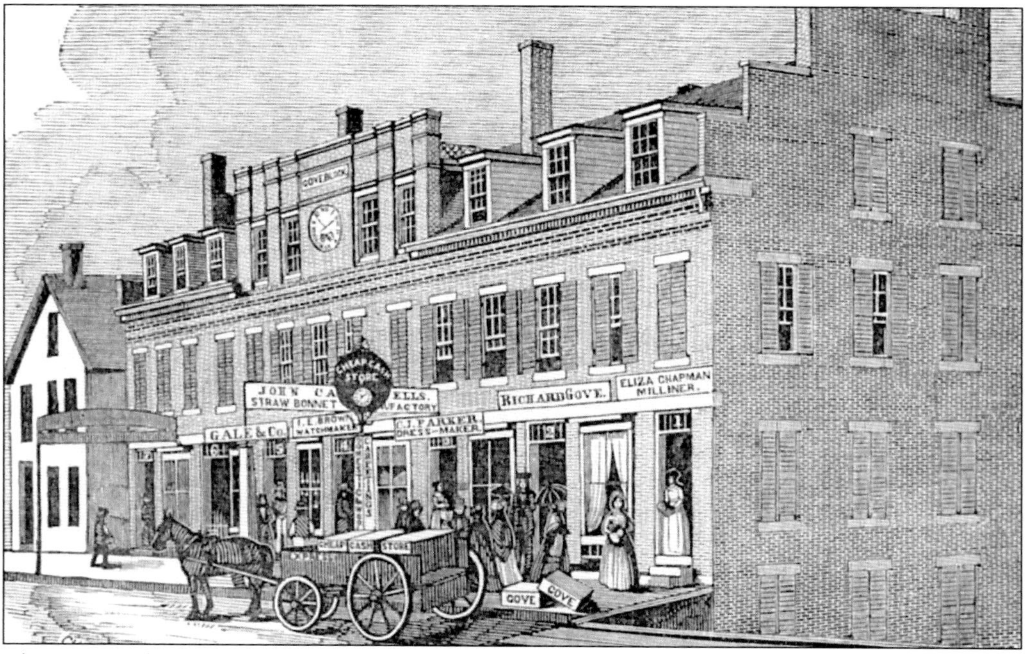


The Gove Block, on the east side of Main Street, before 1860. Eliza Chapman (milliner), Richard Gove's Cheap Cash Store, a straw bonnet factory, I.E. Brown (watchmaker), and Gale & Co. occupied this building, another casualty of the Great Fire of 1860. The Folsom Opera House and "Lower Bank" were its replacements.

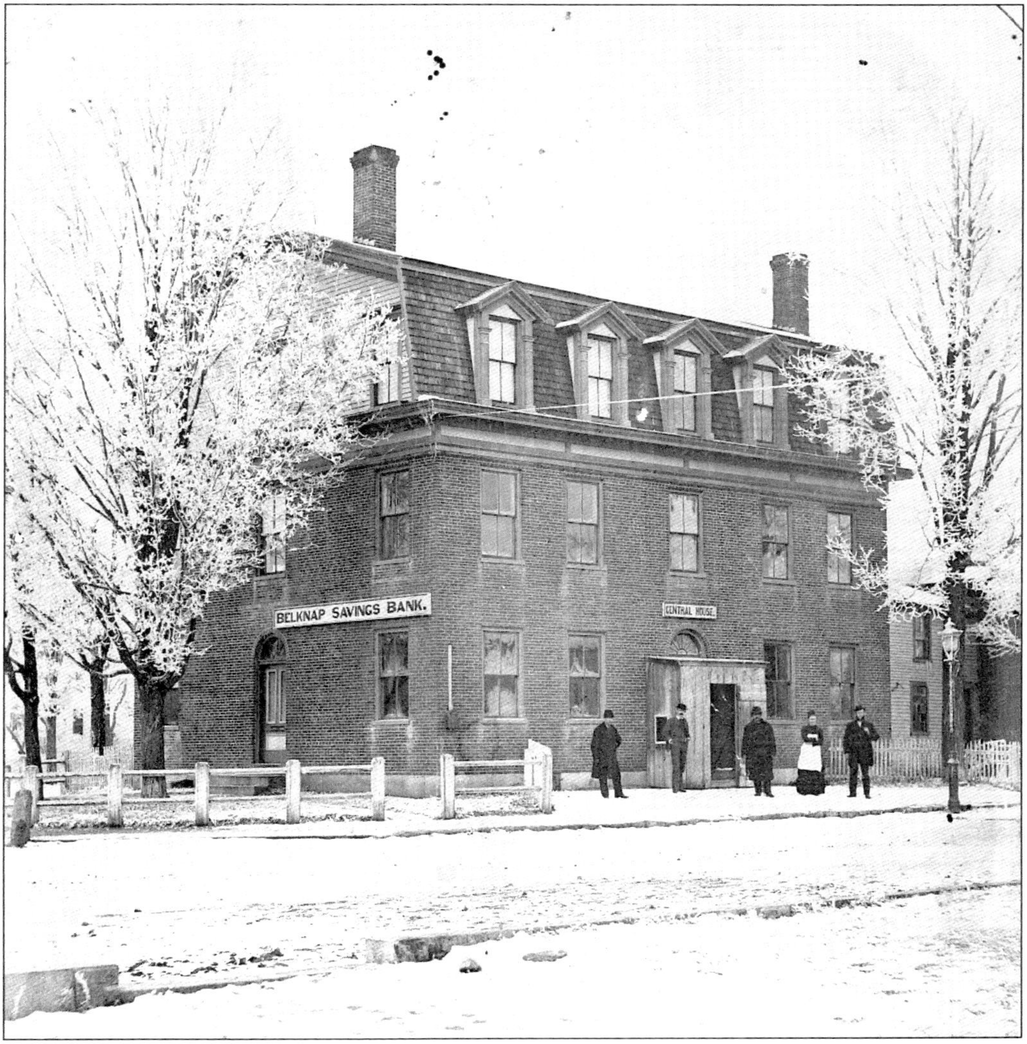

The Belknap Savings Bank and Central House, c. 1872, after the gabled roof replaced the original flat one. Located on the current site of the Sundial Shop, this building dates from 1831. Later, much expanded, the structure housed the Eagle Hotel, and was torn down in 1937 to make way for the new F.W. Woolworth store, which later became Benjamin's Clothing, and eventually the Sundial Shop.

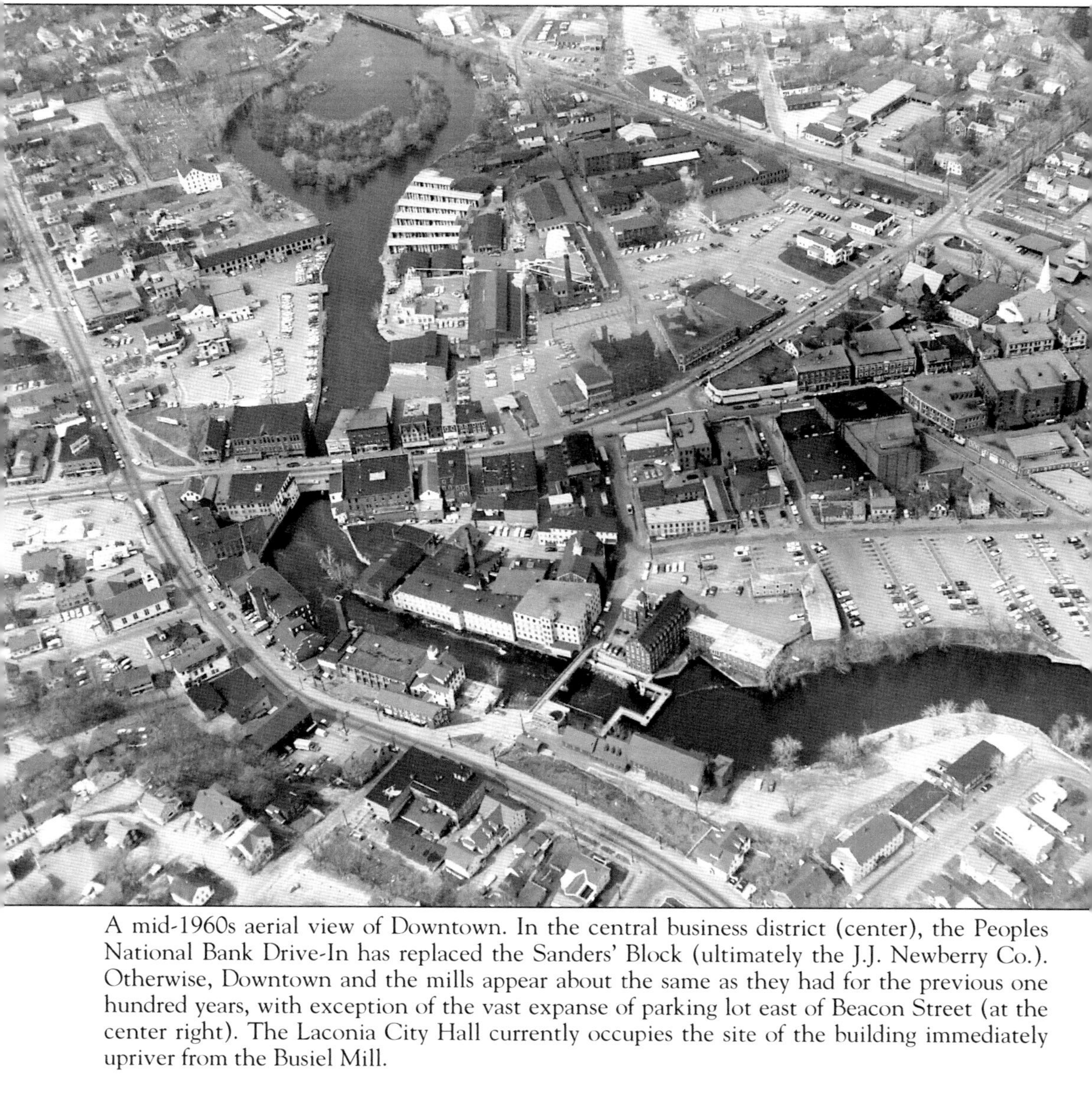

A mid-1960s aerial view of Downtown. In the central business district (center), the Peoples National Bank Drive-In has replaced the Sanders' Block (ultimately the J.J. Newberry Co.). Otherwise, Downtown and the mills appear about the same as they had for the previous one hundred years, with exception of the vast expanse of parking lot east of Beacon Street (at the center right). The Laconia City Hall currently occupies the site of the building immediately upriver from the Busiel Mill.

# *Three*

# River and Mills

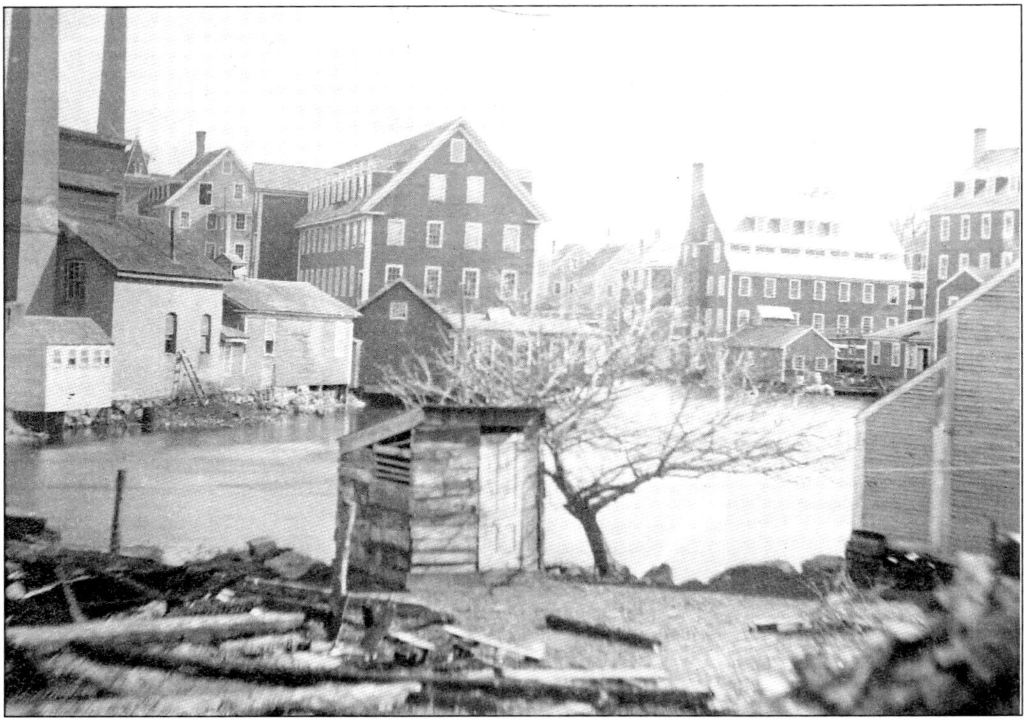

Looking up the Winnipesaukee River in the mid-1870s. This photograph was taken from the area of today's Stewart Park, looking toward the Mill Street Bridge. The buildings on the left were part of the Belknap Mill complex, with the Lewis F. Busiel Mill at the top center of the group. The buildings on the right were part of Pitman Hosiery Co.

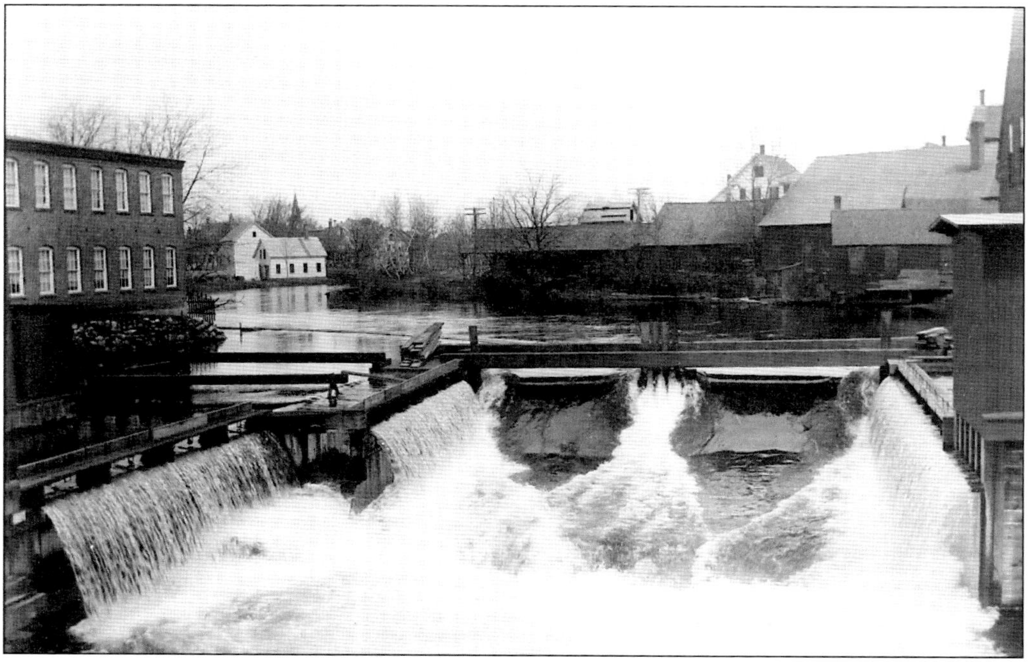

Avery Dam, from the Mill Street Bridge, prior to 1949.

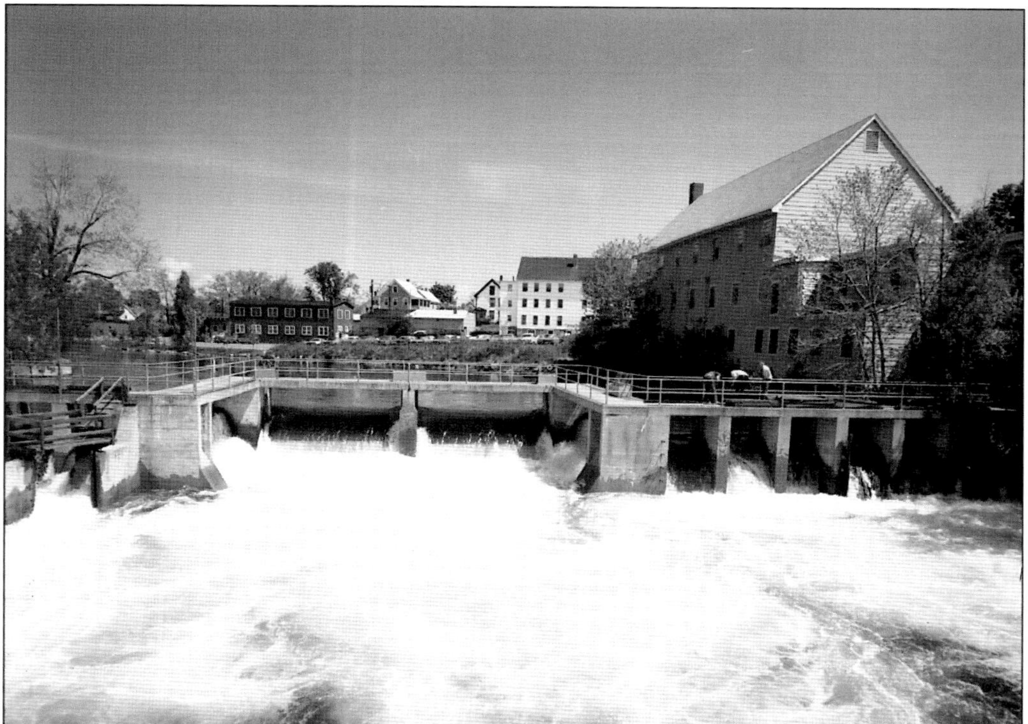

The new Avery Dam, built in 1949. Both photographs give an indication of the tremendous waterpower available to the mills.

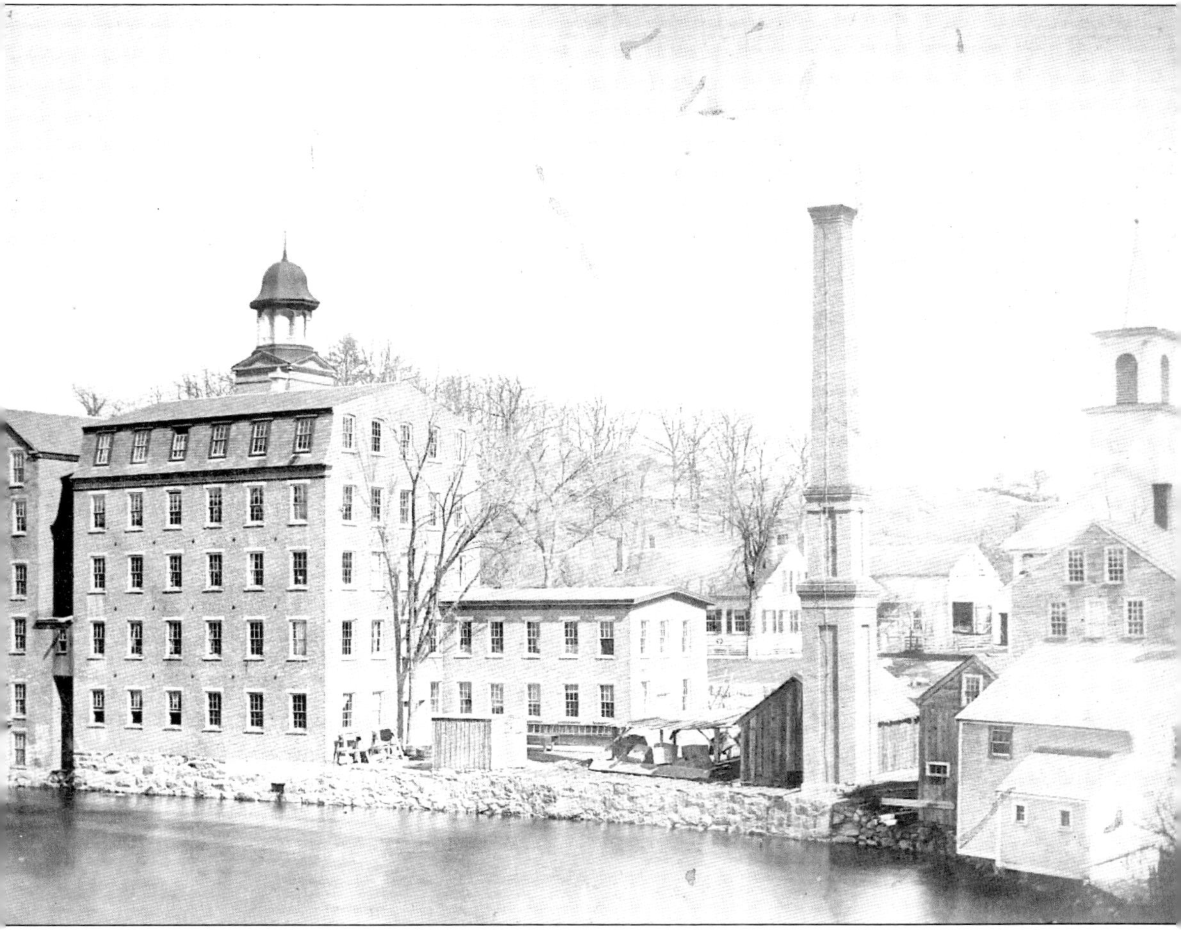

An early view of the Gilford Hosiery Mill (later, the Clow Mill), showing the First Methodist Church (on the right) at the site of today's Sunrise Towers. The church was built c. 1838 by the Universalists (later, the Unitarians), who sold it to the Methodists in 1869 upon the completion of their new church on Main Street in Bank Square. The mill site is now part of Stewart Park. The Baldwin House (visible at the left of the large chimney) was located on site of today's Southgate Terrace Condominiums. At the time of this photograph, Avery Hill (in the background) was largely pasture land.

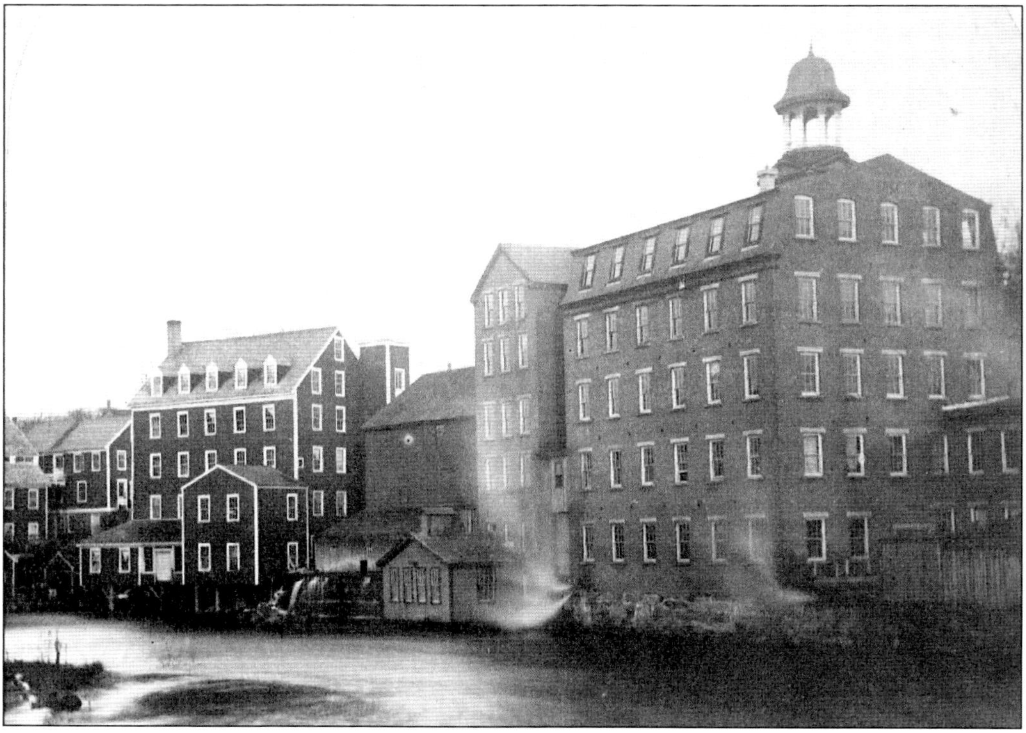

The Gilford Hosiery Mill, from downriver. Pitman Hosiery is on the left.

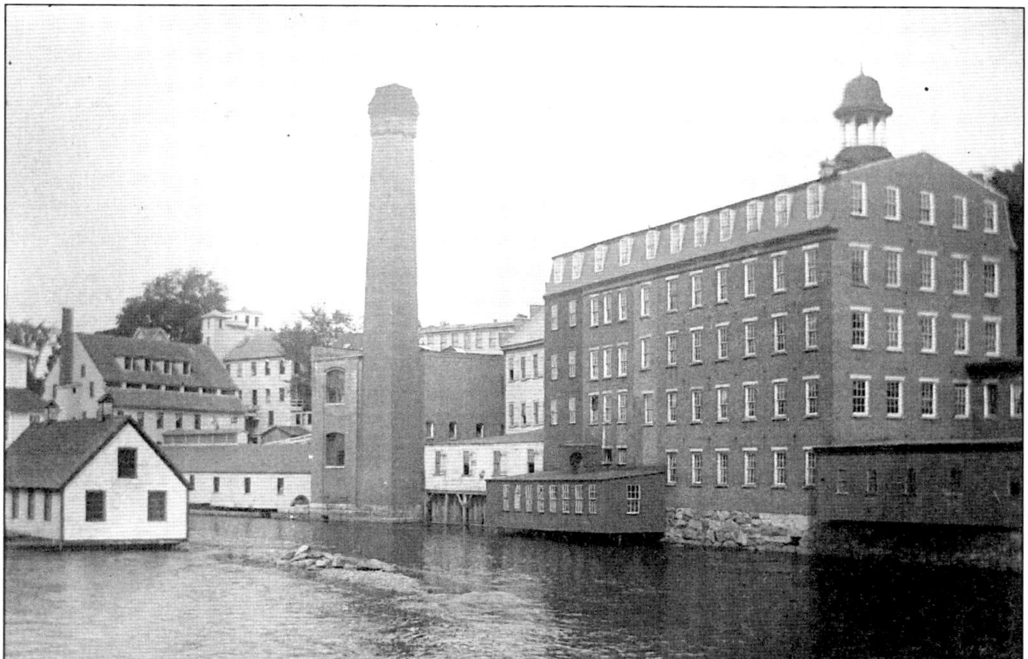

Another view of the Gilford Hosiery Mill, looking upriver from the Main Street Bridge. The old gristmill is on its immediate left, and then the Pitman Hosiery buildings.

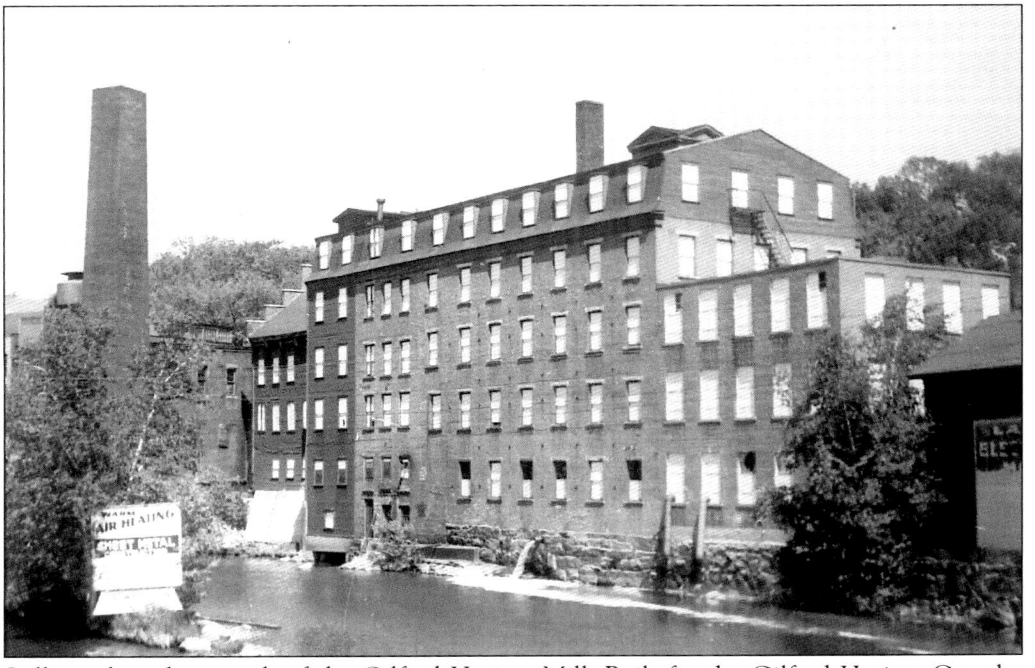

Still another photograph of the Gilford Hosiery Mill. Built for the Gilford Hosiery Co., the building later became the Clow Mill and then Cormier Hosiery before its demolition during Urban Renewal in the late 1960s.

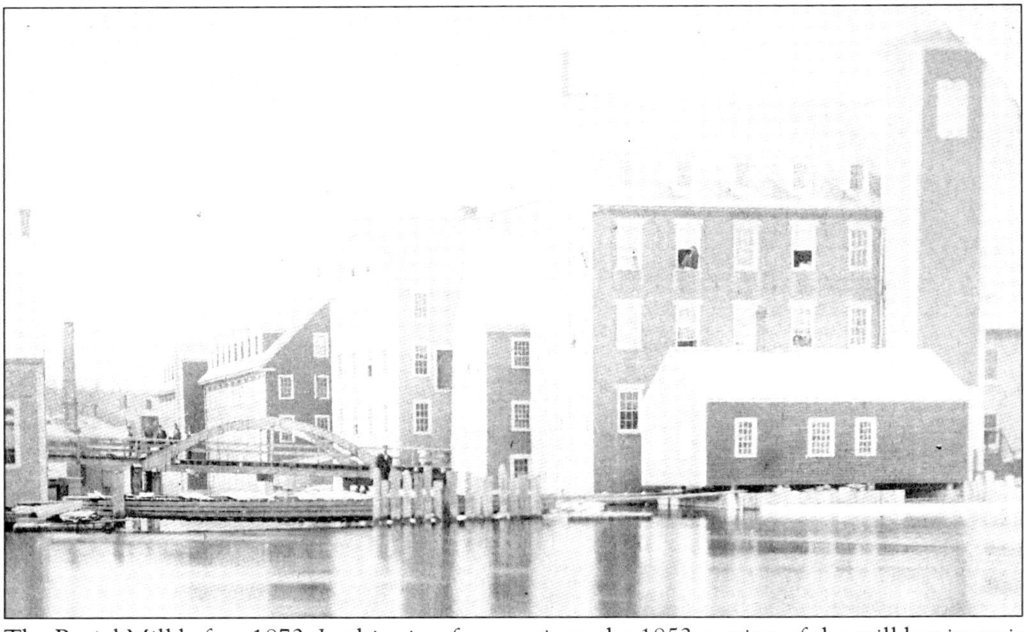

The Busiel Mill before 1873. In this view from upriver, the 1853 portion of the mill has its stair tower on the opposite side from where it is today. The stair tower was relocated when the mill was doubled in size, in 1877–1878. Earlier, beginning in 1873, a number of ancillary buildings were also added.

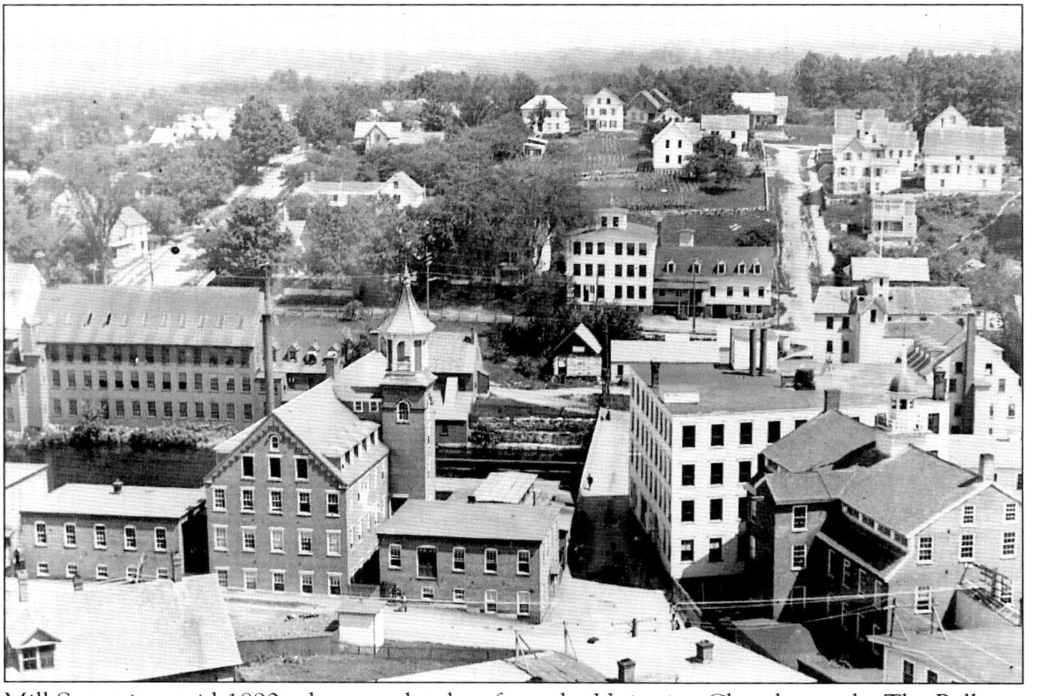

Mill Street in a mid-1890s photograph taken from the Unitarian Church steeple. The Belknap Mill (1823) is on the right, adjoining the Esty Mill (originally the hosiery mill of Lewis F. Busiel, a brother of J.W. Busiel, whose holdings occupy the lower left of photograph). Across the river, the W.D. Huse & Sons machine shop appears before the building was enlarged in 1907.

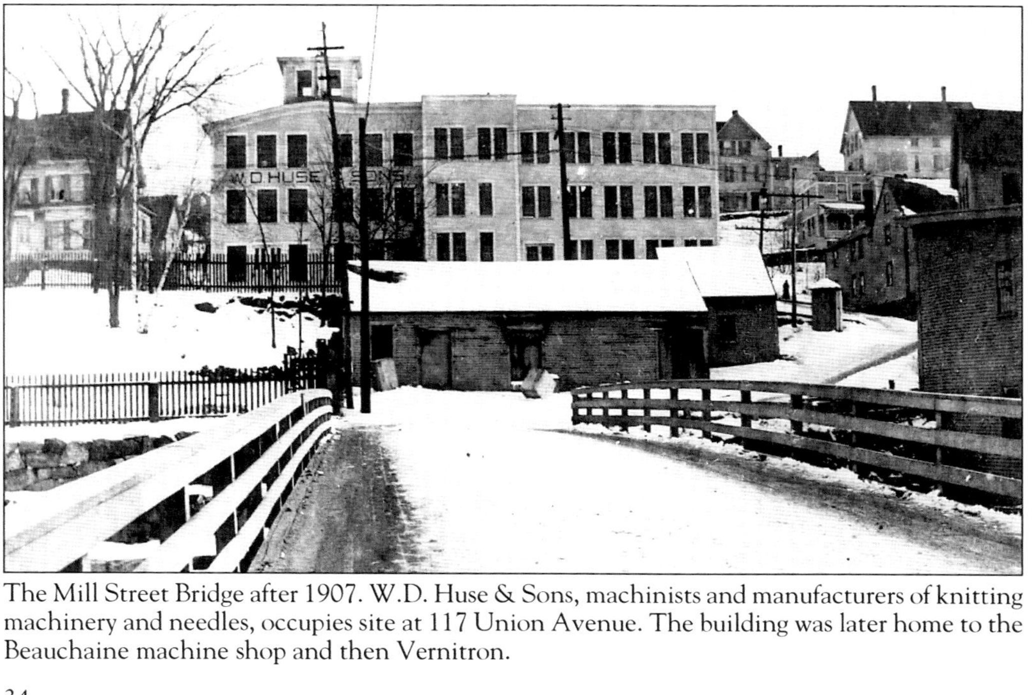


The Mill Street Bridge after 1907. W.D. Huse & Sons, machinists and manufacturers of knitting machinery and needles, occupies site at 117 Union Avenue. The building was later home to the Beauchaine machine shop and then Vernitron.

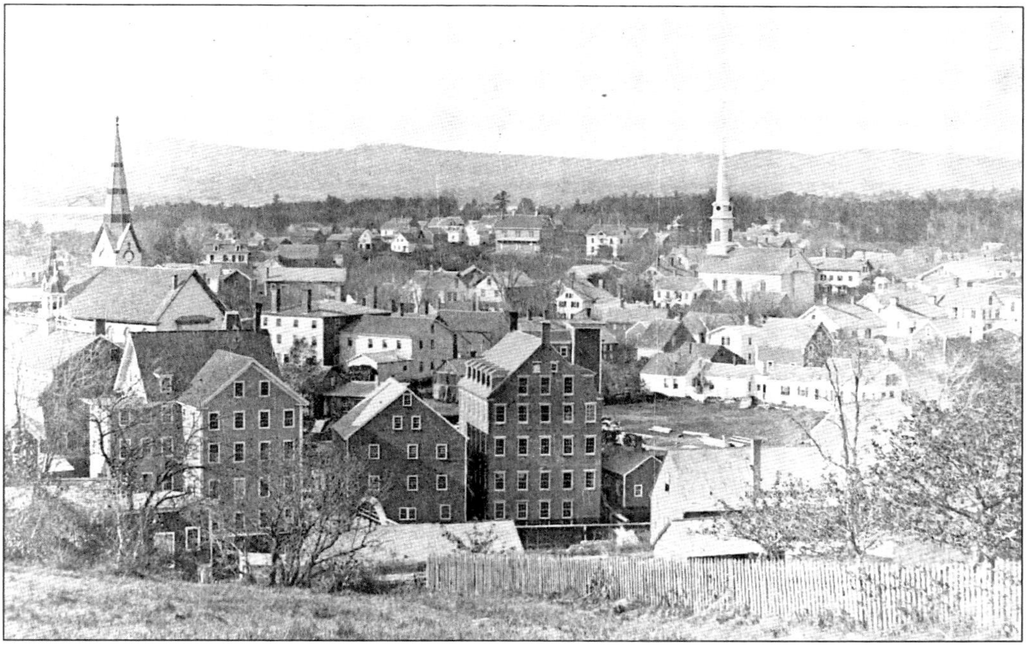

The mills and downtown, c. 1868–1873. The Busiel Mill (center) has yet to be enlarged and the Lewis F. Busiel Mill (left) still has gable roofs. The frame building between the two Busiel mills was later removed. The Belknap Mill can be seen at the extreme left. The spire on the left is that of Unitarian Church; on the right, that of Old North Church (Congregational), located on the modern site of the library's flagpole.

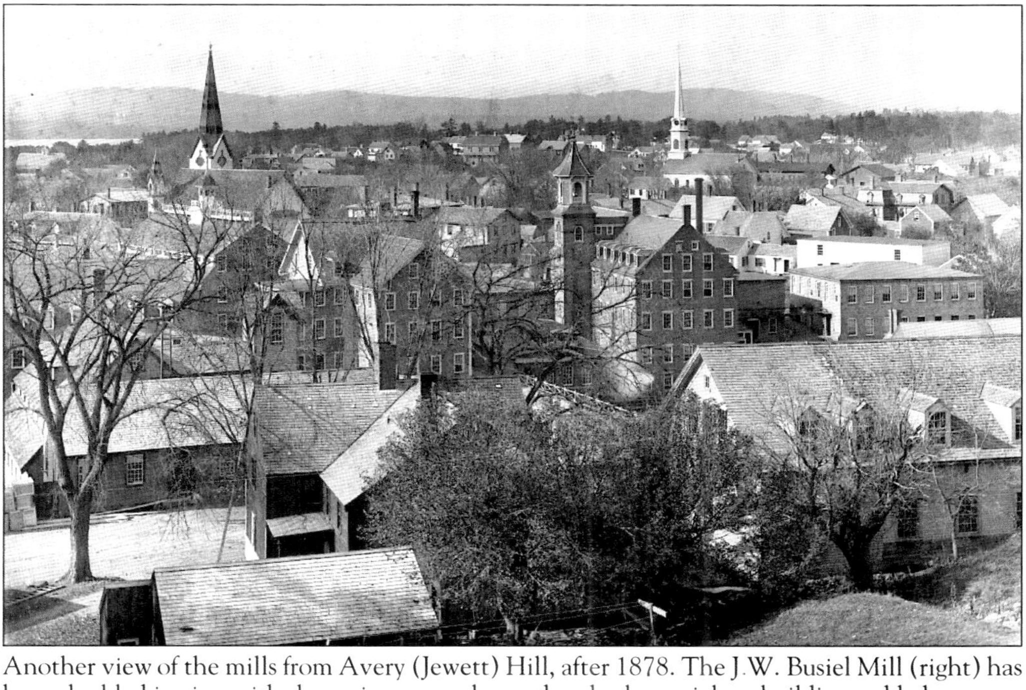

Another view of the mills from Avery (Jewett) Hill, after 1878. The J.W. Busiel Mill (right) has been doubled in size, with the stair tower relocated and substantial outbuildings added.

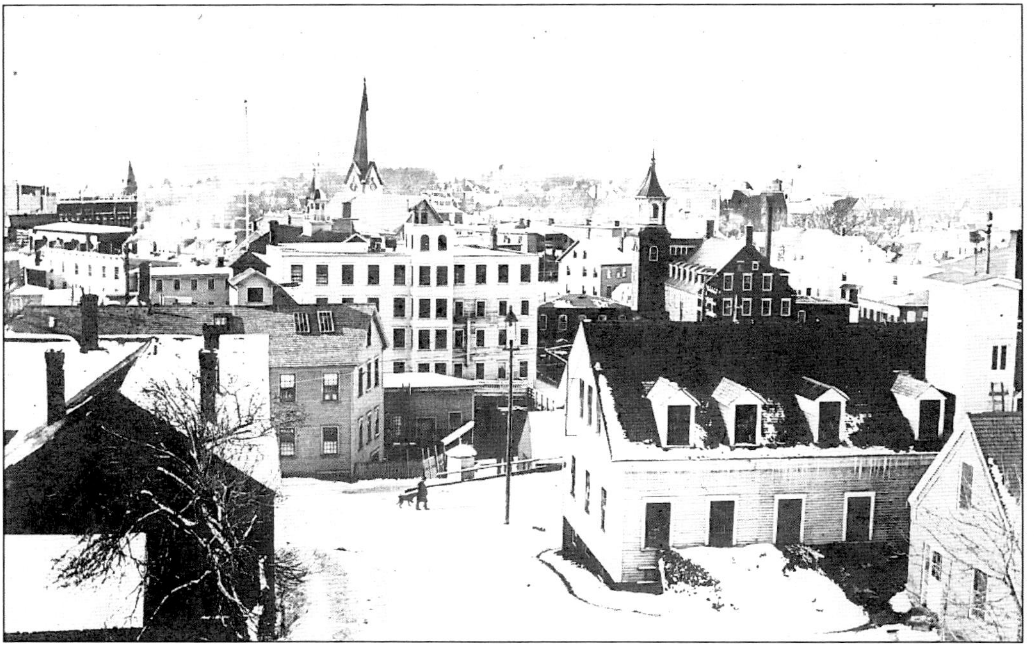

A 1906 view of the mill buildings. Across the river, the Esty Mill (the former Lewis F. Busiel Mill) has been considerably enlarged, eliminating the gables.

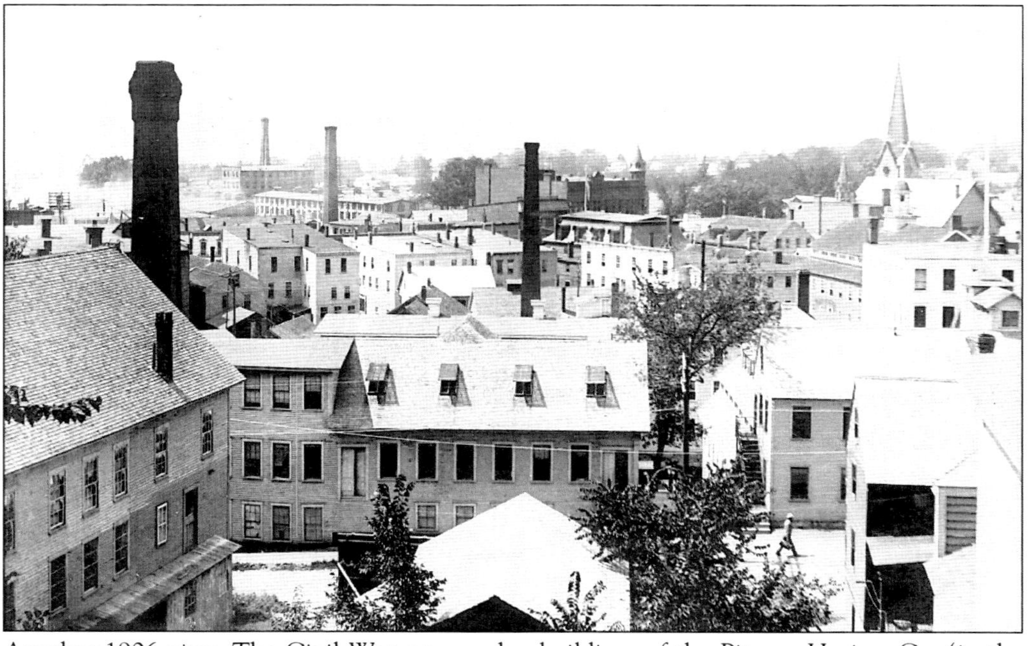

Another 1906 view. The Civil War-era wooden buildings of the Pitman Hosiery Co. (in the near center) were demolished in the early 1940s, but the building to the right of them, fronting on Union Avenue, remains today. The building at the near left, taken over by Laconia Needle Co. in 1907, is now J.H. Valliere Plumbing & Heating. The rooming house at the near right has been demolished.

# *Four*

# Main Street to Bank Square

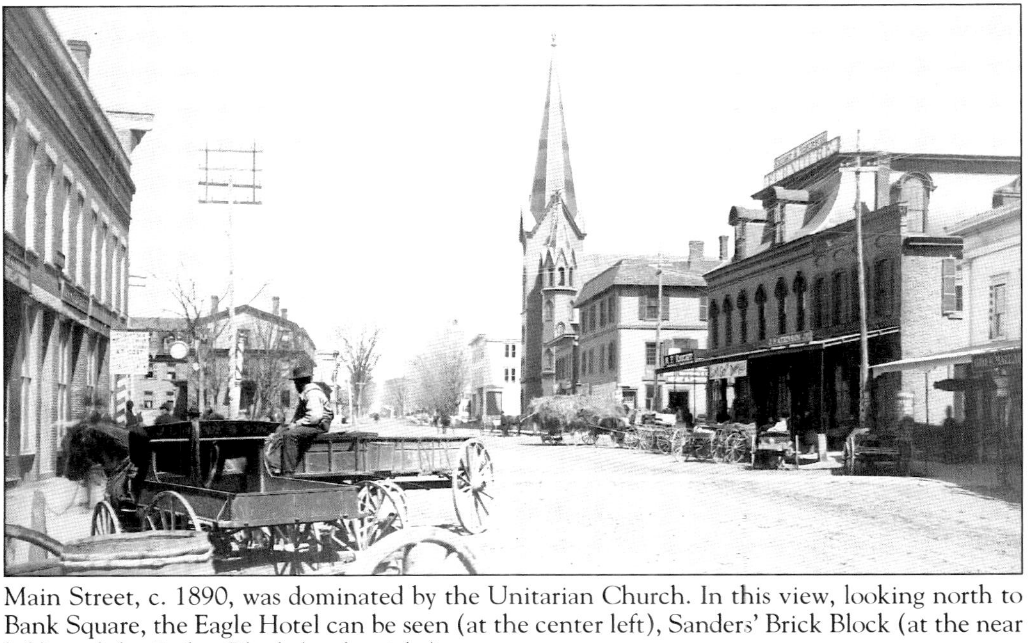

Main Street, c. 1890, was dominated by the Unitarian Church. In this view, looking north to Bank Square, the Eagle Hotel can be seen (at the center left), Sanders' Brick Block (at the near left), and the Parker Block (at the right).

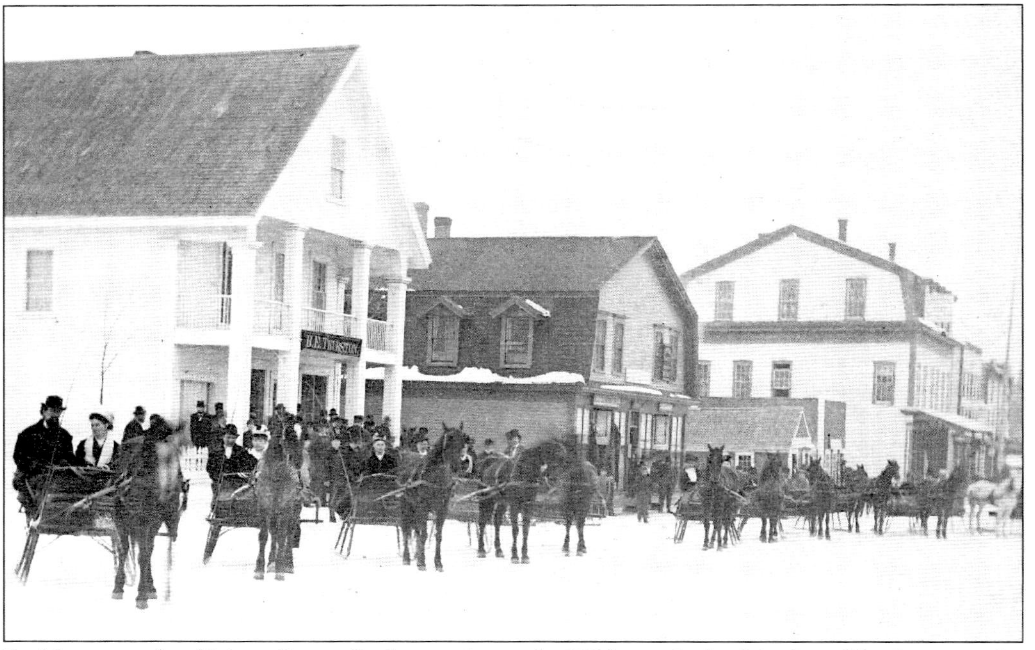

Buildings south of Main Street Bridge in the early 1880s, with the Moulton Block across the river on the right. This photograph was taken from the Main Street-Union Avenue-Court Street intersection, looking north. The middle building was later moved to Mill Street when the Smith Block (later the Tilton Block) was built here in 1886. The building on the left later became Harry Sanborn's grocery store and then Laflamme's Bakery. The site is now occupied by the Landmark Inn.

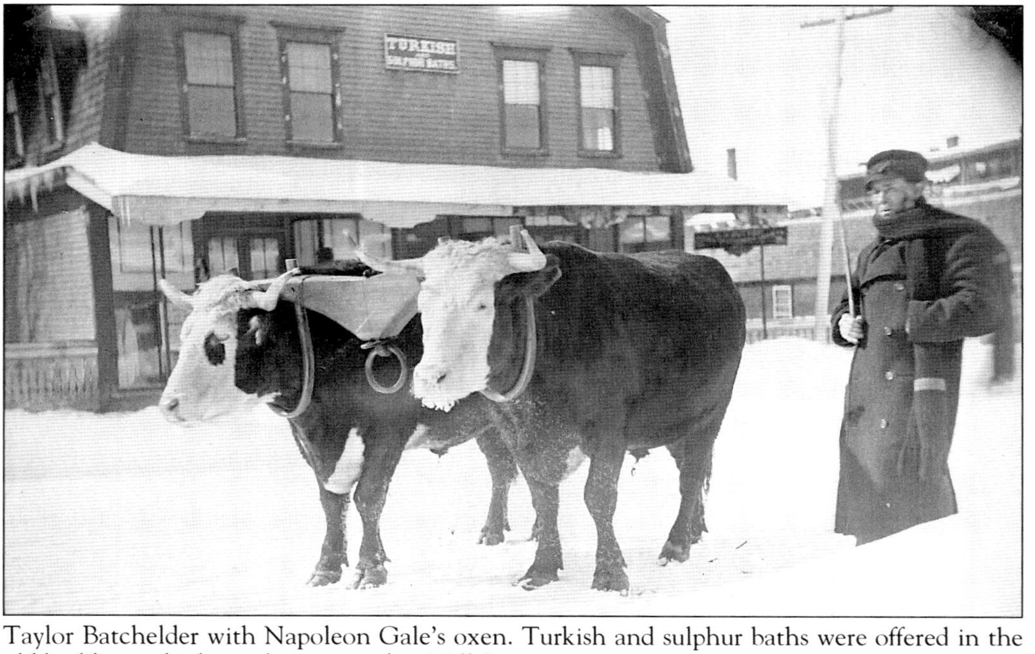


Taylor Batchelder with Napoleon Gale's oxen. Turkish and sulphur baths were offered in the old building, which was later moved to Mill Street.

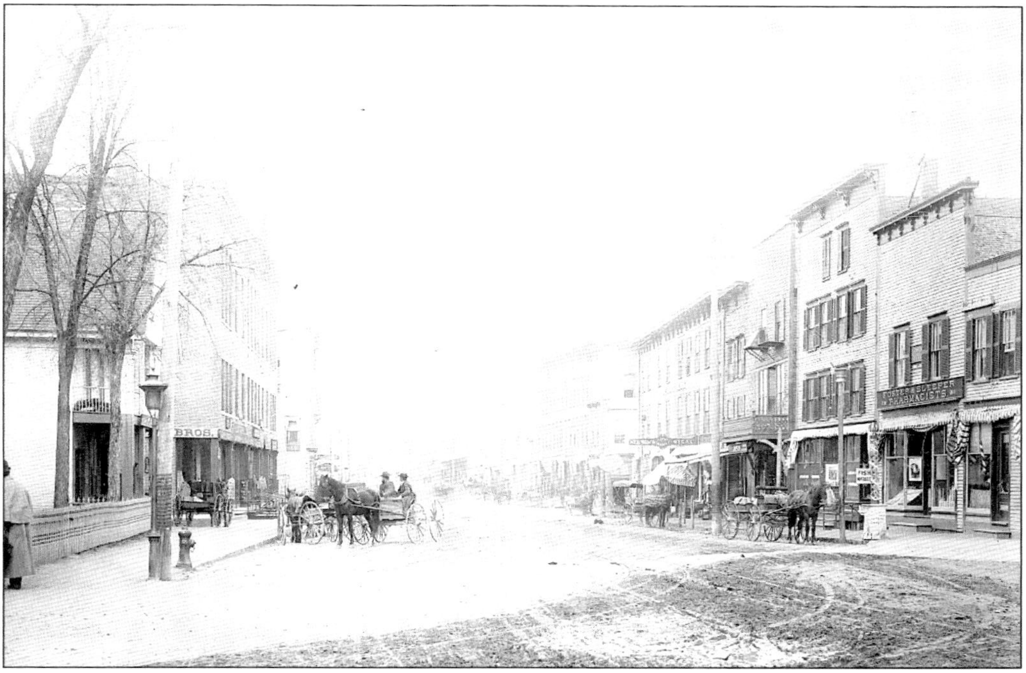

Main Street, looking north to Bank Square in the late 1880s or early 1890s. The Smith Block (on the left) was occupied for decades by the Lougee Bros. department store (later the Oscar A. Lougee Co.).

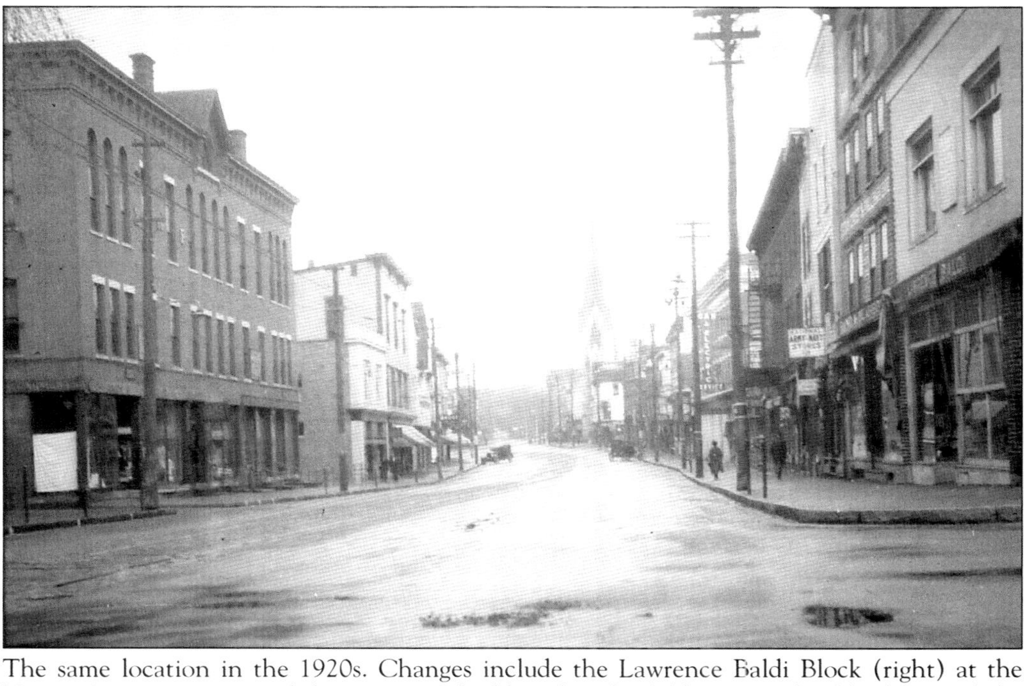

The same location in the 1920s. Changes include the Lawrence Baldi Block (right) at the Union Avenue corner and the two-story building (on the left) just north of bridge. And the automobile has replaced the horse.

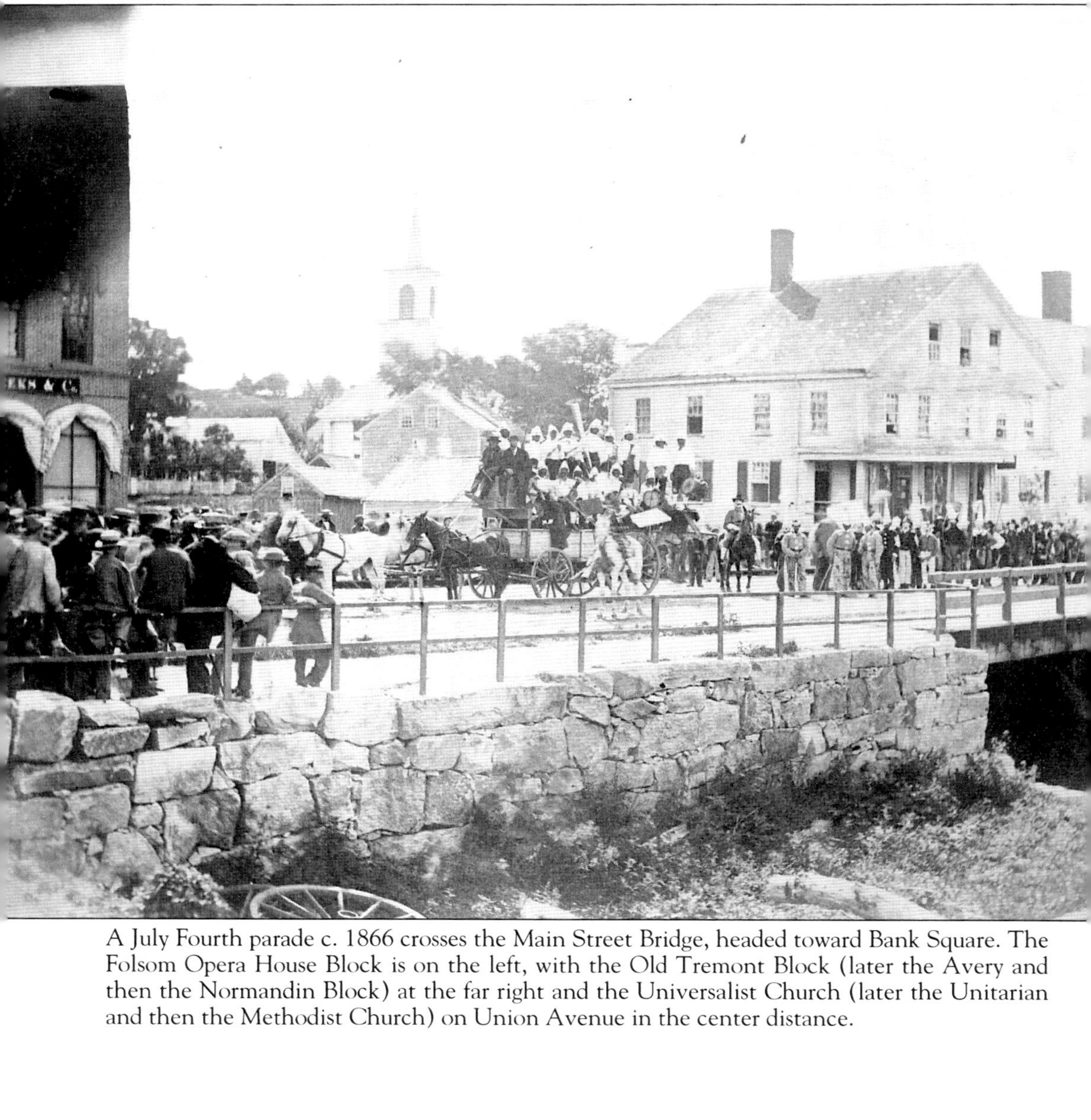

A July Fourth parade c. 1866 crosses the Main Street Bridge, headed toward Bank Square. The Folsom Opera House Block is on the left, with the Old Tremont Block (later the Avery and then the Normandin Block) at the far right and the Universalist Church (later the Unitarian and then the Methodist Church) on Union Avenue in the center distance.

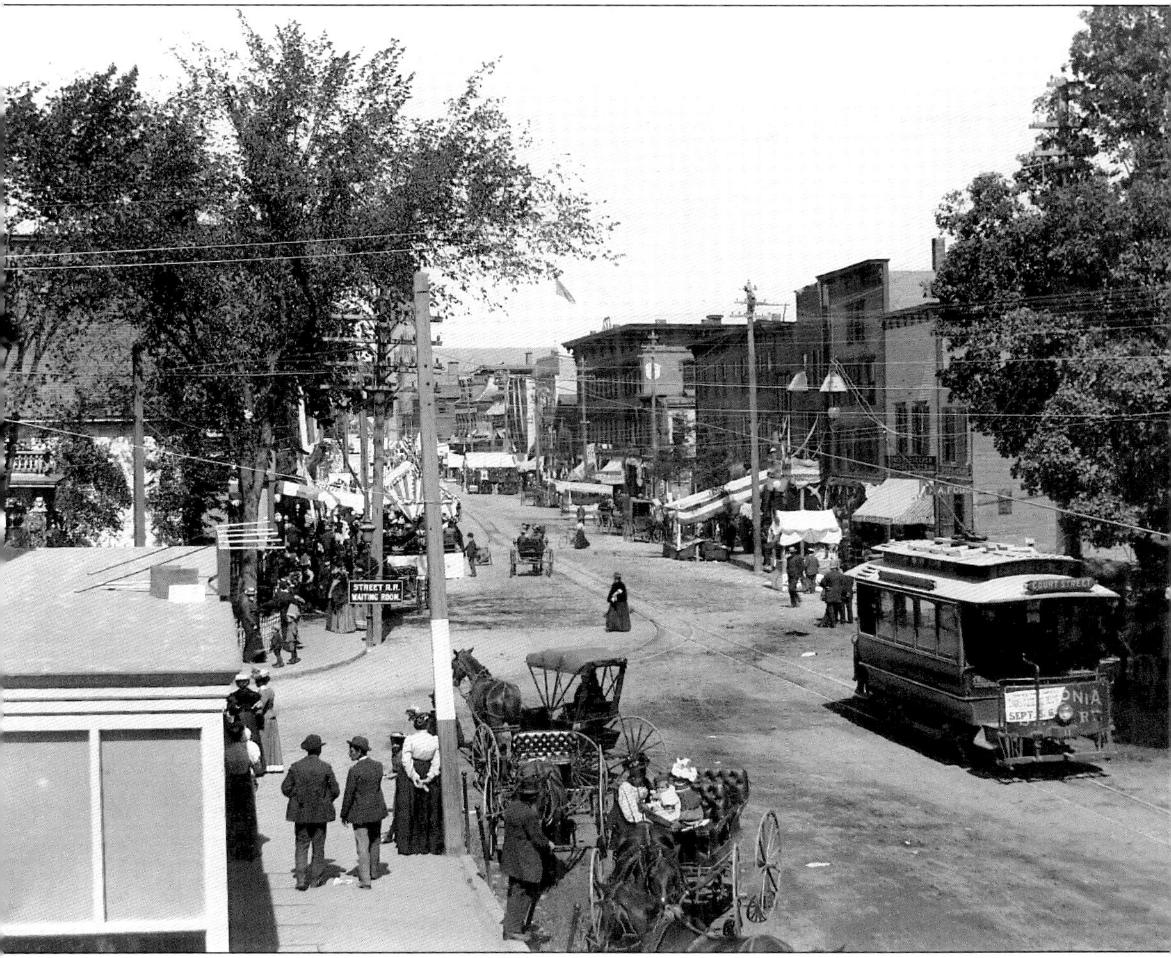


The bustling Main Street-Union Avenue-Court Street intersection, c. 1900. The narrow-gauge trolley car heads down South Main Street (despite its "Court Street" sign). The building at the near left is John Parker Smith's Old Corner Store.

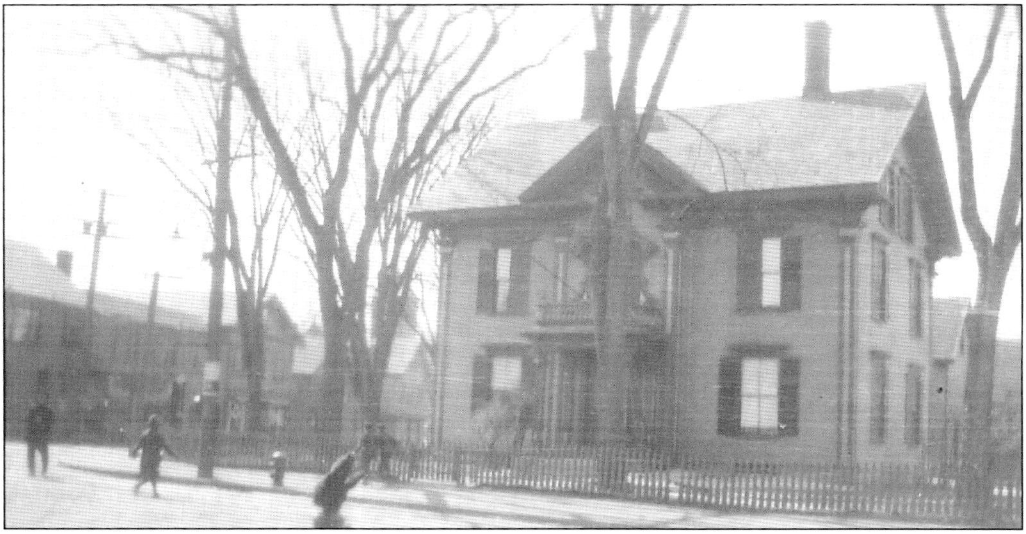

The General Knight House at the corner of Main Street and Union Avenue, in the late 1920s. Actually, the imposing residence was built by Daniel A. Tilton on the site of the former home of early local physician, Dr. Zadock Bowman. The house was moved to Rowe Court in the late 1940s, and it is now the office of the Labbe Oil Co. Its original site is currently part of the parking lot for the Landmark Inn.

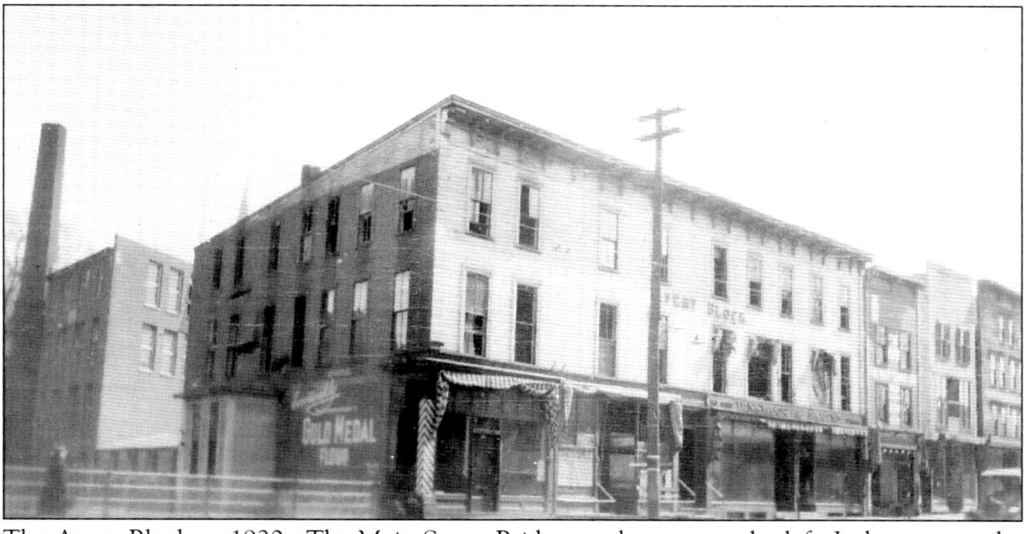


The Avery Block, c. 1920s. The Main Street Bridge can be seen on the left. In later years, the Avery Block was known as the Normandin Block. All of these buildings were razed during Urban Renewal to create Stewart Park.

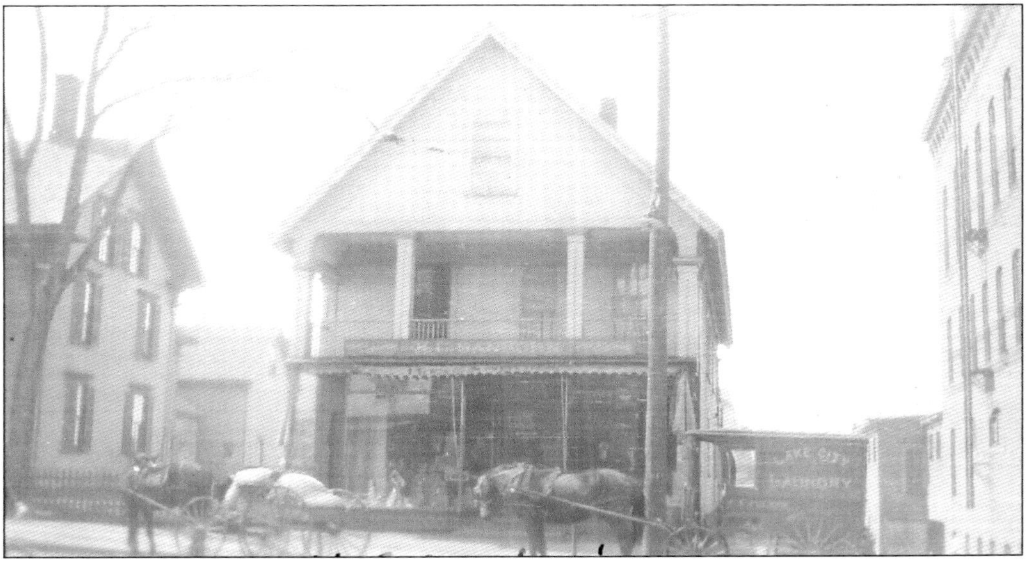

Harry Sanborn's market, c. 1920s. The General Knight House is on the left with the Smith Block (later, the Tilton Block) on the right. From the late 1940s to the late 1960s, the Sanborn building was occupied by Laflamme's Bakery.

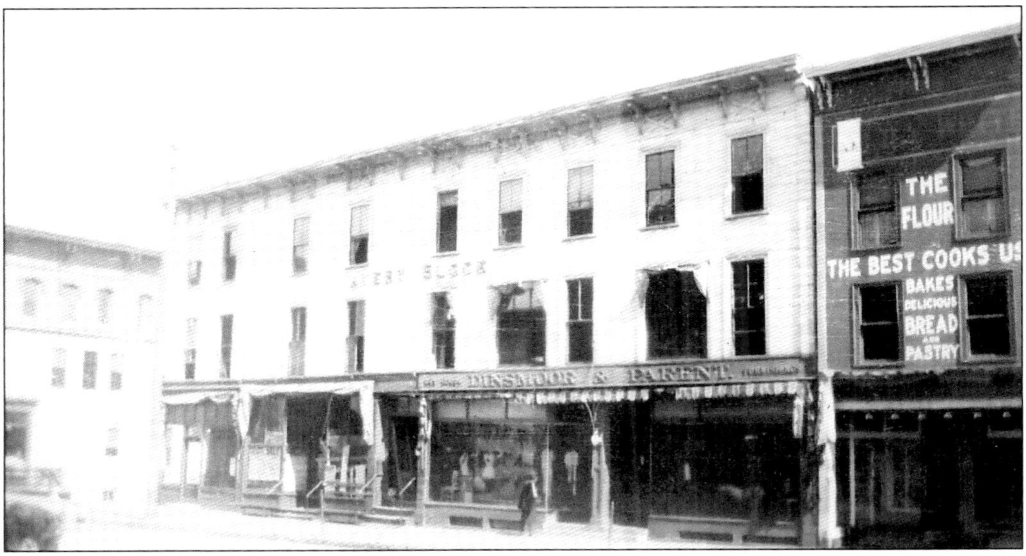


Another c. 1920s view of the Avery Block.

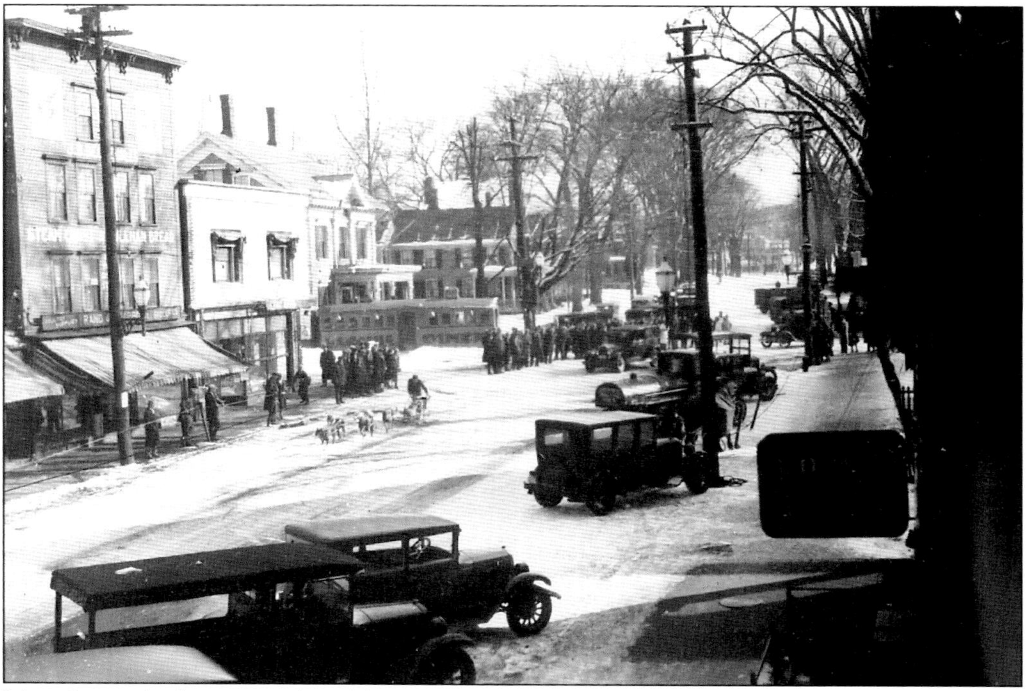

Main Street, looking toward "Baldi's Corner" (center left) in the 1920s. An early diner occupies the southeastern Union Avenue corner before the Bessie Clow House was moved back.

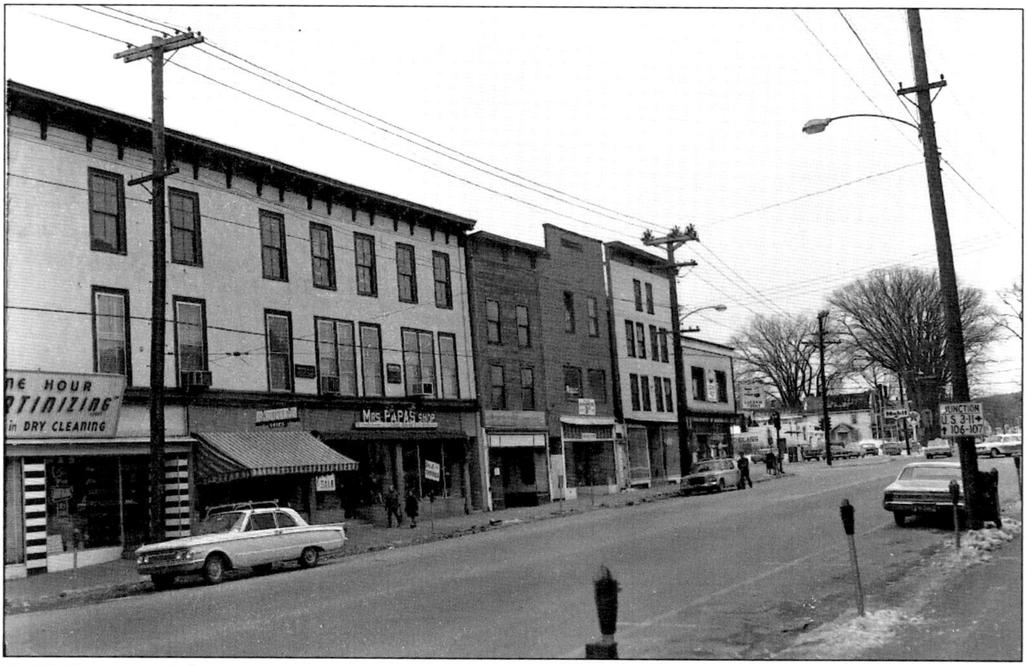


A 1960s view of the same area, now part of Stewart Park. Laconia Fruit Co., the last occupant of "Baldi's Corner," closed its doors at Christmas in 1966, on the eve of Urban Renewal.

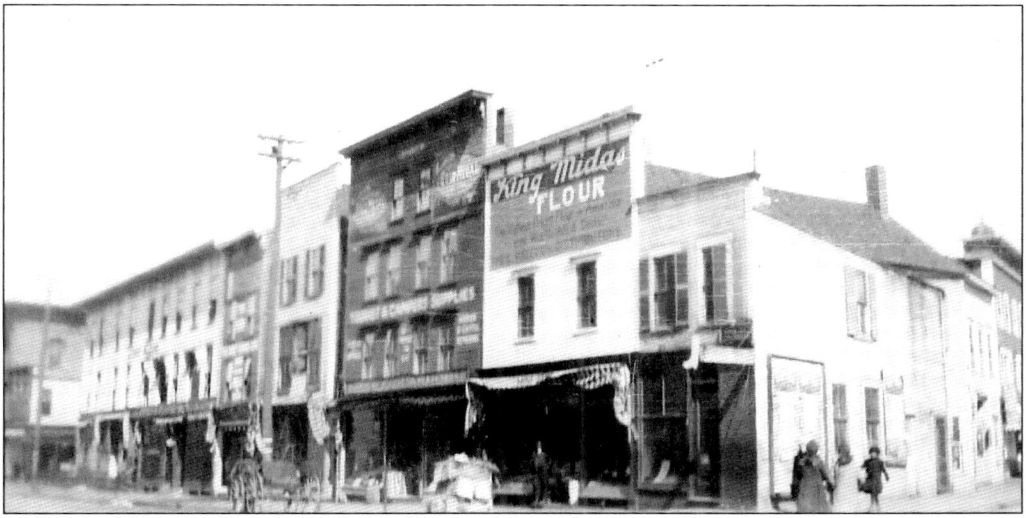


Another view of the Main Street-Union Avenue corner in the 1920s, as seen from South Main Street.

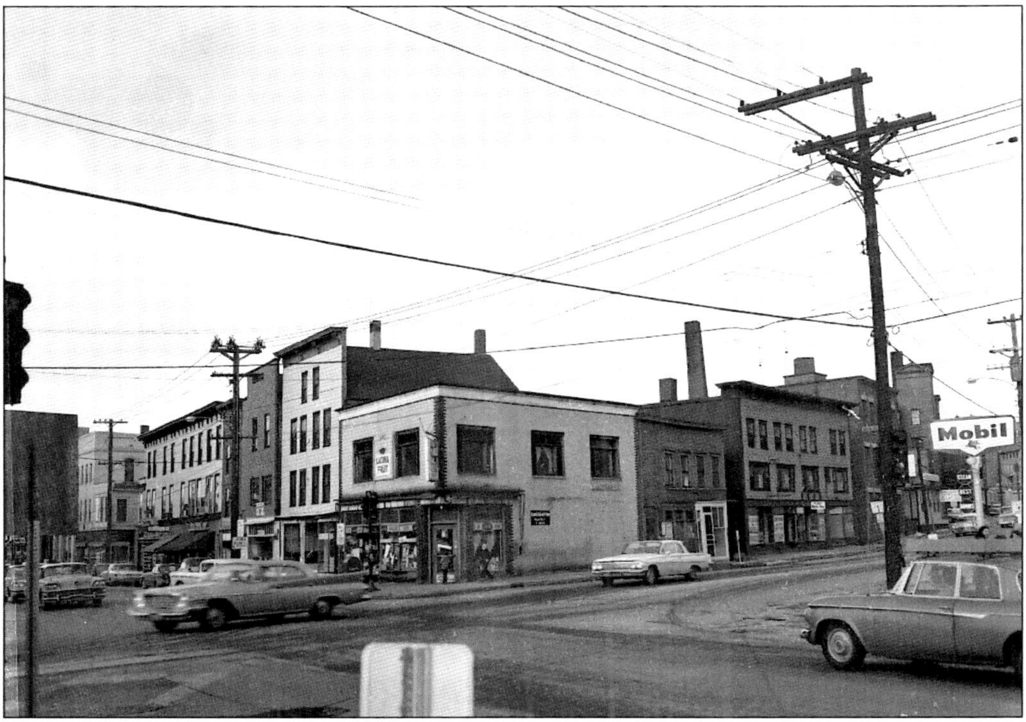


The same corner in the 1960s.

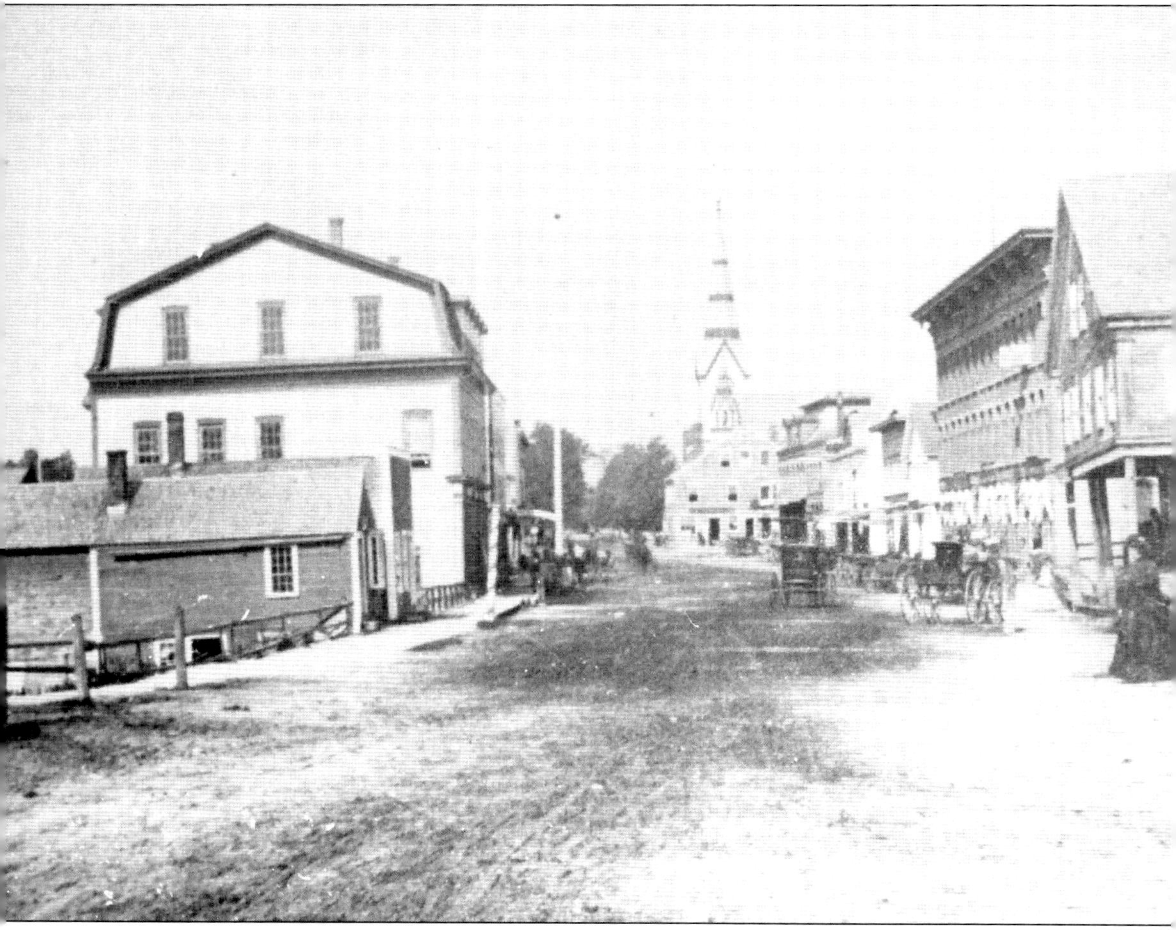

Main Street, looking north, in the 1870s.

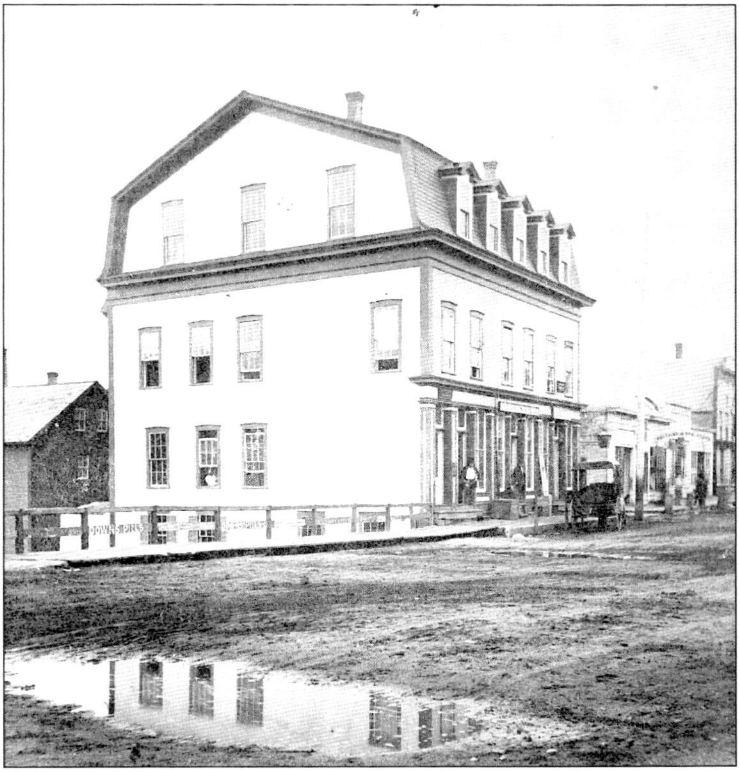

Moulton's Block, just north of the Main Street Bridge, c. 1870. This was the building erected after the Great Fire of 1860, replacing those north of the river in the photograph on p. 25.

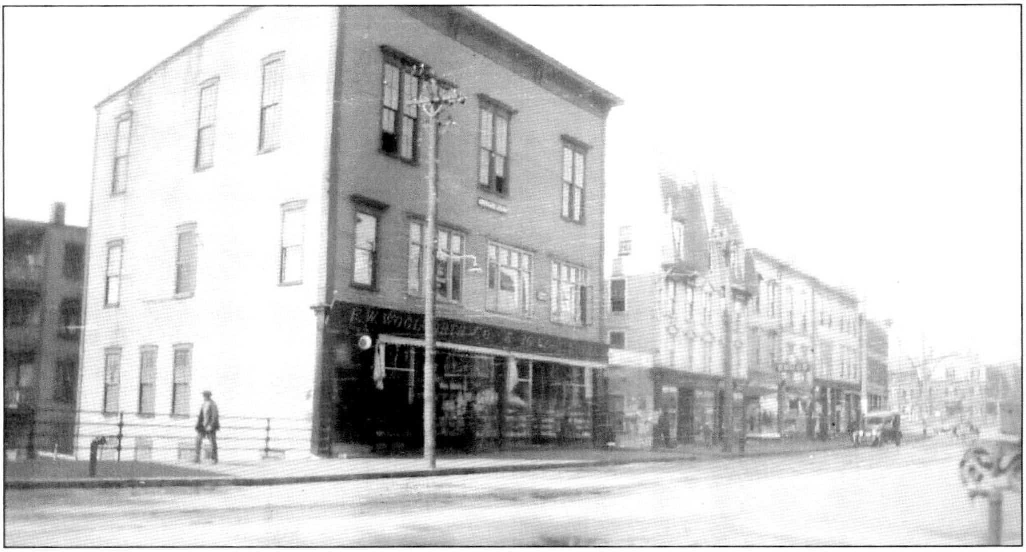

The same building, considerably remodeled, c. 1920. When the F.W. Woolworth Co. came to Laconia, this was its first location. In later years, the structure was known as the Wein Block.

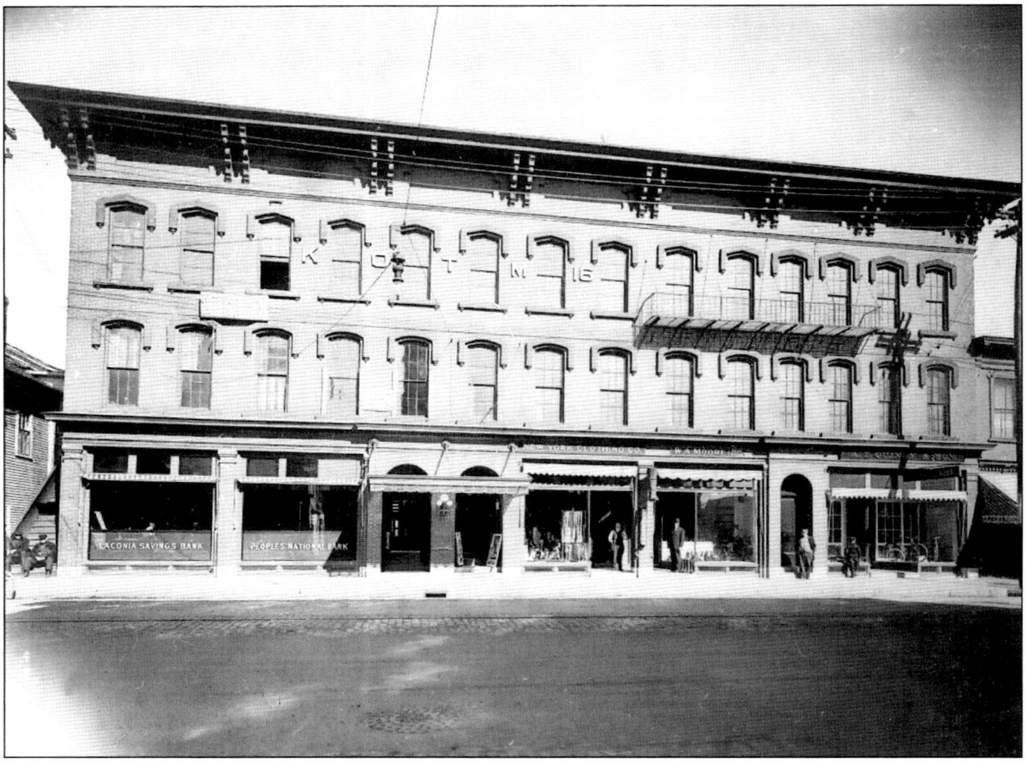


An early view of the Folsom Opera House Block, built in 1861. Among the ground-floor tenants were the Laconia Savings Bank and Peoples National Bank.

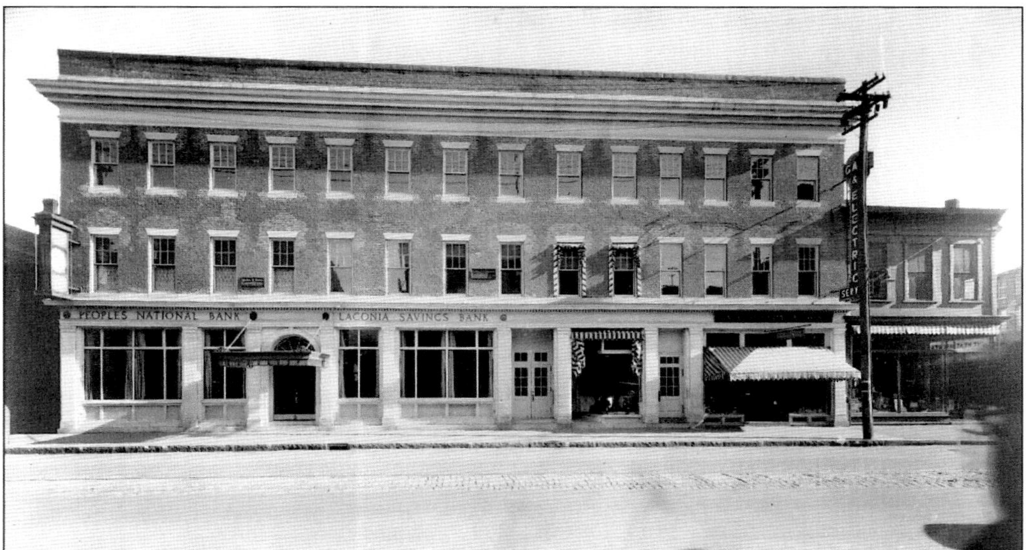


The "Lower Bank" building after remodeling, with the addition of its signature "chime clock" on the left. The Laconia Gas & Electric Co. occupied the addition at the right, next to the river.

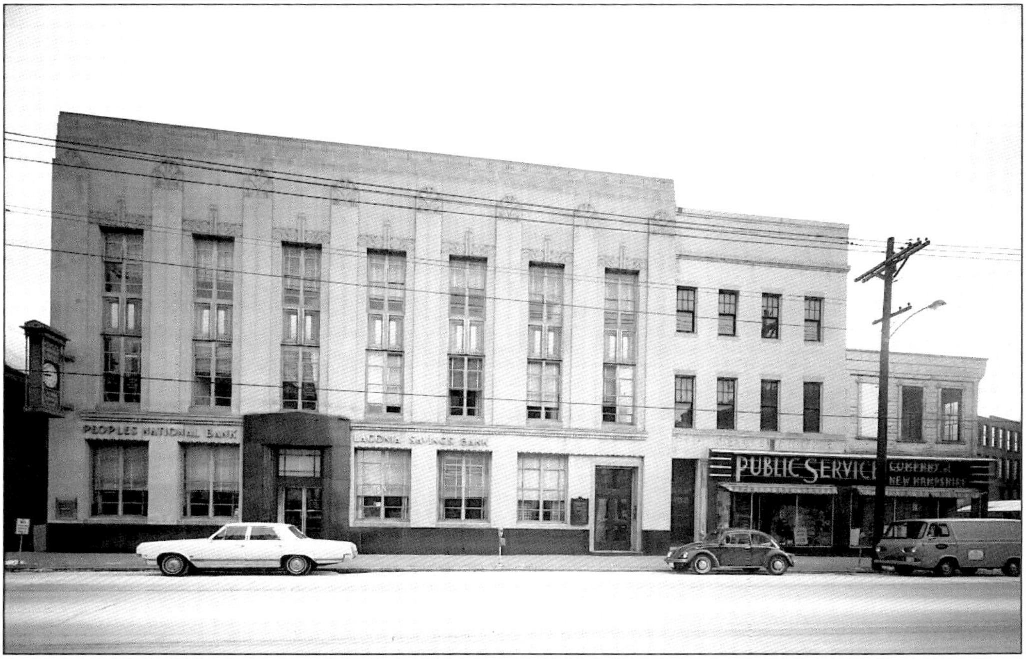


Another view of the "Lower Bank" building, after remodeling and the installation of a granite facing in 1939.

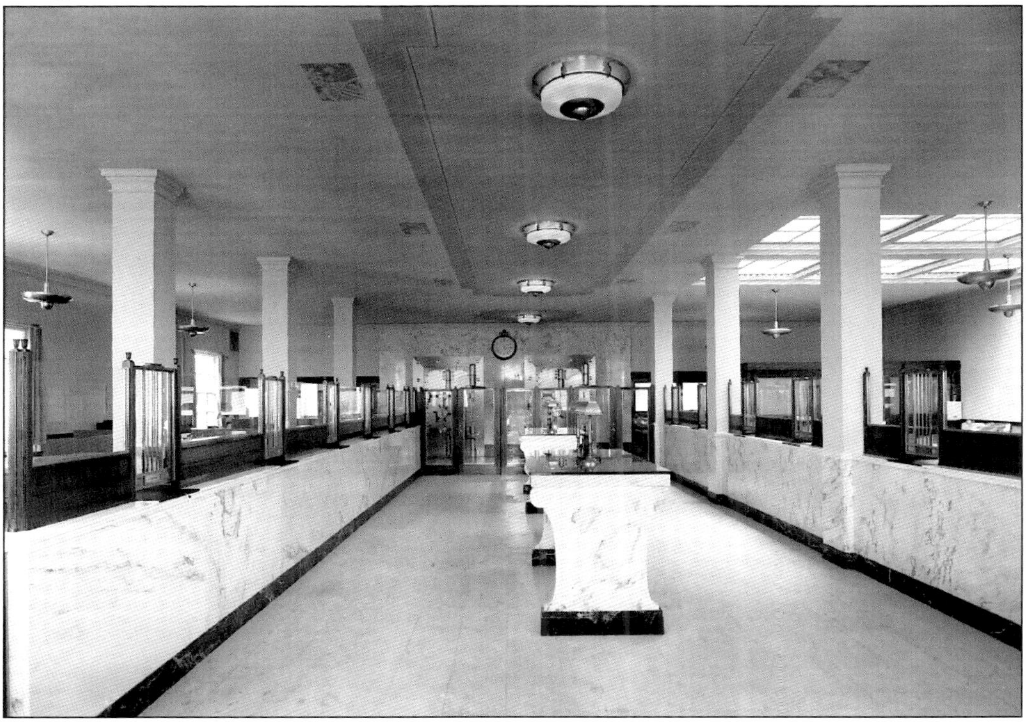

The interior of the remodeled bank building. Peoples National was located on the left and Laconia Savings was located on the right.

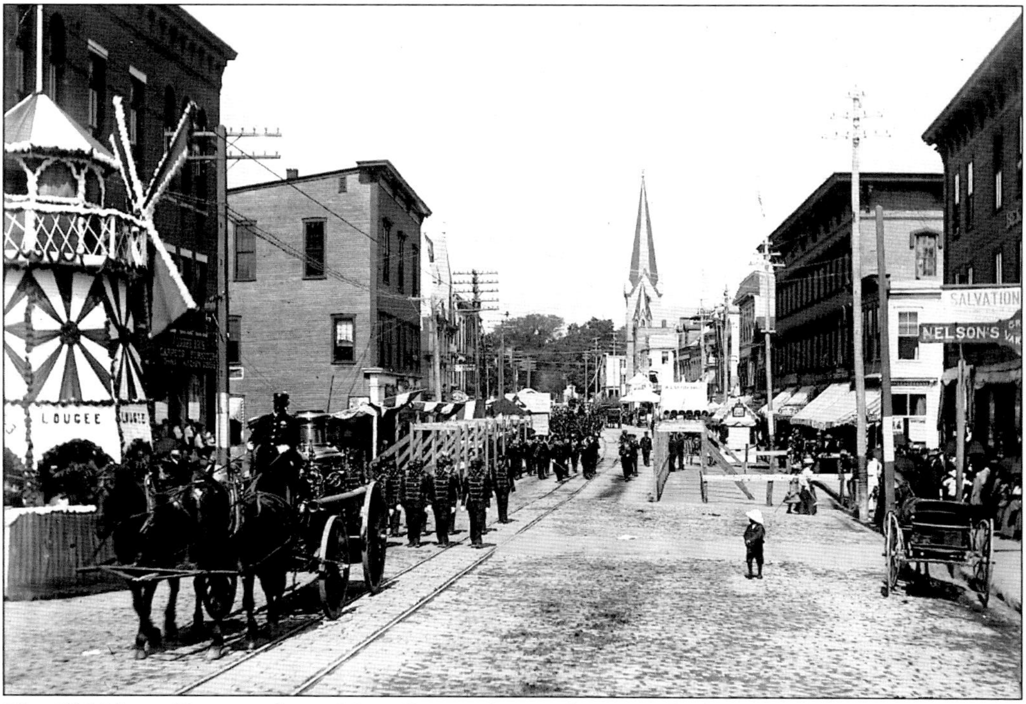


The Old Home Day parade on Main Street, August 31, 1901, looking north. By this time, mud had been replaced by cobblestones, though trolley cars still ran on narrow-gauge tracks.

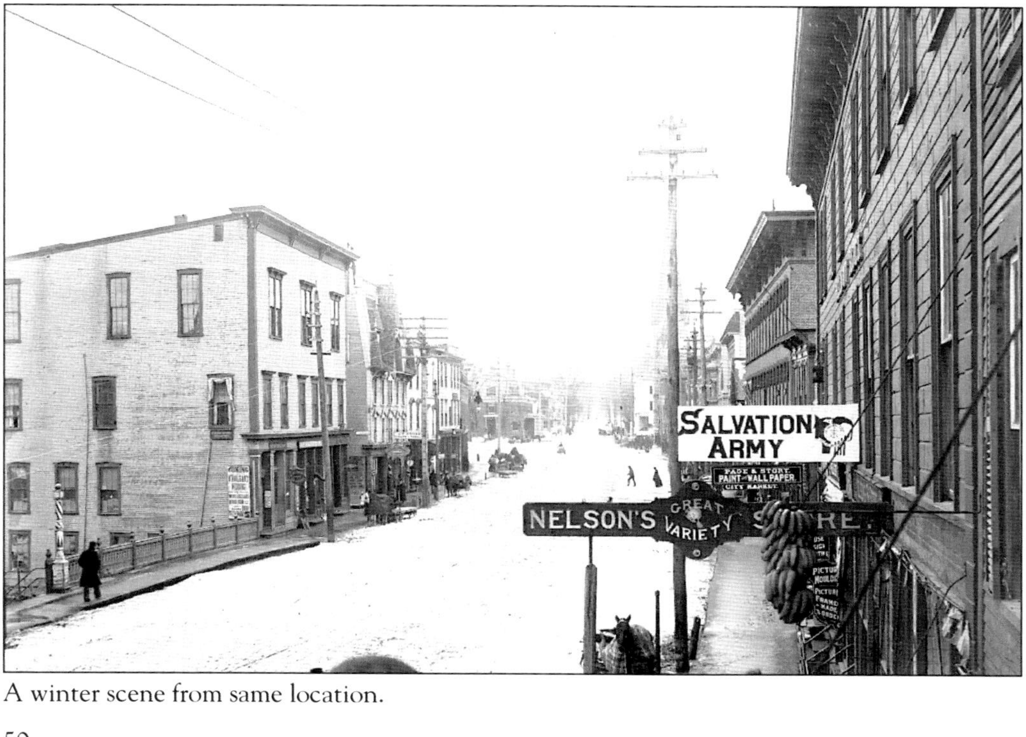


A winter scene from same location.

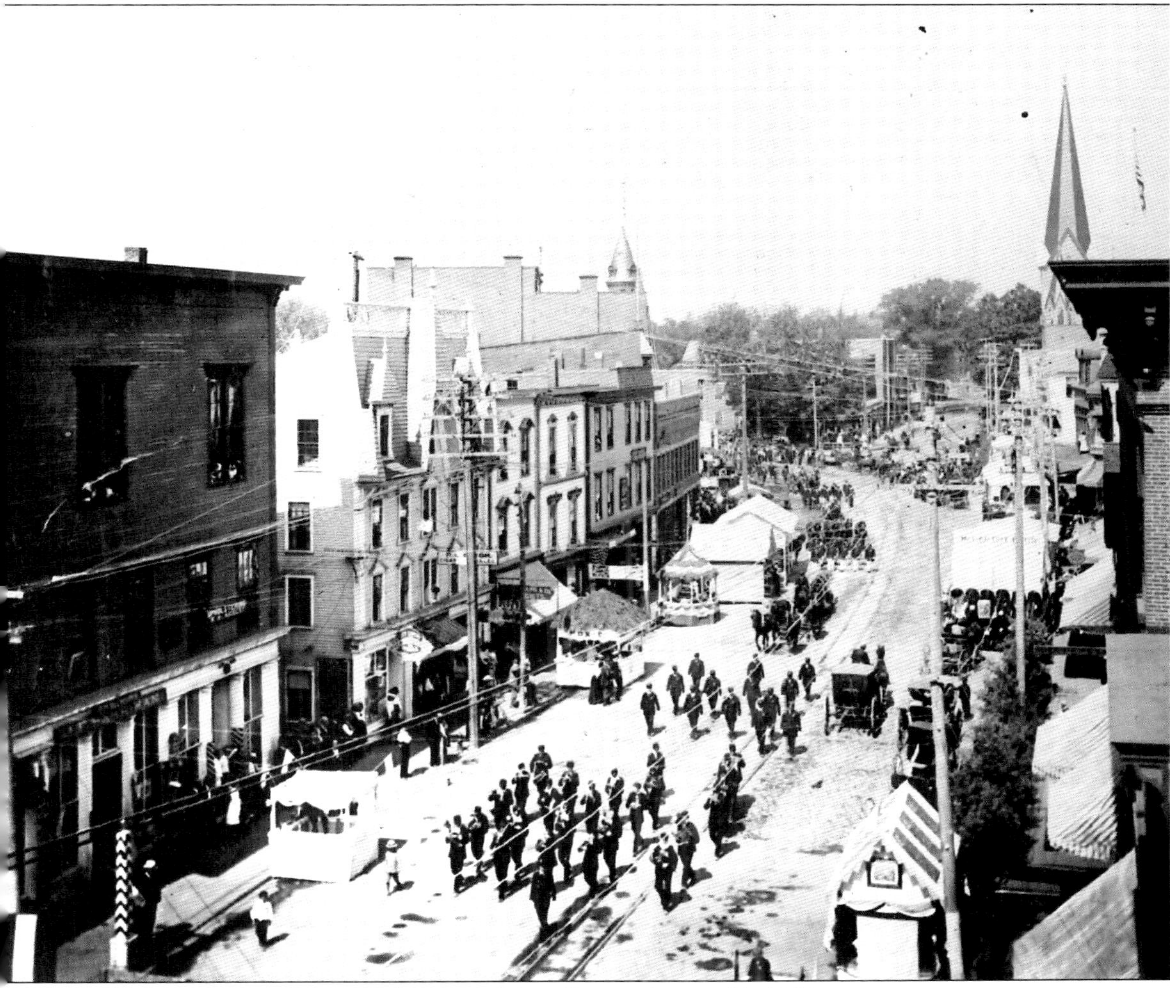

The Old Home Day parade marches down Main Street, August 31, 1901.

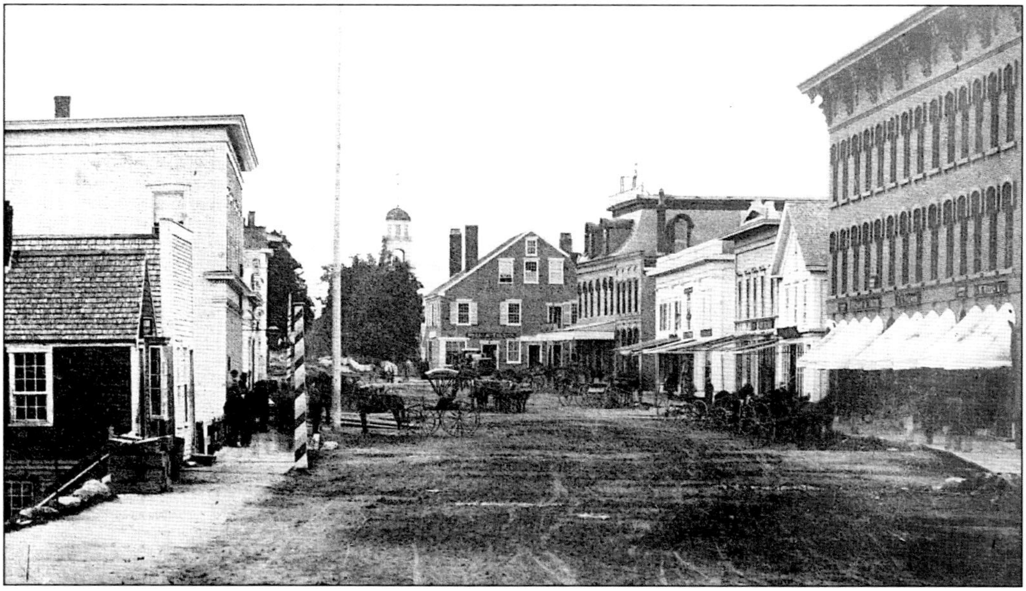

Main Street, c. 1860s. The Old North Church (Congregational) still has its "pepper-box" steeple and the building at the intersection with Mill Street (center right) still extends into Main Street. This photograph was taken from the bridge, with the Folsom Opera House on the right.

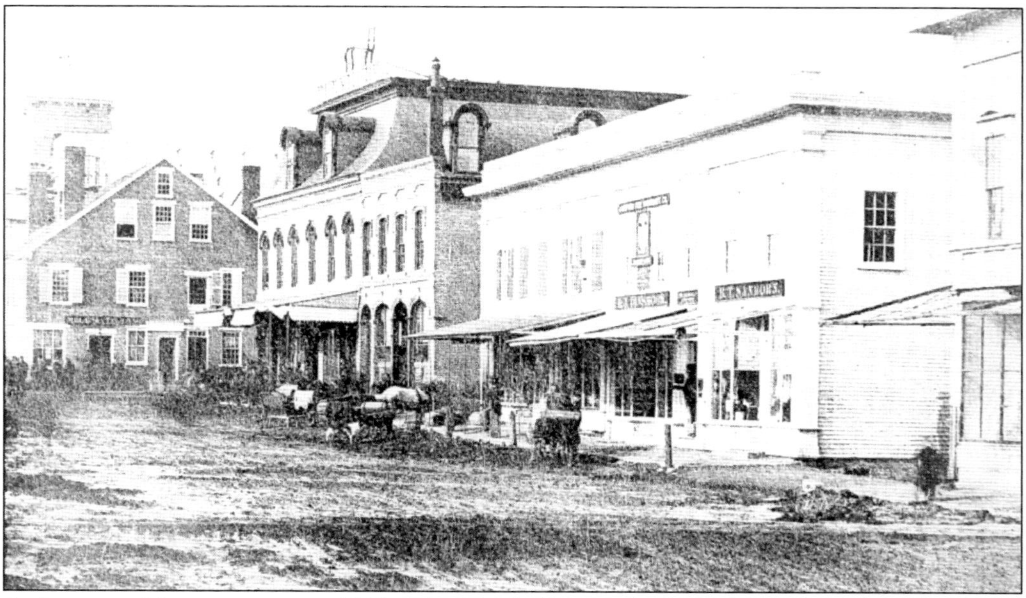

A close-up of the same area, c. 1860s. The Mitchell & Mallard Block (on the right) would later be expanded to true Victorian splendor.

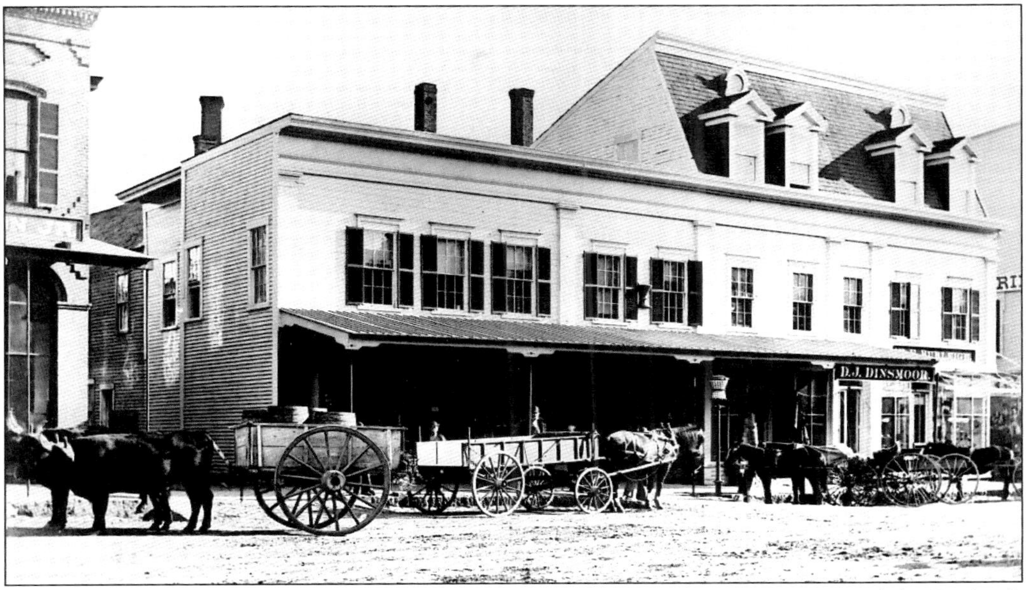


The Mitchell & Mallard Block, c. 1861. Other occupants were D.J. Dinsmoor and the Burleigh store, on the right.

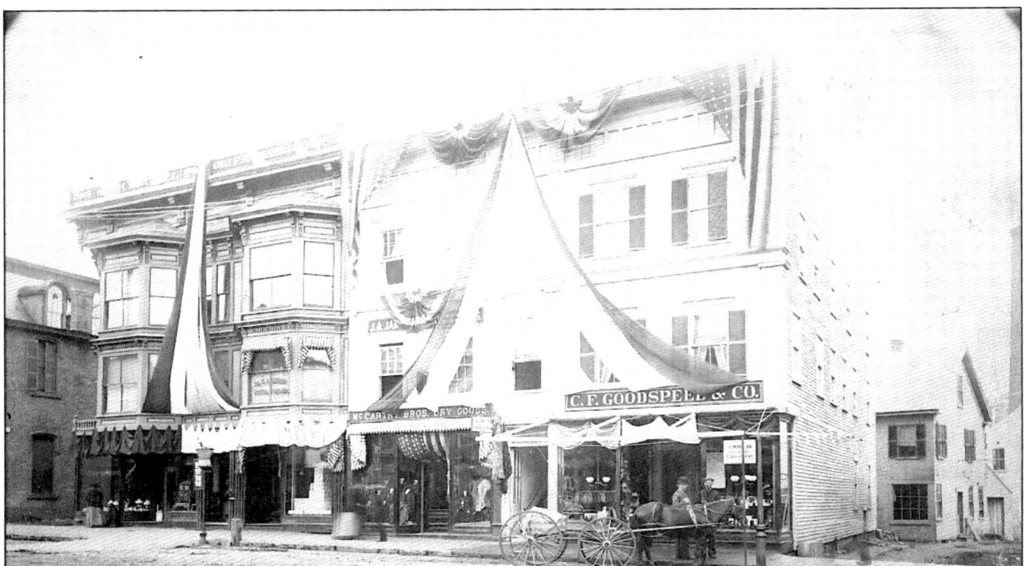


The Mitchell & Mallard Block, c. 1891. By this time the McCarthy Bros. and C.F. Goodspeed & Co. had replaced Dinsmoor and Burleigh.

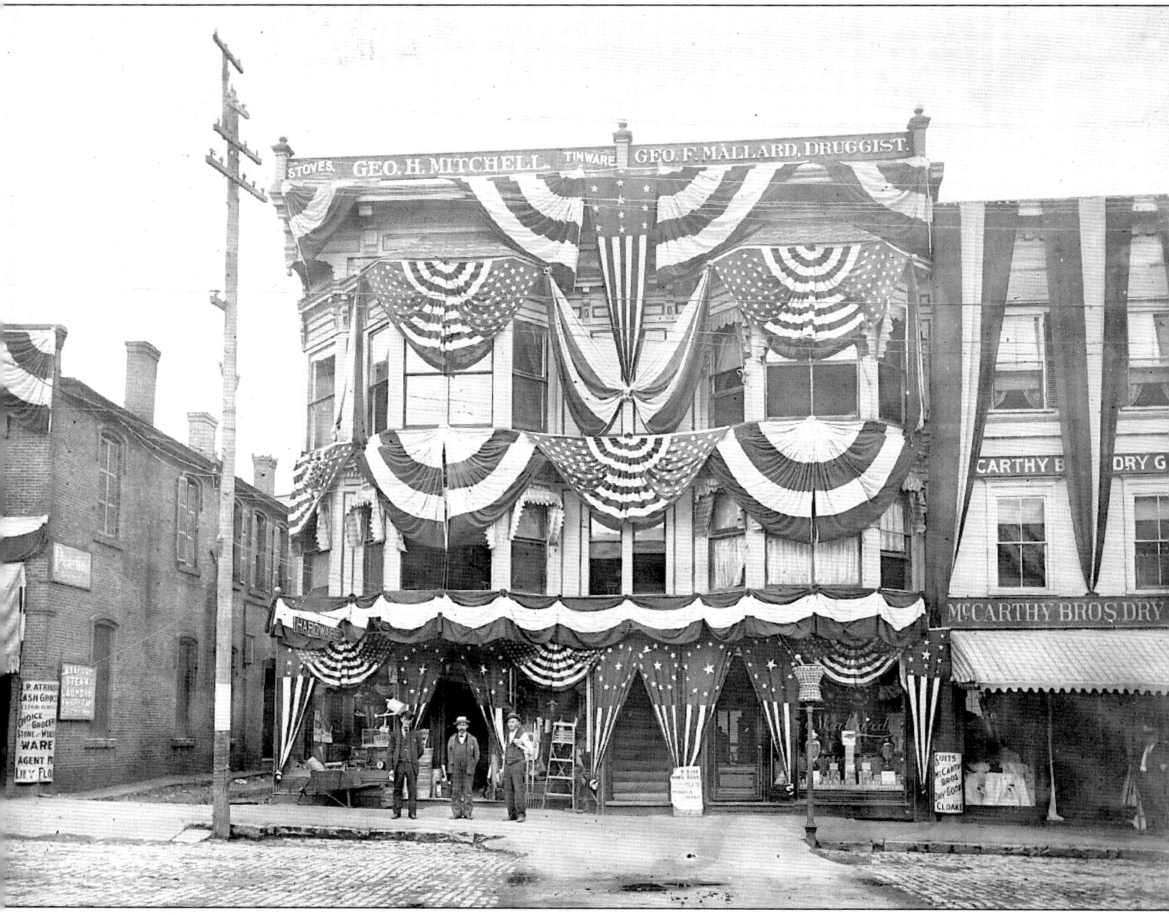

One last view of the Mitchell & Mallard Block, in full patriotic finery, c. 1890s.

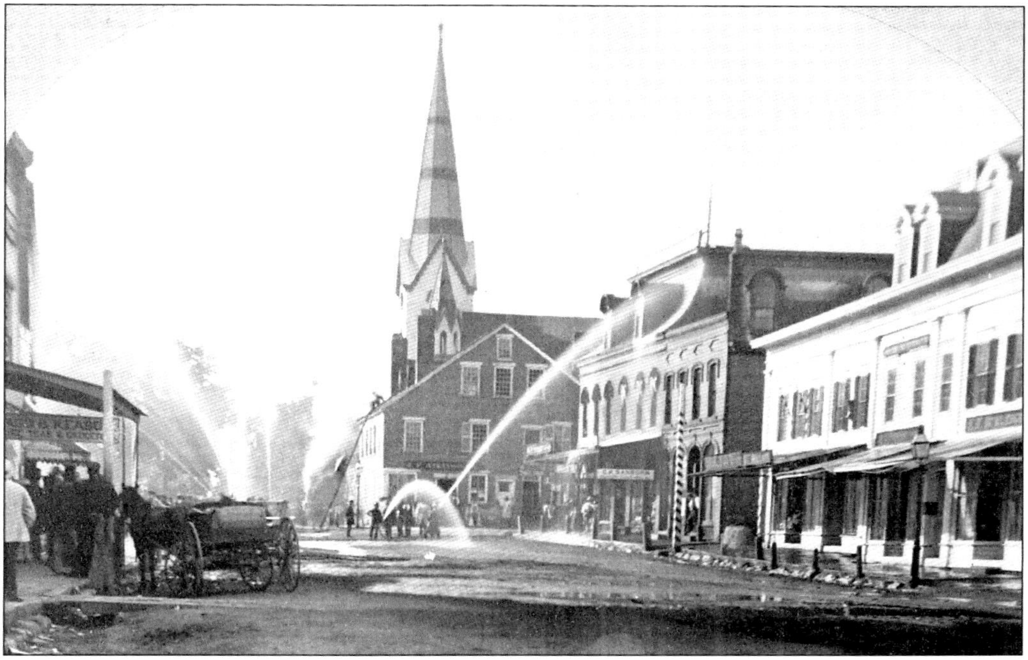

A fireman's hand pump drill and demonstration in Bank Square, c. 1880s.

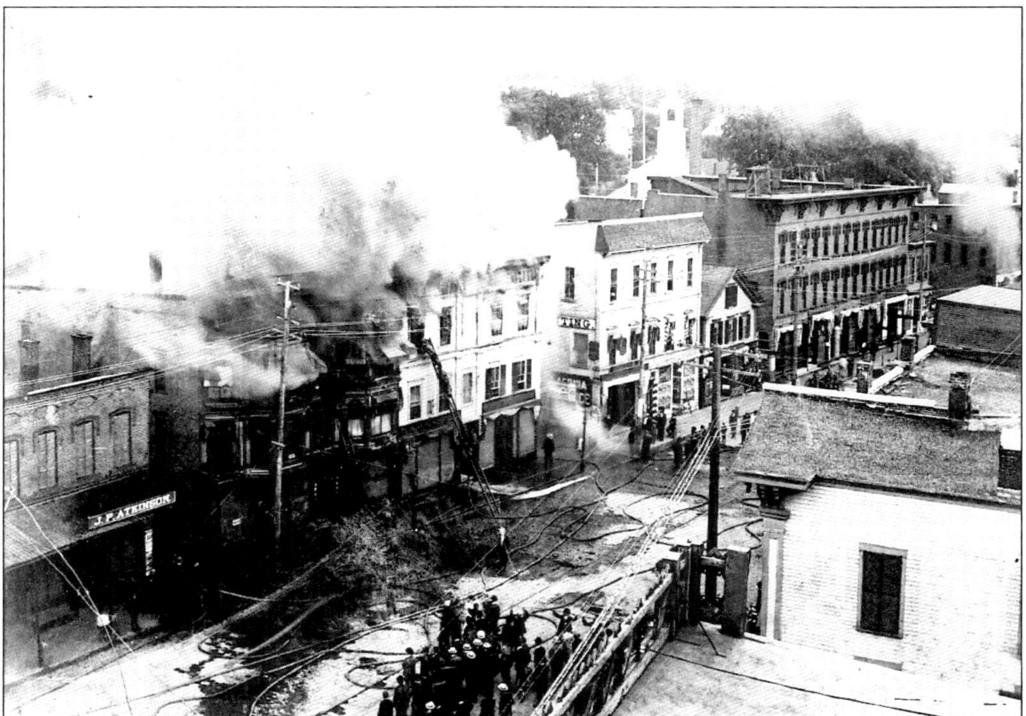


A real fire at the same location in 1904. The Methodist Church, at the corner of Baldwin Street and Union Avenue, can be seen in the distance.

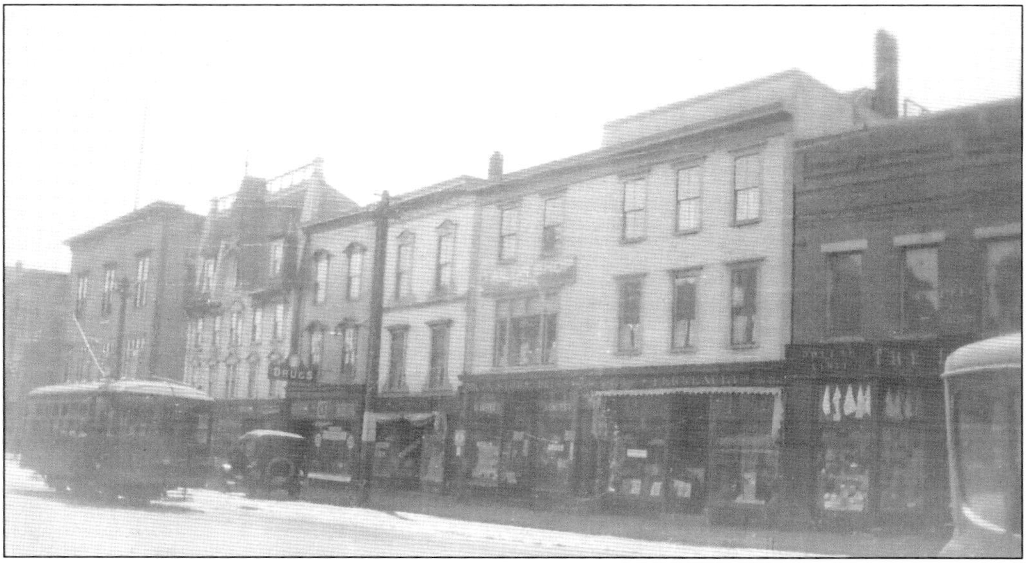


Main Street in the early 1920s. The trolley car heads toward Bank Square, past wooden buildings built in the 1860s, with the Sanders' Brick Block on the right.

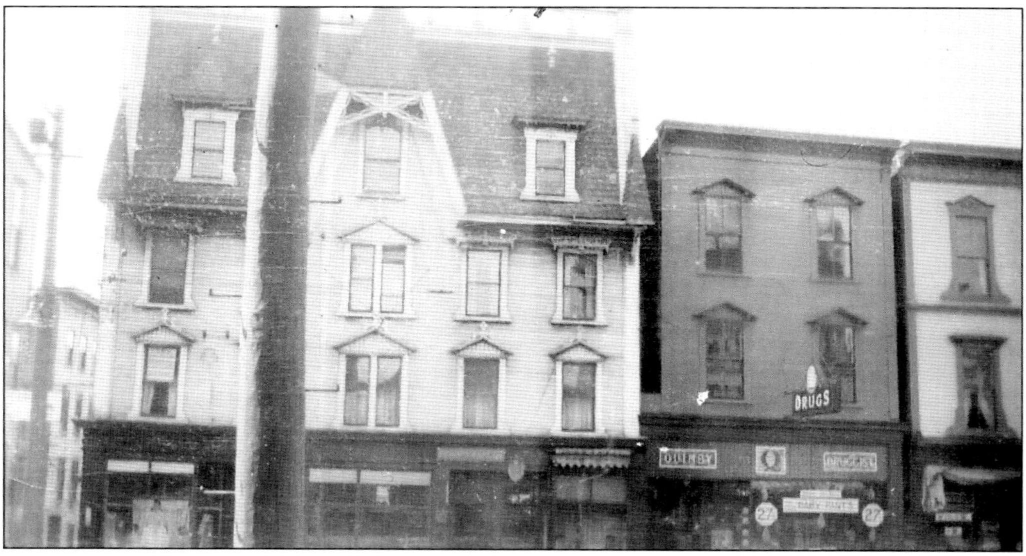


Main Street in the early 1920s. Quimby Drug Store is on the right.

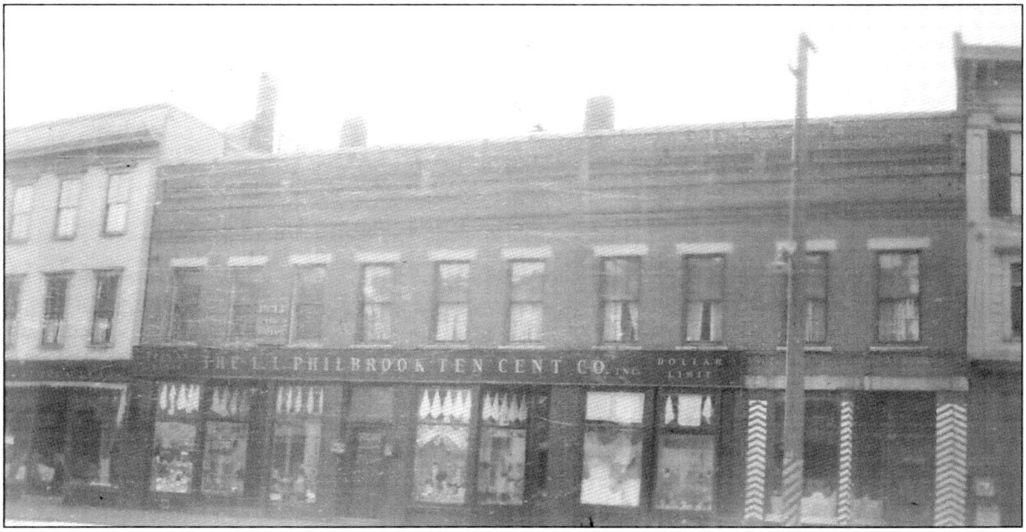


The Sanders' Brick Block in the early 1920s. Here, the merchant is the L.L. Philbroda Ten Cent Co., which was ultimately succeeded by the J.J. Newberry Co.

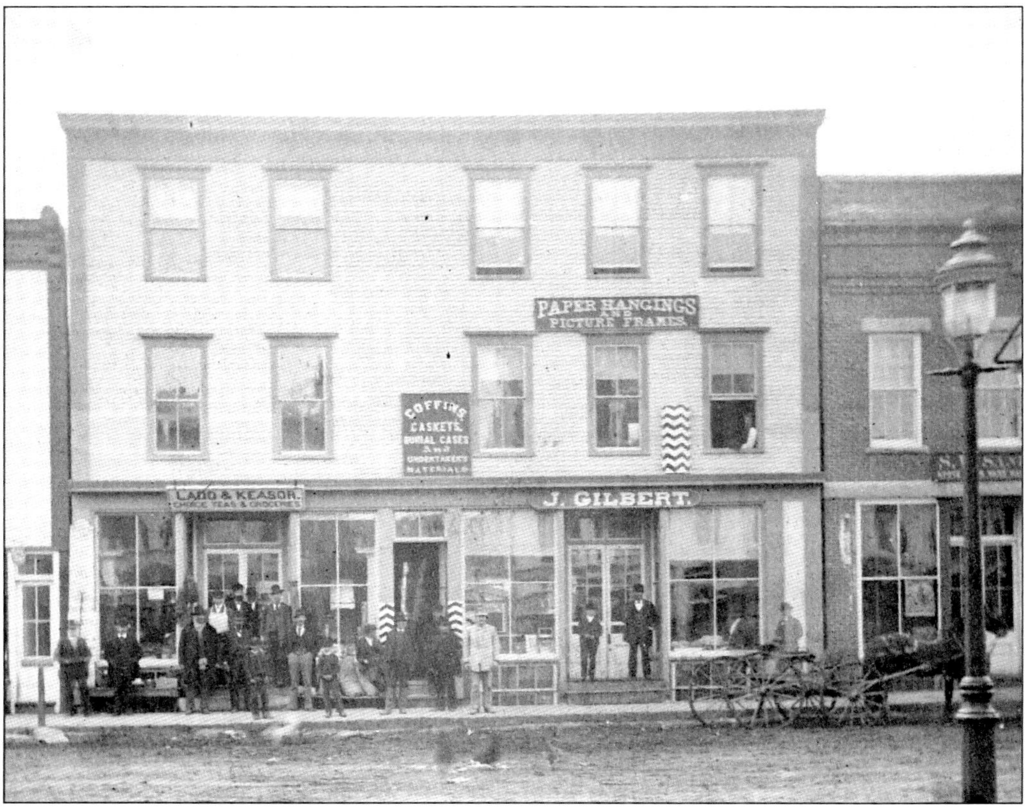


Main Street, c. 1880s, with a gas light on the right. Ladd & Keasor (left) was later replaced by Story's Drug Store. Jefferson Gilbert (next to Sanders' Brick Block) was an undertaker, the early predecessor of today's Wilkinson-Beane.

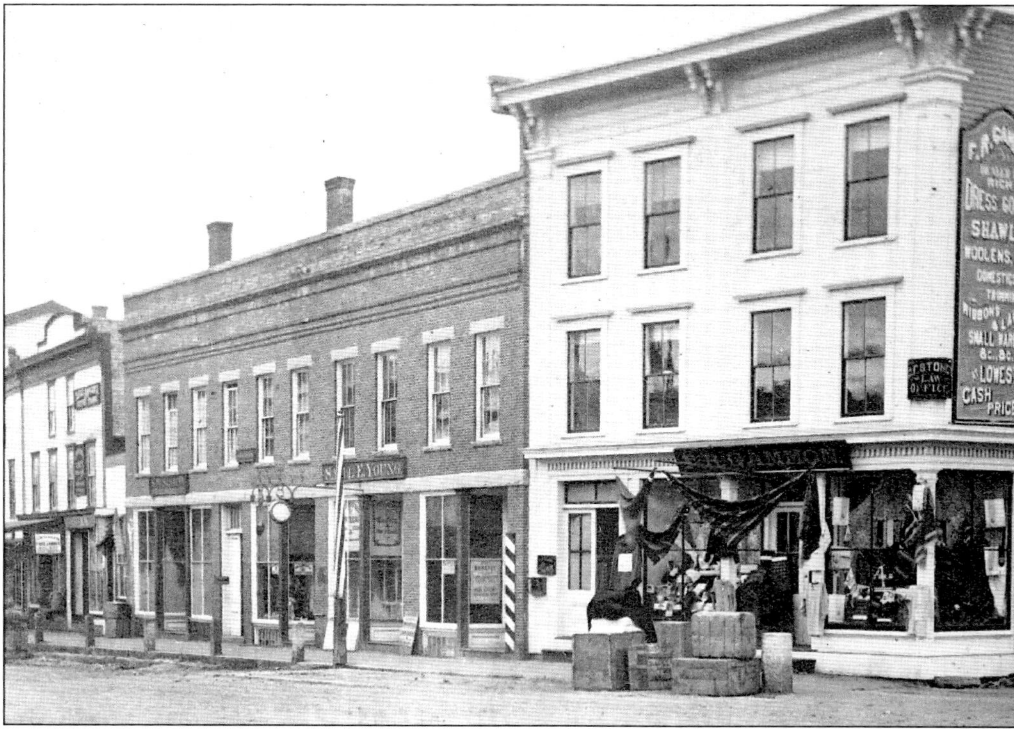


Main Street in the 1880s.

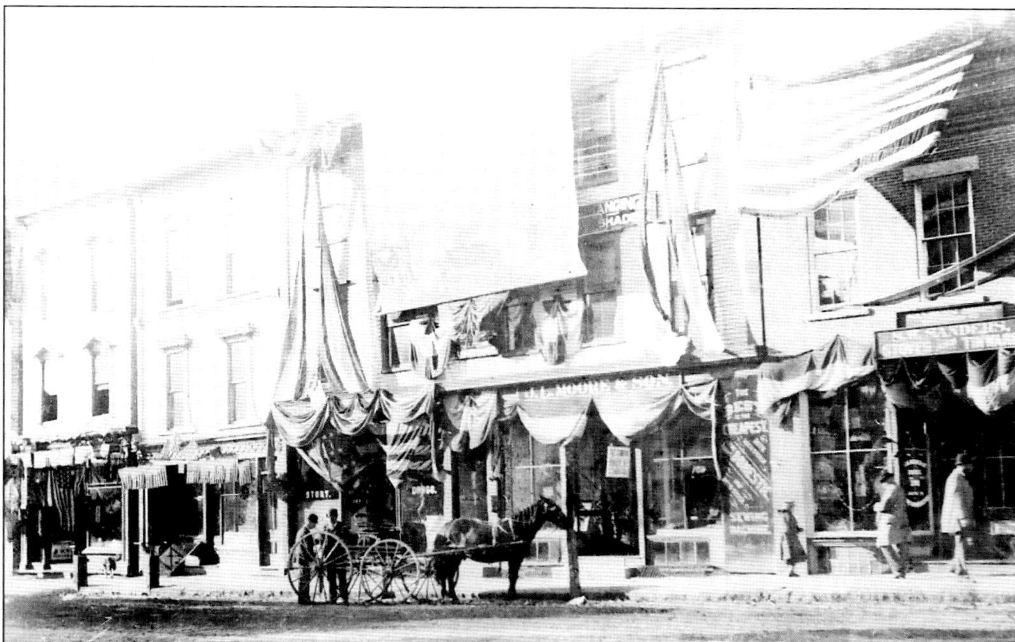

Decorations for tradesman's parade, October 22, 1892. Story Drug Store is on the left, behind the wagon wheels.

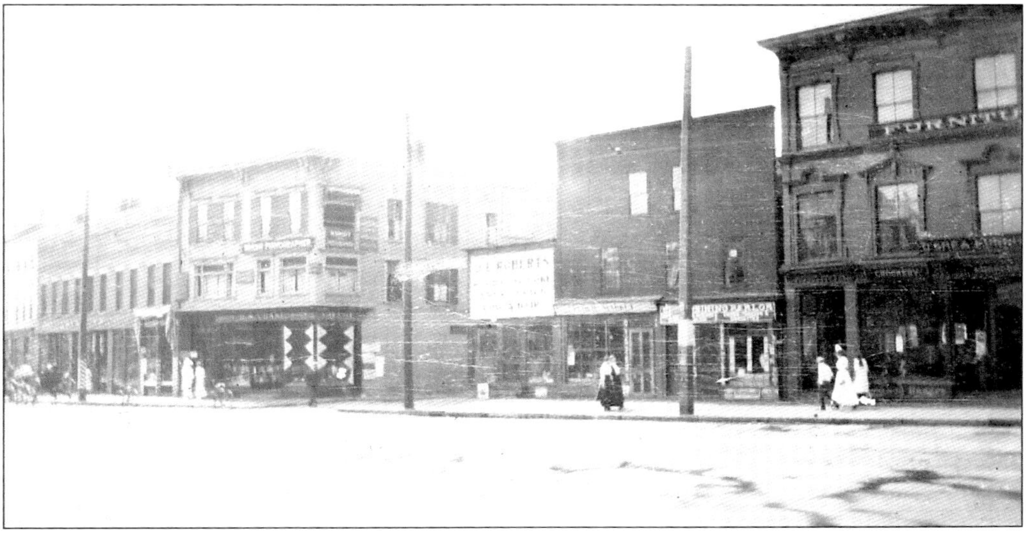

Bank Square in the 1920s. The furniture store on the right was part of O'Shea Bros.

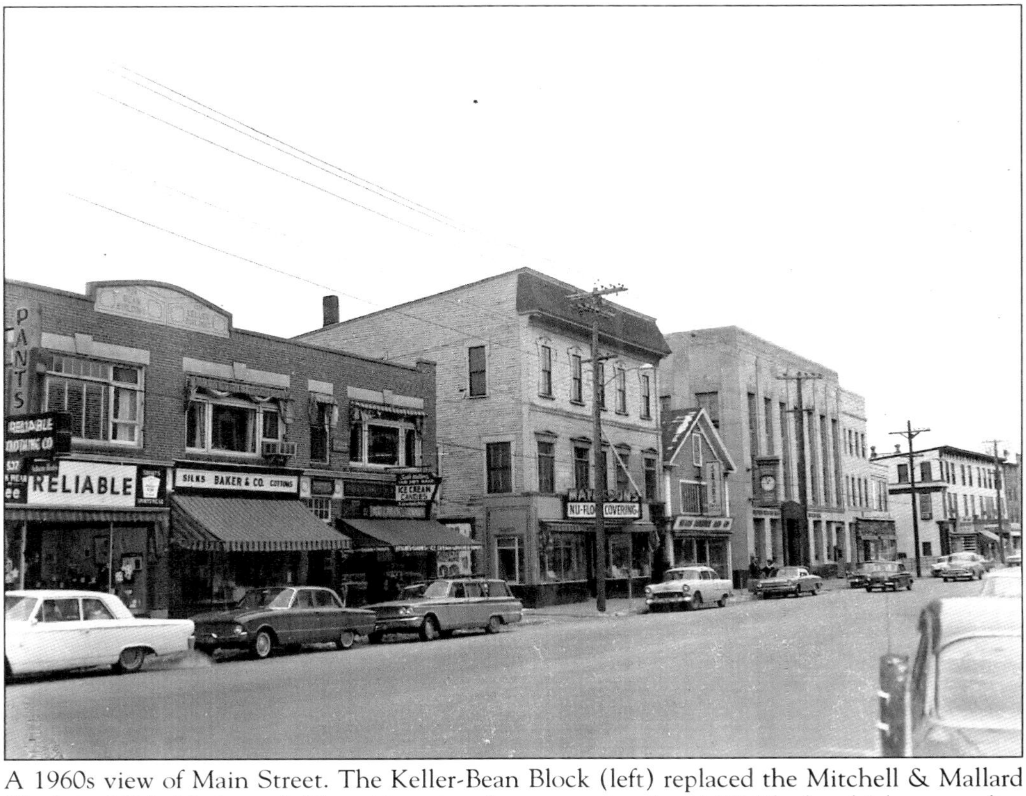


A 1960s view of Main Street. The Keller-Bean Block (left) replaced the Mitchell & Mallard Block in 1928. Matheson's Floor Coverings here occupies the GAR Block, which was earlier home to the Crystal Cafe; and Sears had replaced Pitman Hardware, next to the "Lower Bank." The Normandin Block can be seen in the distance.

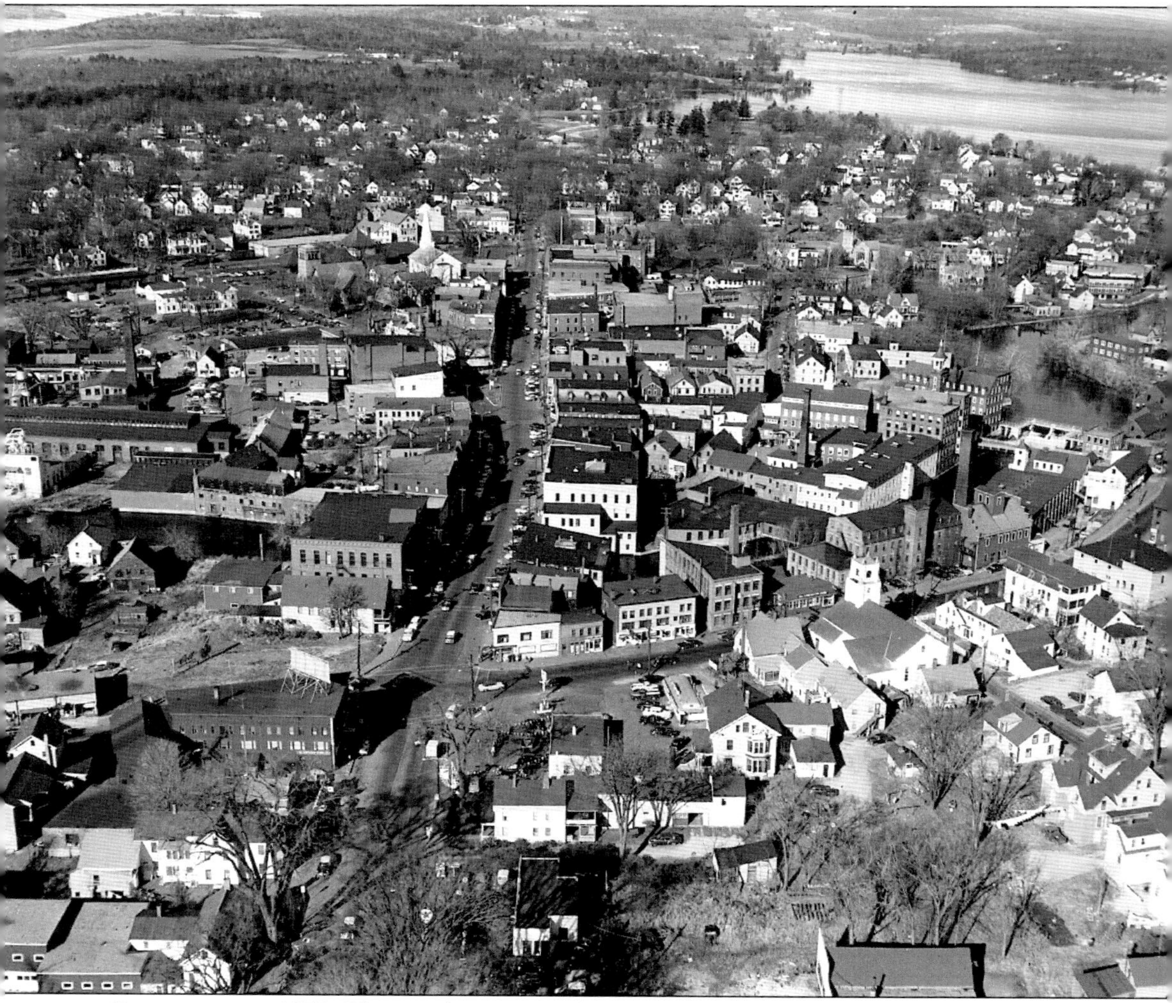

Downtown, c. 1950. The northern part of Lake Winnisquam can be seen in the upper left, while Lake Opechee is in the upper right. This photograph captures Main Street and the mills, much as they had appeared for nearly one hundred years prior to the Urban Renewal program of the late 1960s and early 1970s. Today, Sunrise Towers has replaced the Methodist Church (lower right) and several adjacent buildings. Across Union Avenue, from the Cormier Mill and the adjacent Laconia Gristmill, the space all the way to "Baldi's Corner" is now part of Stewart Park. All the buildings in the lower left corner are now gone, as is the Smith Block (later, the Tilton Block) and the Harry Sanborn-Laflamme's Bakery frame structure above them, next to the river. Likewise, all but the Belknap and Busiel Mills were razed in the tightly-packed industrial section along the river. In the upper left, Laconia's City Hall from 1926–1970, the white-frame John Adams Harper House (with additions), is visible.

# Five

# Bank Square and Vicinity

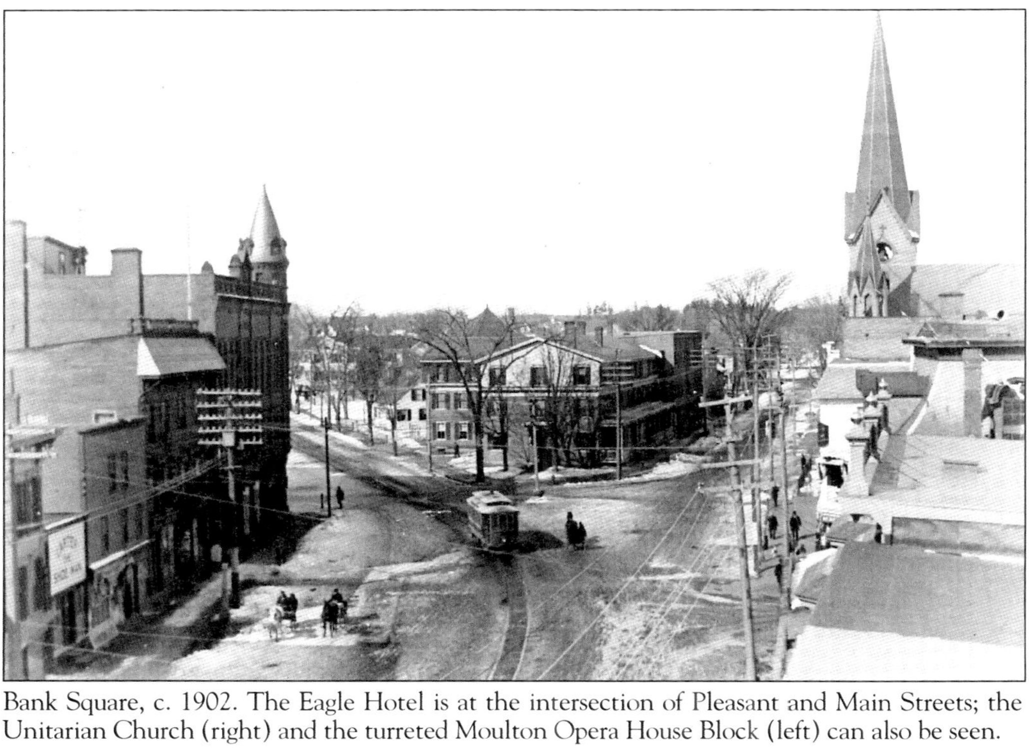

Bank Square, c. 1902. The Eagle Hotel is at the intersection of Pleasant and Main Streets; the Unitarian Church (right) and the turreted Moulton Opera House Block (left) can also be seen.

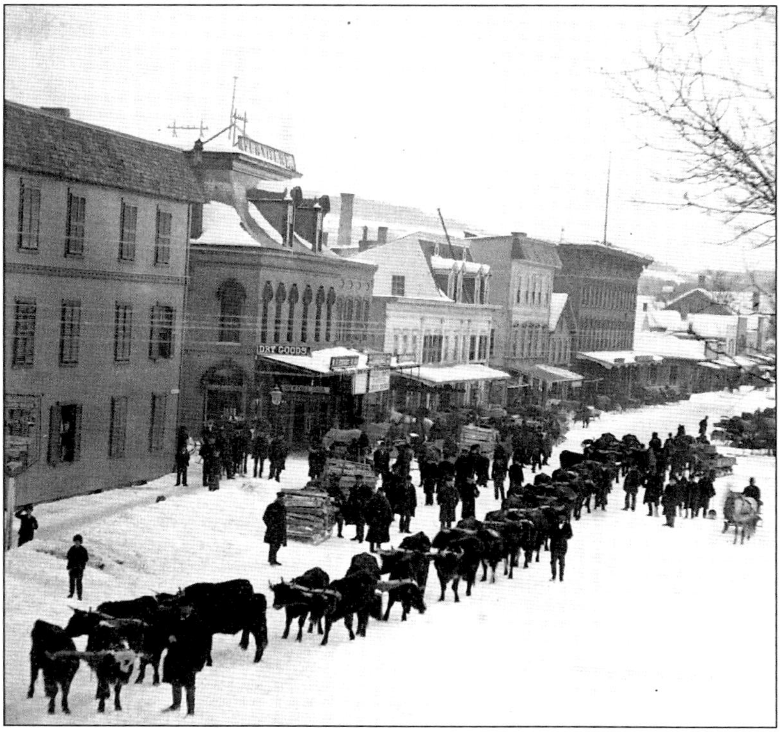


Oxen in Bank Square, c. 1880.

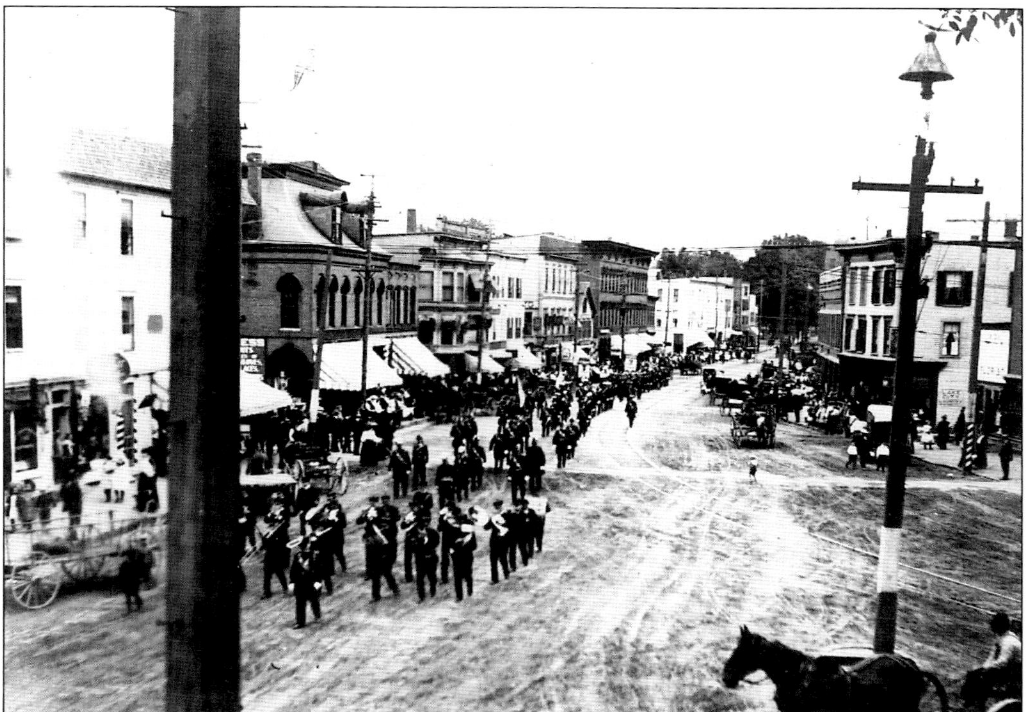

A parade moving up Main Street in the early 1890s.

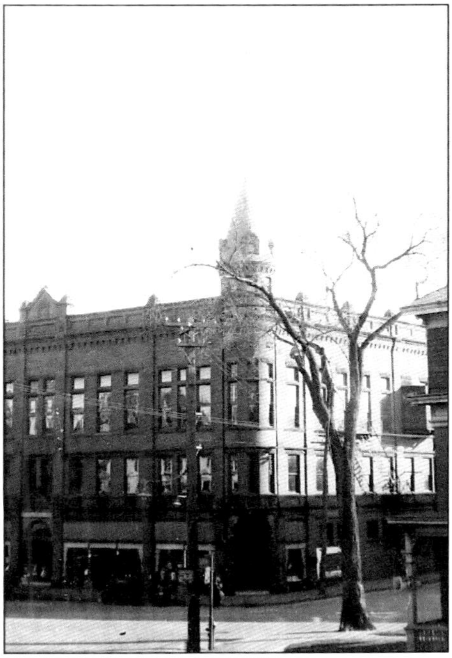

The Moulton Opera House Block, built in 1886 as the new home of O'Shea's Department Store (founded in 1875). The massive brick structure containing the opera house on the second and third floors loomed over Bank Square at the corner of Water Street until it was demolished during Urban Renewal in 1970. The Eagle Hotel is on the right in this c. 1925 photograph.

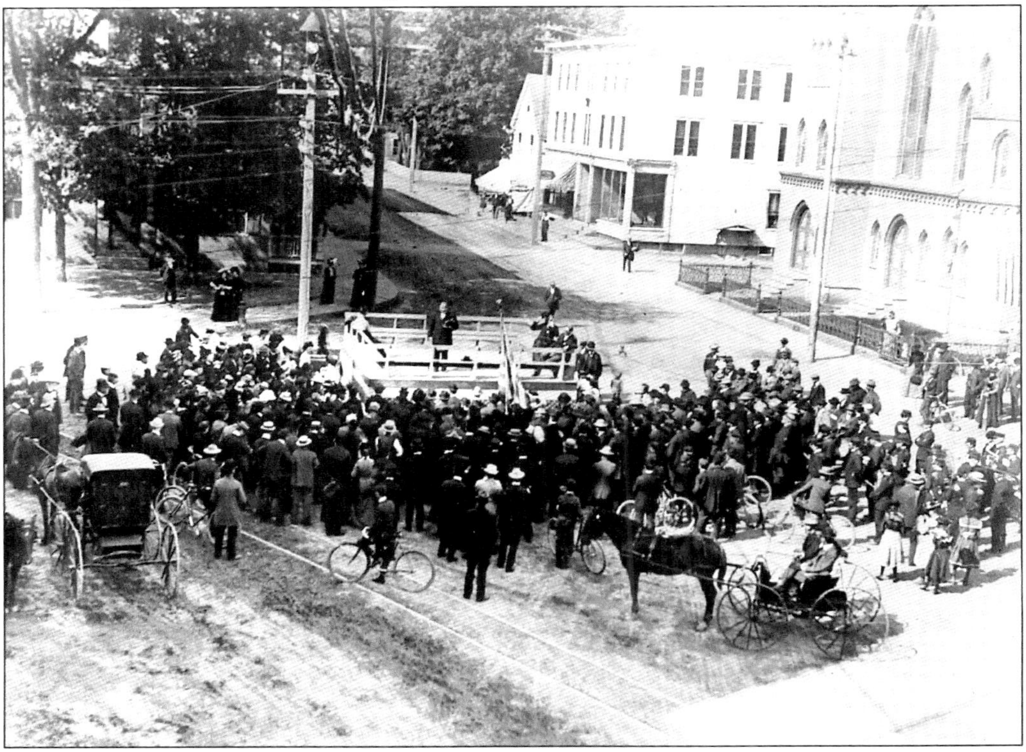

A political rally in Bank Square, 1890s. The Unitarian Church is on the right, followed by the Perley Block (site of today's J.J. Newberry Co.) and dwelling houses (which were replaced by the Colonial Theater Block in 1913–1914).

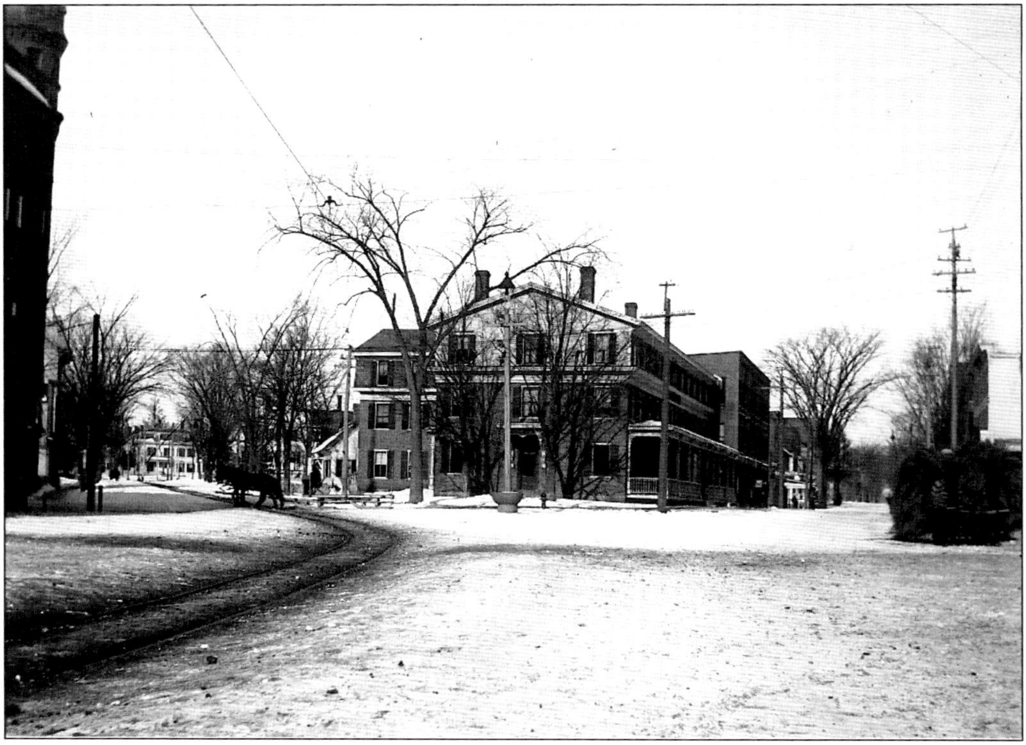

An early 1900s photograph of the Eagle Hotel in Bank Square. The adjoining Cook Block (right) was built in 1898.

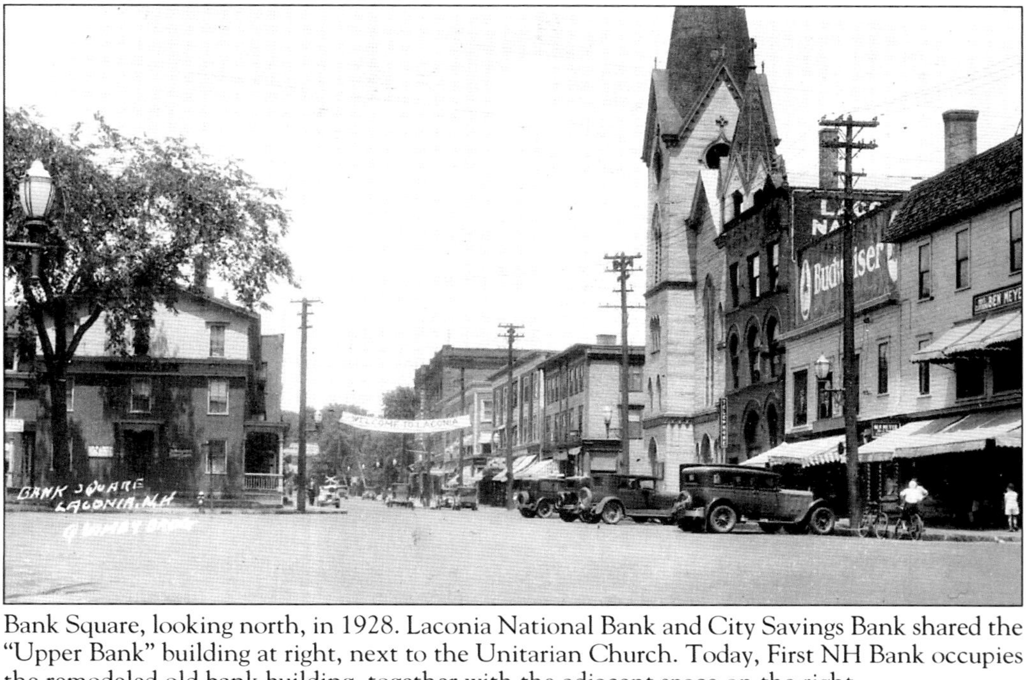


Bank Square, looking north, in 1928. Laconia National Bank and City Savings Bank shared the "Upper Bank" building at right, next to the Unitarian Church. Today, First NH Bank occupies the remodeled old bank building, together with the adjacent space on the right.

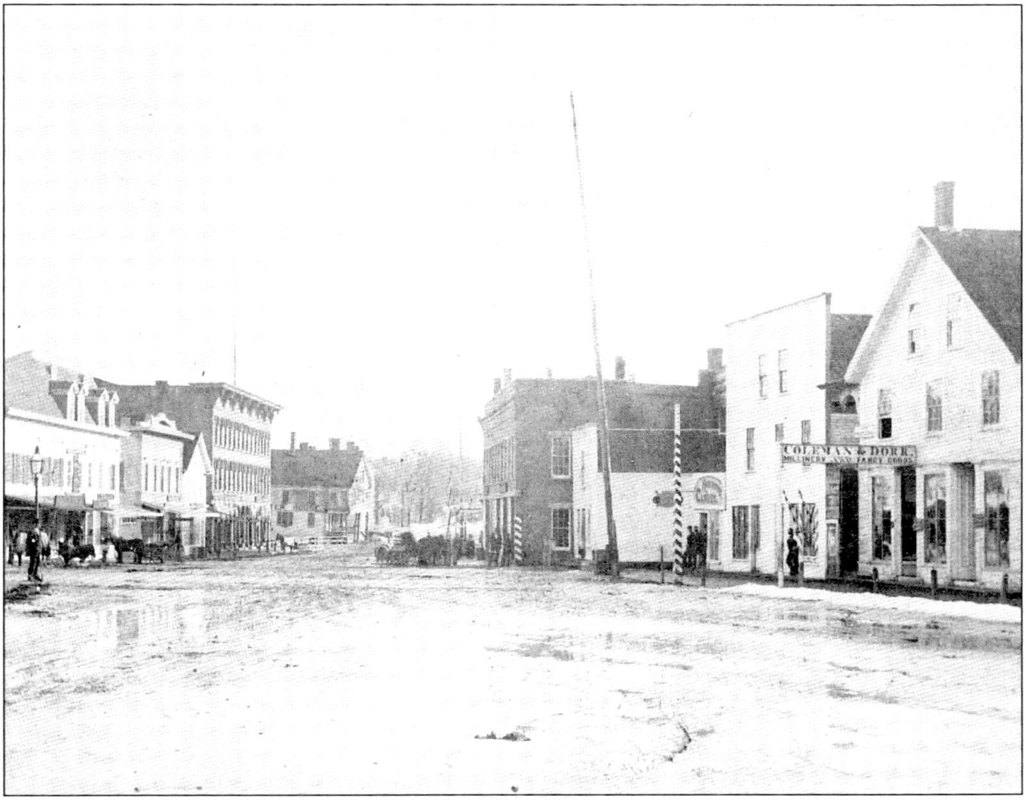


Bank Square, looking south toward the river, c. 1870s.

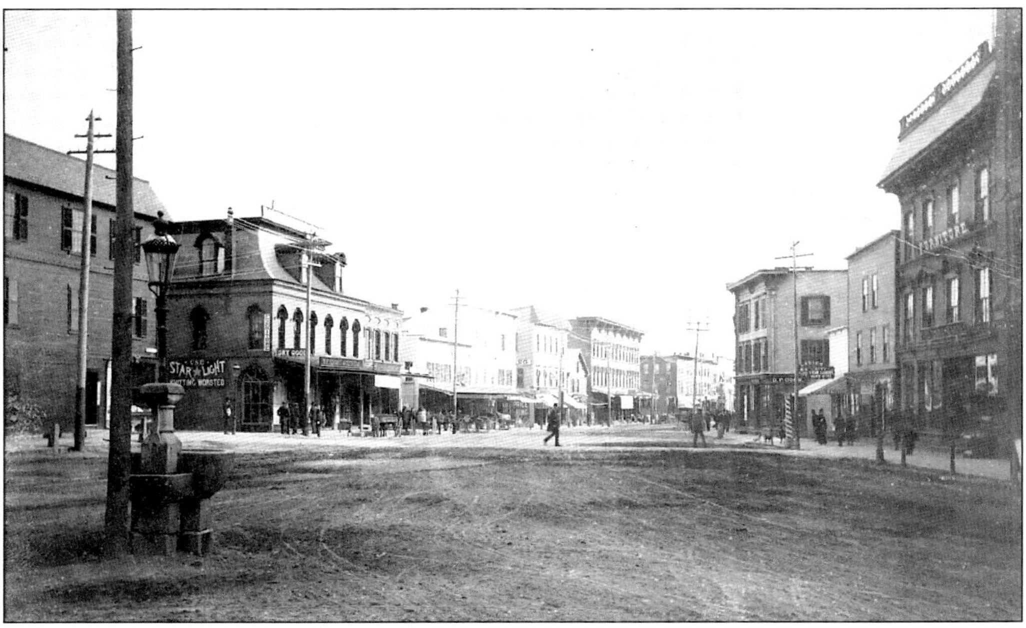


The same view in the late 1880s.

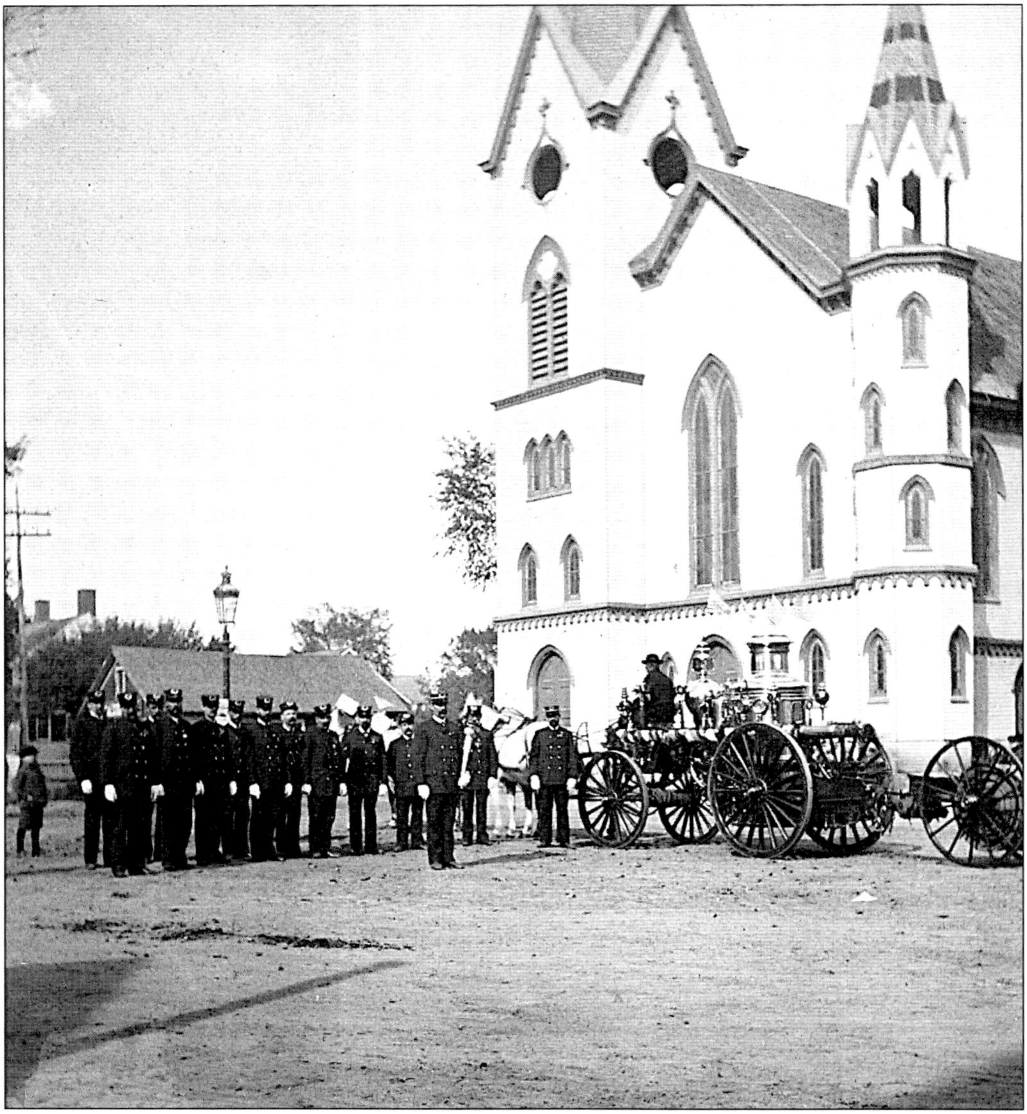

The Laconia Fire Department in the early 1880s. Small boy, firemen, and an Amoskeag steamer (acquired in 1875) line up in front of the Unitarian Church. Beyond the gaslight on the left, the building preceding the Perley Block (1885), and dwelling on the site of today's Colonial Theater, may be seen.

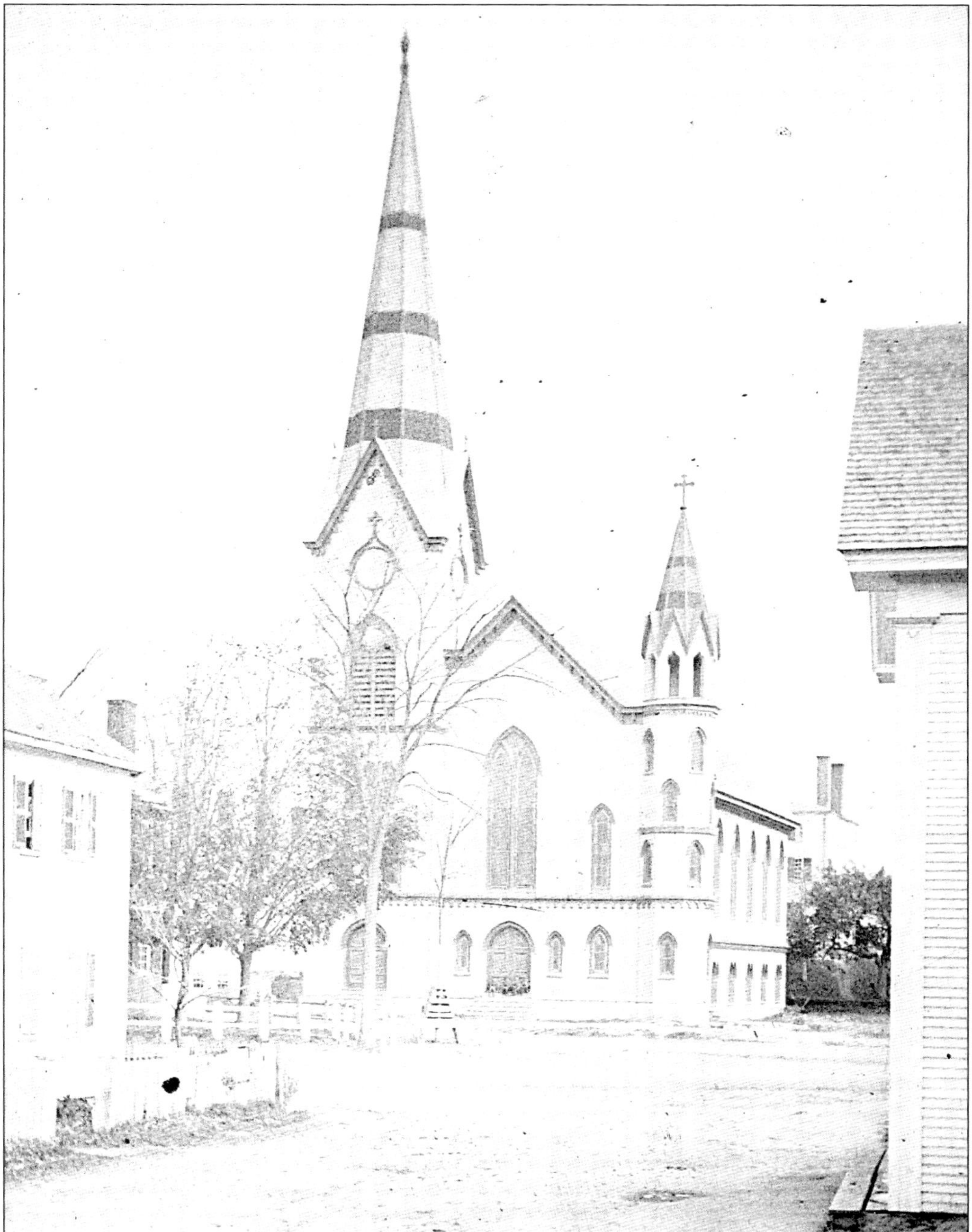

An early 1880s photograph of the Unitarian Church, taken from Water Street. The house on the left was replaced by the McIntyre Block in 1915. In the distance on the right, beyond the church, part of the boarding house known as the Mansion House is visible.

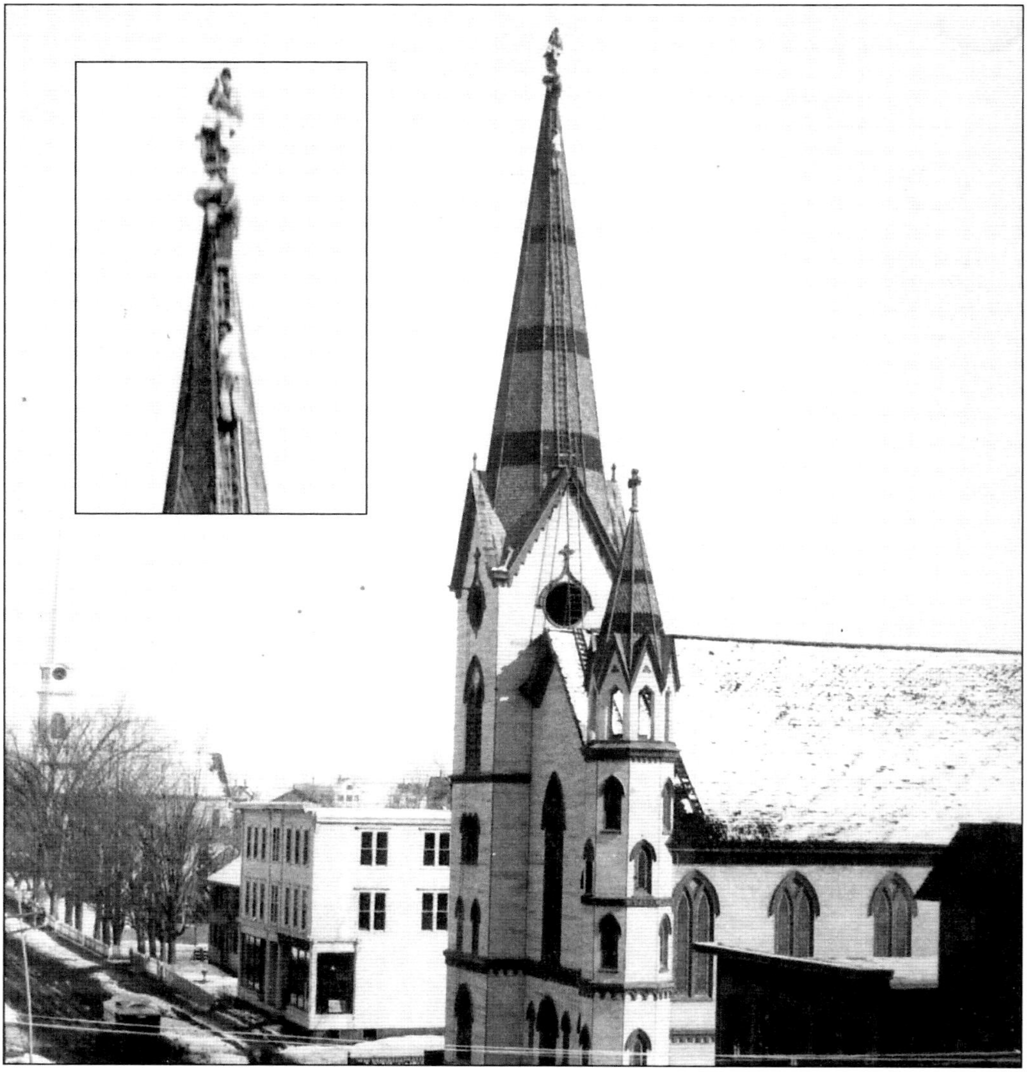

The Unitarian Church, Bank Square, April 1888. Ezra Page was painting the steeple of the Unitarian Church. According to The Laconia Democrat: "It is customary to build a staging for jobs of this kind, but of course this about doubles the expense of the work, and Mr. Page will in this case spread the paint without the aid of a staging. The top of the steeple is some 130 or 140 feet from the ground, but Ezra fixed a narrow board to the topmost ladder and after 'straddling the plank' kicked up his heels and appeared as comfortable as though merely astride a sawhorse on 'terra firma.' It looks rather a risky job and certainly excites the mingled horror and admiration of the small boys, but Mr. Page says he is never troubled with dizziness and feels as much at home up in the air as when painting a back-yard fence. Ezra has a good reputation as a first-class painter, but it strikes us that this job will come under the head of 'high art.' " The horse car (lower left) provided transportation between the South End and Lake Village (Lakeport) until the line was electrified in 1898 and the tracks were rerouted over Pleasant Street from Bank Square instead of Main Street. Here Truland Bros., printers, occupies the space to the right of the church. In July 1888, construction of the Laconia National Bank began, and the bank moved into its new quarters in May 1889.

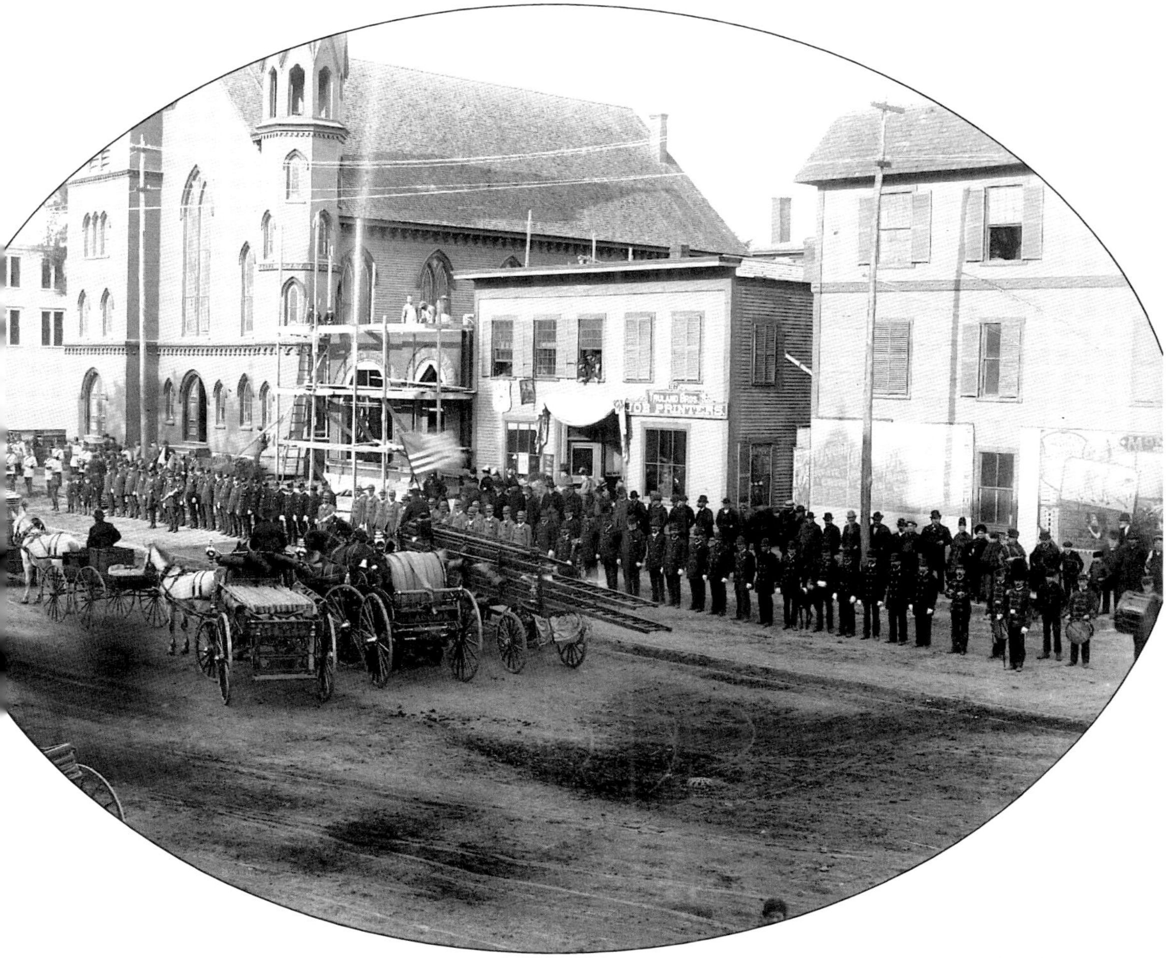


Firemen muster in Bank Square, 1888, with an Amoskeag steamer, hose wagons, and a hook and ladder. The Laconia National Bank building is under construction, between the Unitarian Church and Truland Bros. (right). From 1889–1903, the Laconia Public Library was located in the bank building.

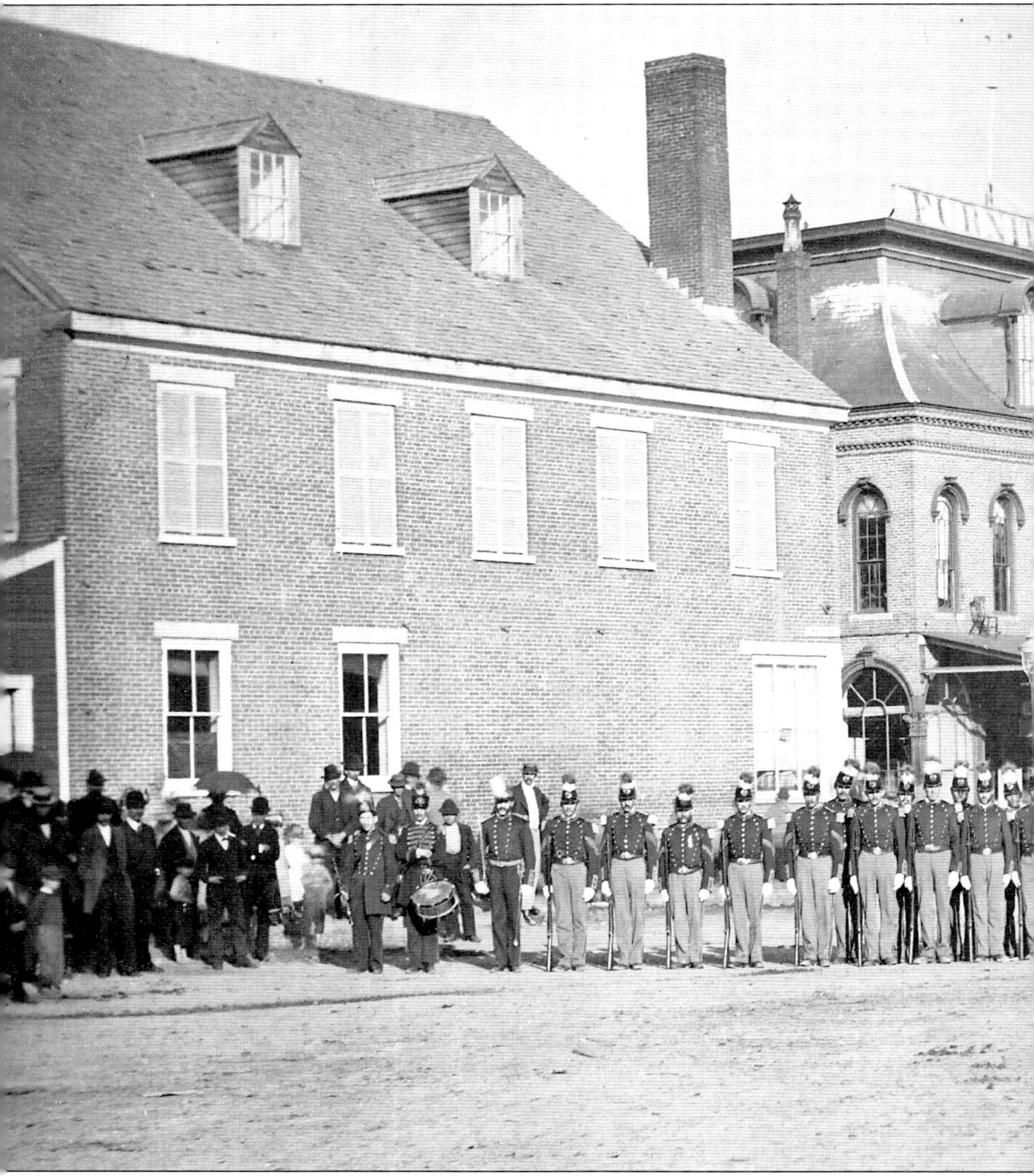

The Belknap Rifles (Company K, 3rd Regiment, New Hampshire National Guard) on parade in Bank Square, c. 1879. It is believed that this photograph recorded the unit's first full-dress parade—to show off its new regulation regimental uniforms which The Laconia Democrat called "very showy and dashing." In any event, The Democrat reported that shortly after 2 p.m. on Tuesday, May 13, 1879, the company left its armory "with full ranks and marched down main street to some of Ed. Stevens' best drumming. The heat was oppressive and playing soldier must

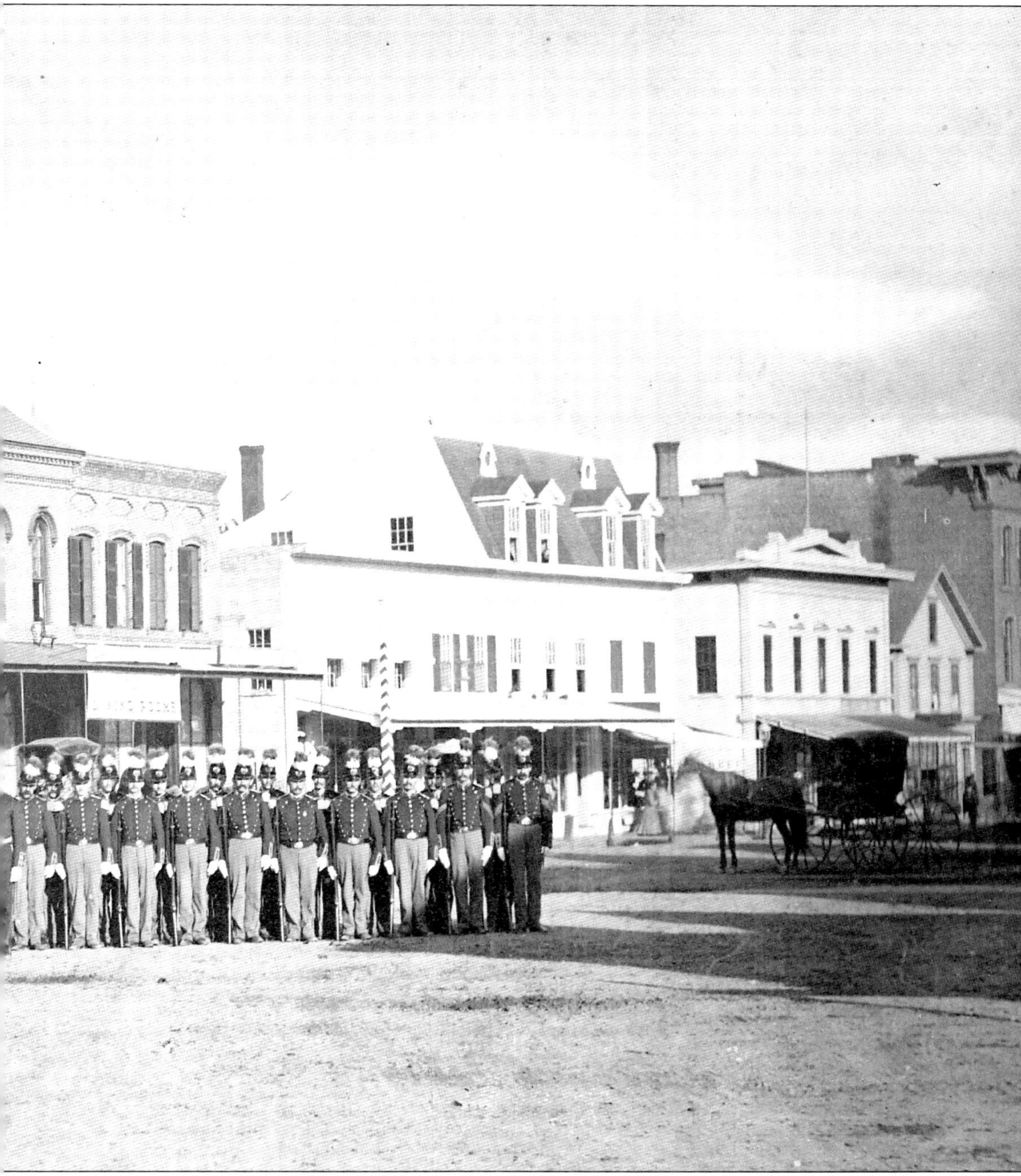

have been anything but fun. We are bound to say, however, that the boys stood up manfully to their work and marched off at a brisk step, presenting a fine military appearance which would have been creditable to a much older organization. All military men whose opinion we could get, spoke in very high terms of Capt. Wheeler's command and predicted that it would be the crack company in the regiment to which it is attached."

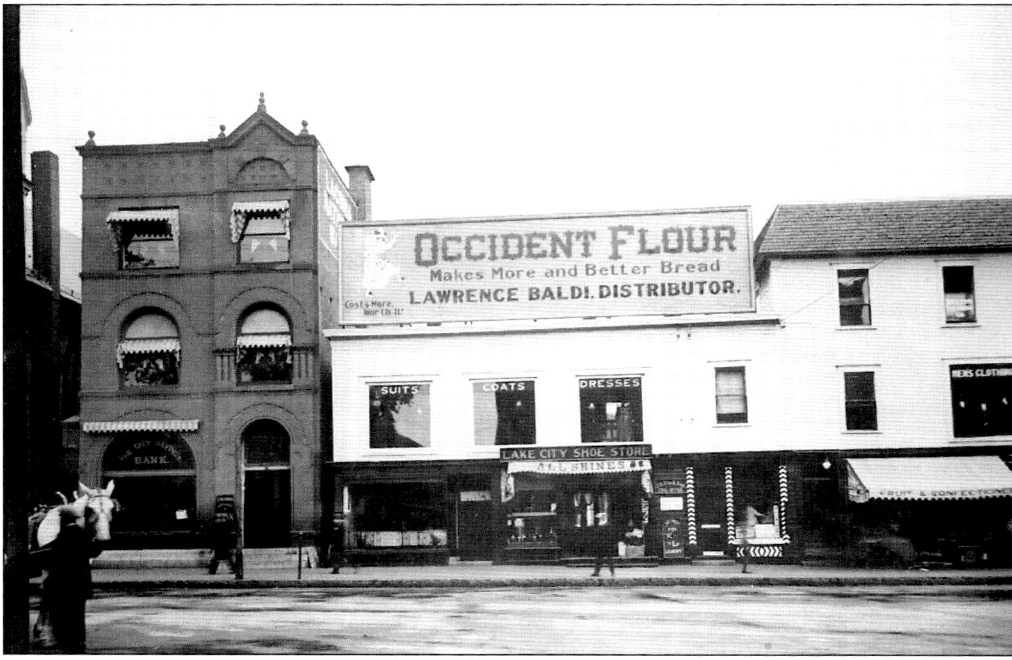


Bank Square, c. 1913–1914. The Laconia National Bank (left), Lake City Shoe Store (center), and Baldi Fruit and Confectionary (right) were among the occupants of the old buildings on the site of today's First NH Bank complex.

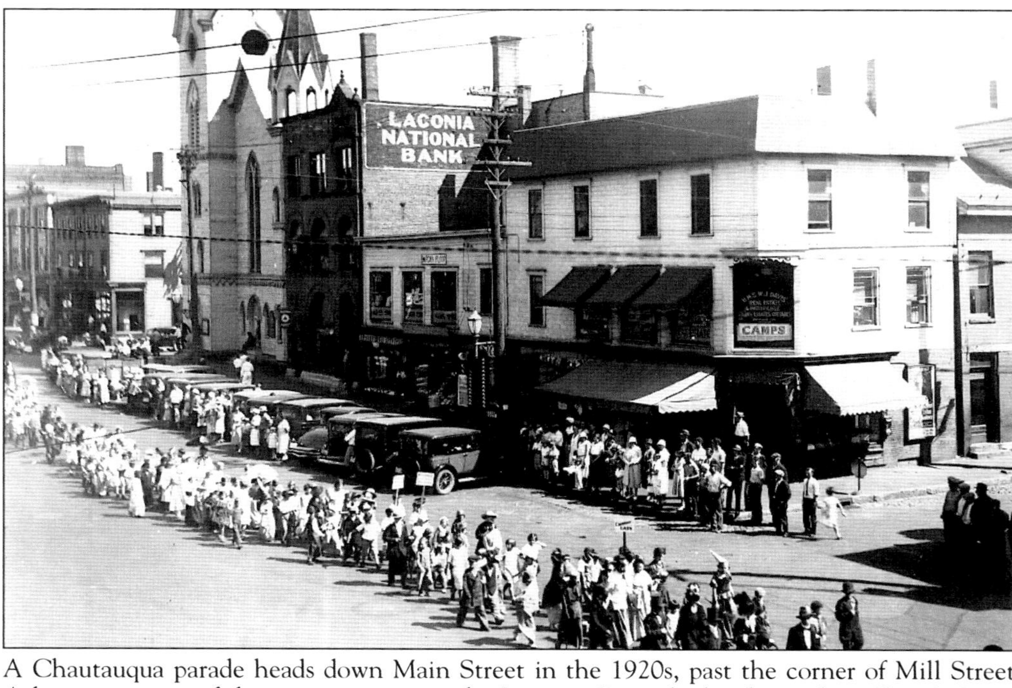


A Chautauqua parade heads down Main Street in the 1920s, past the corner of Mill Street. A later occupant of the corner store was the Laconia Spa, which relocated to Church Street around 1958.

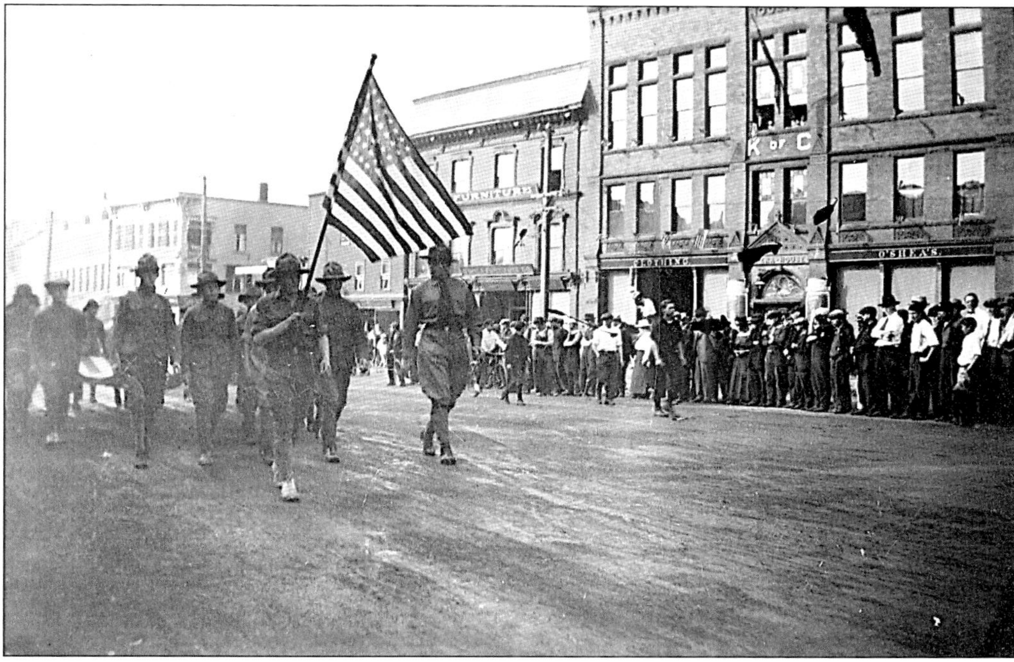


A World War I parade passes through Bank Square. O'Shea's (in the Moulton Opera House Block) is on the right.

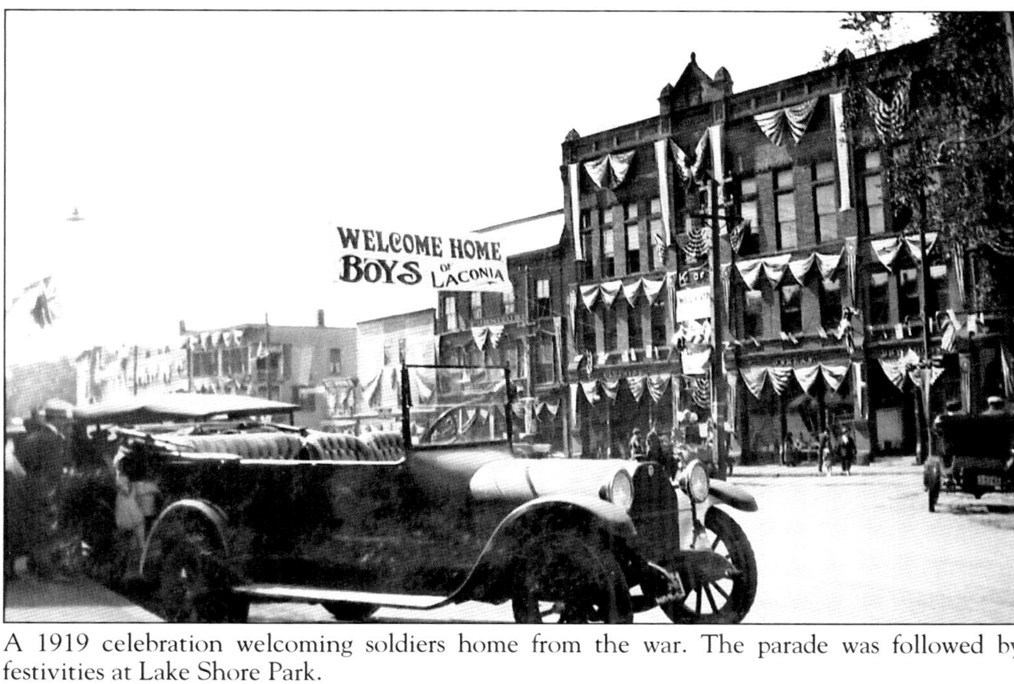


A 1919 celebration welcoming soldiers home from the war. The parade was followed by festivities at Lake Shore Park.

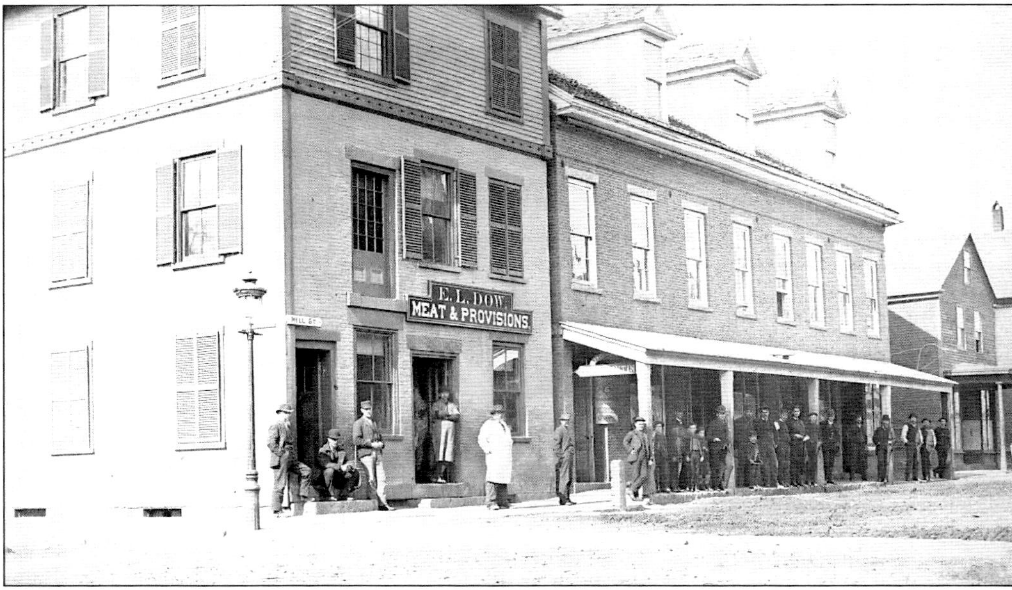


Mill Street, c. 1870s.

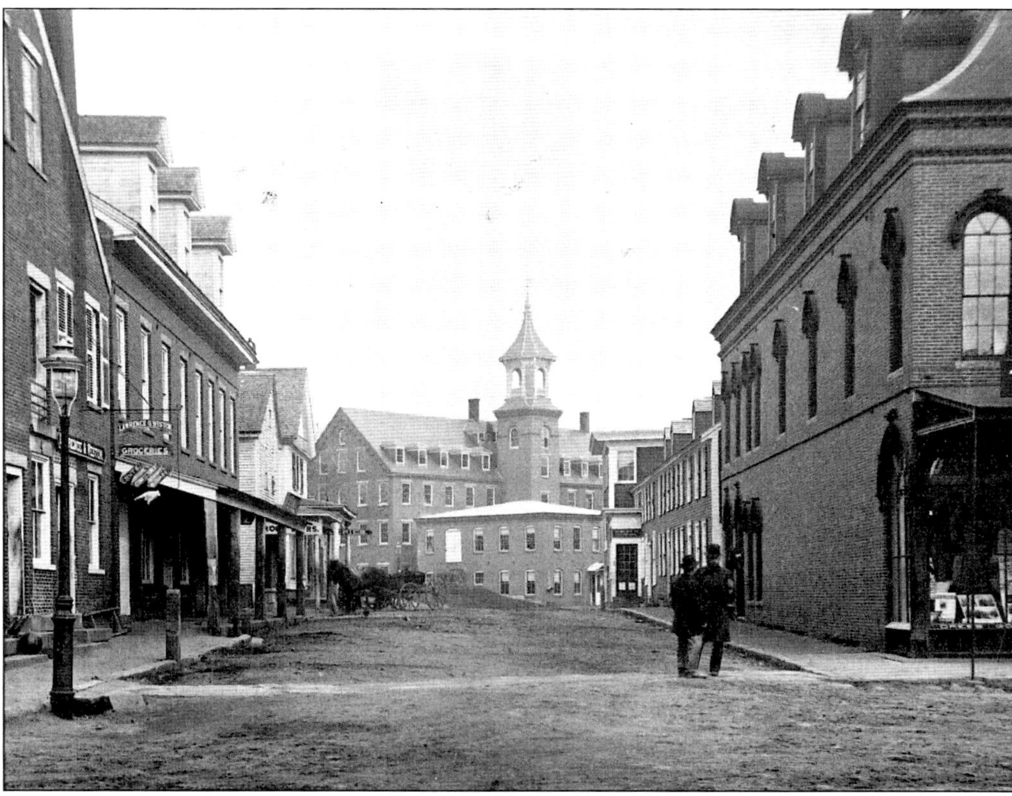

Mill Street, c. 1880s. Parker Block is on the right; the J.W. Busiel Mill can be seen in the distance.

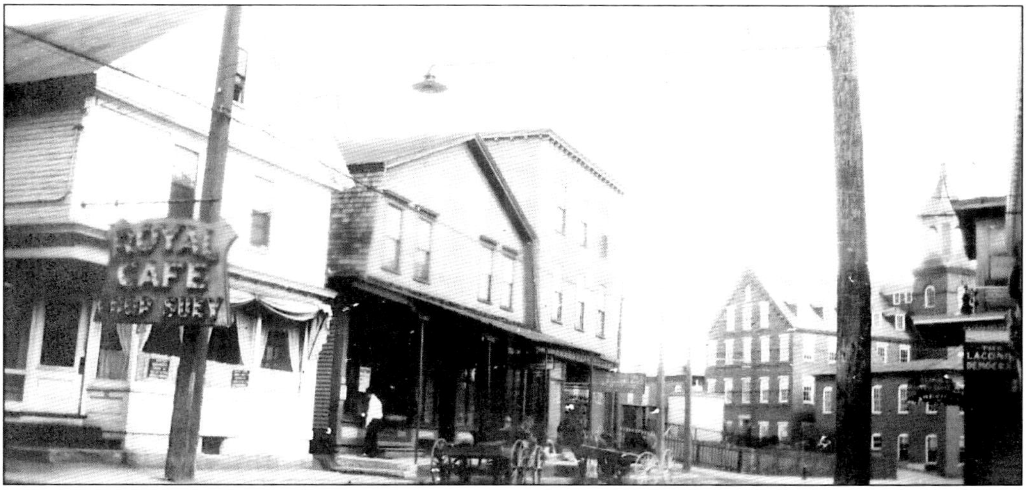


Mill Street in the 1920s. The Royal Cafe (left), a Chinese restaurant, later became the American Cafe of "Ma" Ladd. The middle building was moved to this location from Main Street, near the bridge (see p. 38). The third building from left was, at one time, home of The Laconia Democrat, a weekly newspaper which ceased publication in November 1941. Today, these sites are part of the parking lot behind the First NH Bank.

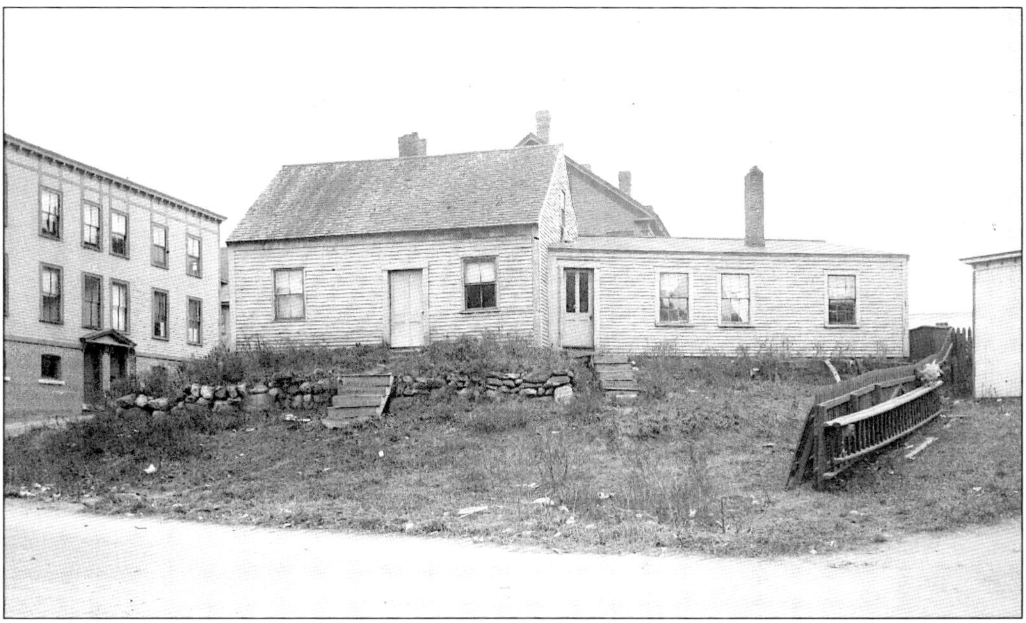

The Old Tucker House on Mill Street, c. 1890, just before it was torn down. Originally the home of Daniel Avery, who had come here around 1790, it was one of the oldest houses in the city. Daniel Tucker was one of the owners of the Avery Mill, which began operating as early as 1813 on the site today occupied by the Belknap Mill (built in 1823). Tucker also owned a blacksmith shop next to the river. The area pictured is now part of the parking lot in front of the Belknap and Busiel Mills.

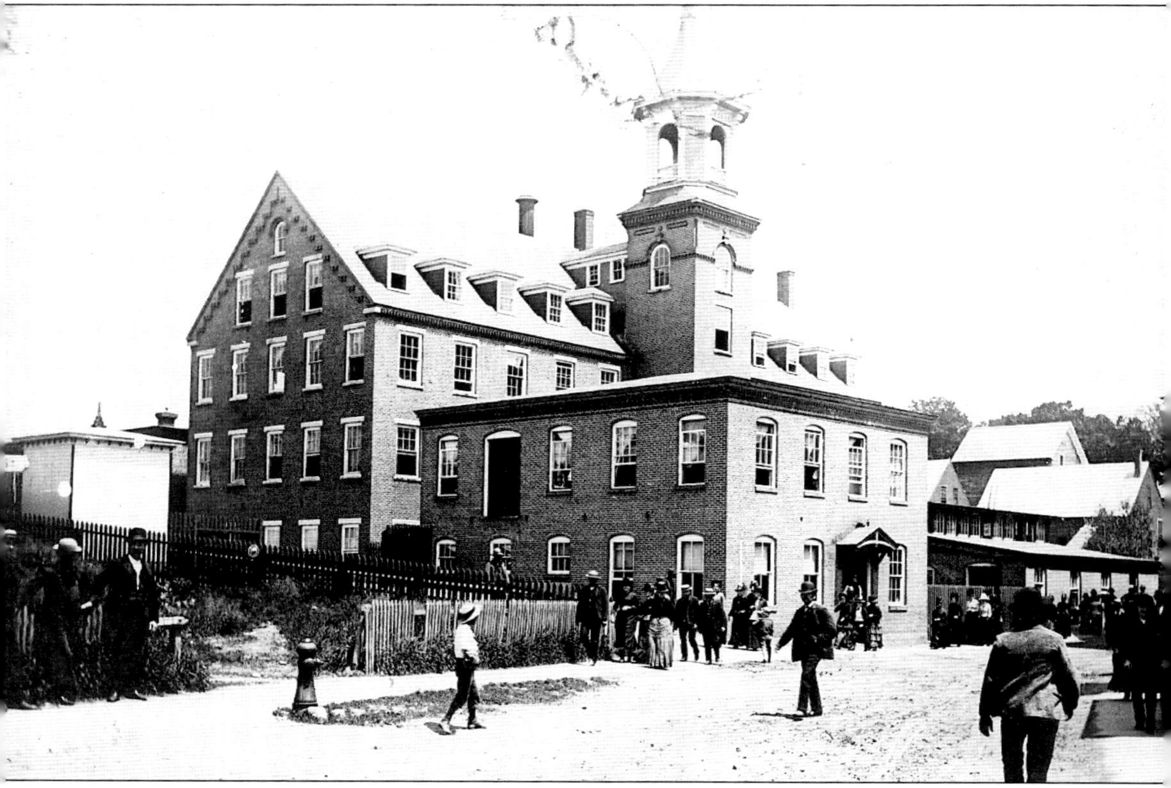

The J.W. Busiel Mill, c. 1880s. The Tucker House stood off the photograph at the left. The two-story office building and dyehouse on the right were razed during Urban Renewal in the late 1960s–early 1970s.

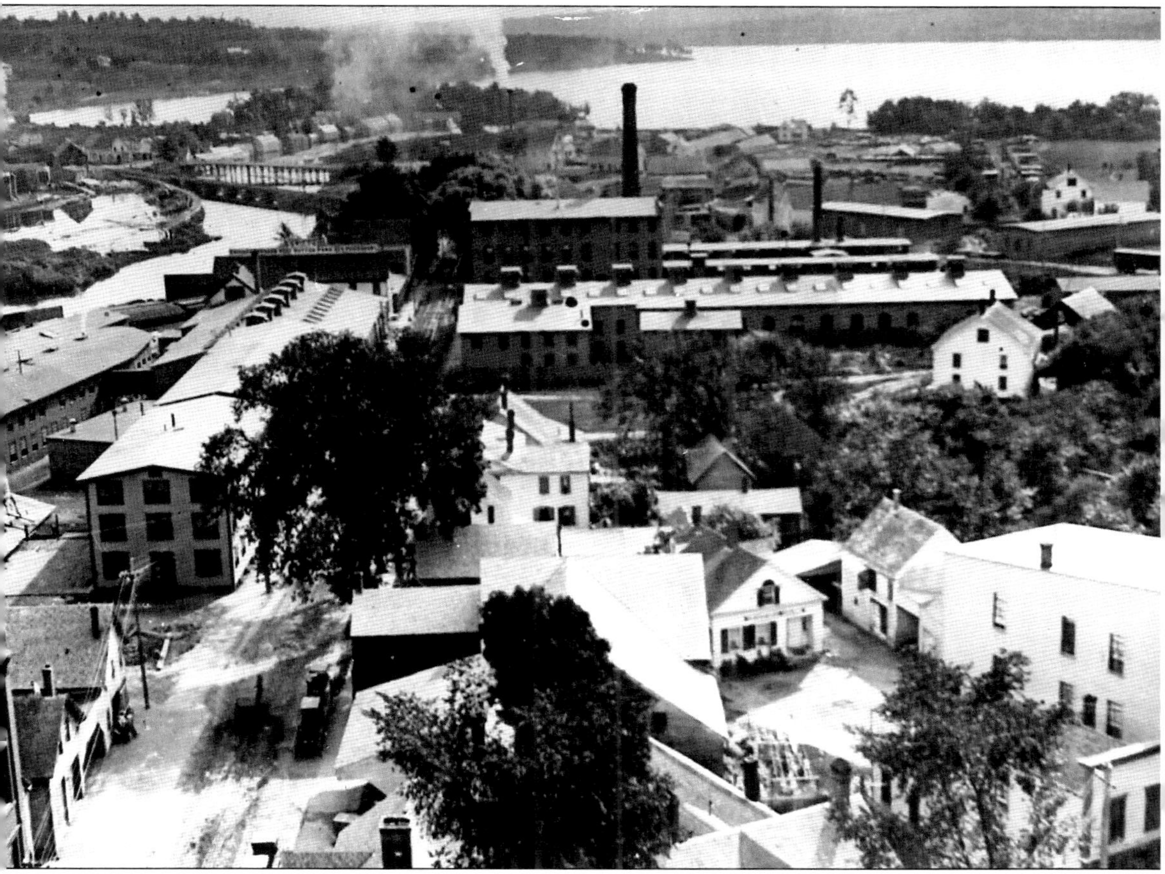

Water Street, 1902, looking toward Lake Winnisquam. Past the Moulton Opera House Block (on the extreme left) was Laconia's early fire station, on the site of what later became the brick Central Fire Station. The industrial buildings were those of the Laconia Car Co., manufacturers of railroad, trolley, and subway cars from 1848 through the early 1930s. Beacon Street West today traverses the lower center of the photograph from right to left. The rectangular wooden building extending out of view on the right was once known as the Hotel Picard. Originally part of the O'Shea Bros. establishment, it was moved to this location when the Moulton Opera House Block was built in 1886. The Hotel Picard was torn down to make way for an automobile dealership and garage, which is now occupied by Laconia Hardware Co.

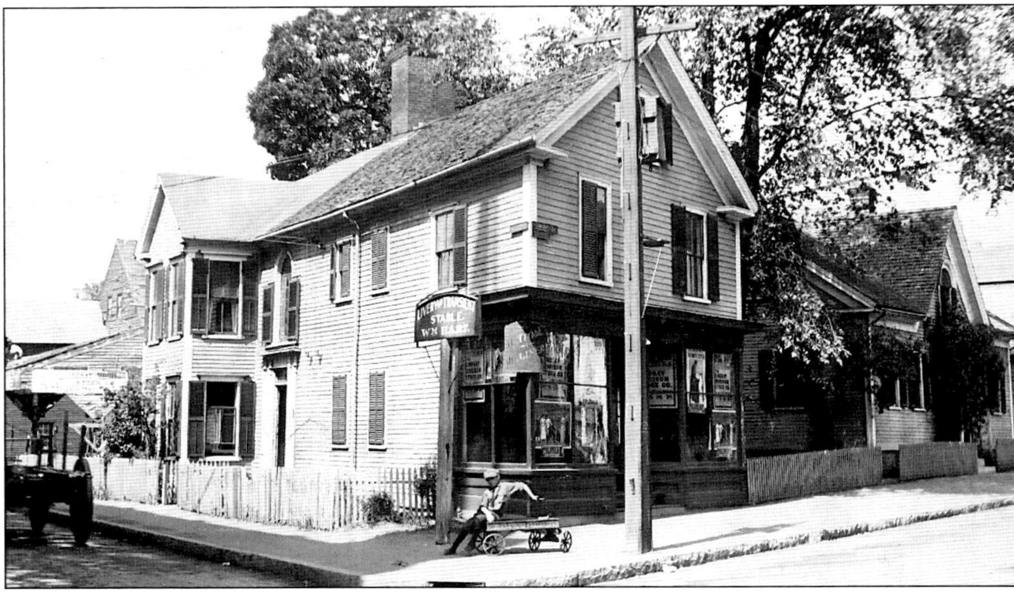

The corner of Water and Pleasant Streets during the summer of 1914. The Josiah Howe House and William Hart stable buildings were torn down when the McIntyre Block was erected, 1914–1915.

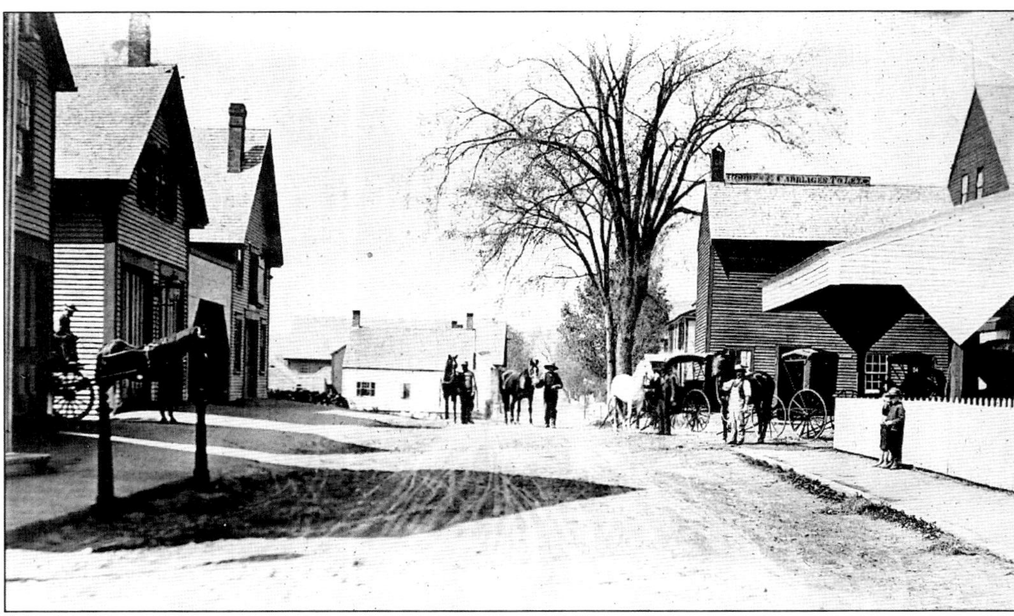

Water Street, c. 1870s, looking west. The early fire station buildings are on the left, with the livery stable on the right. Early Laconia Car Shops buildings are out of sight at left and right.

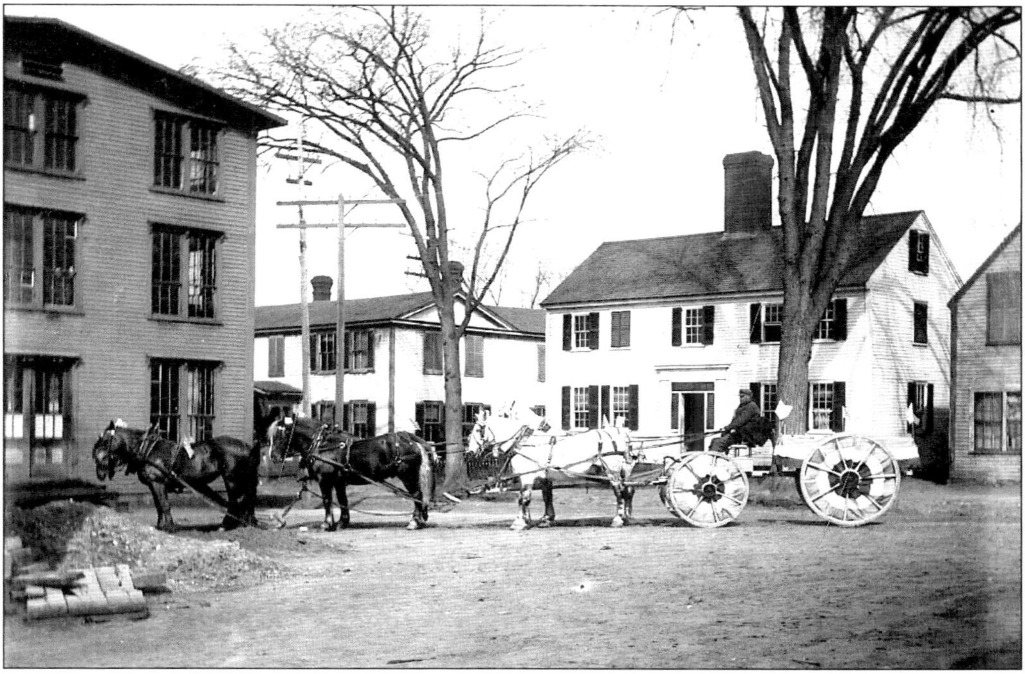

Water Street, c. 1880s. The building on the left was part of the Laconia Car Shops. The livery stable and Main Street were beyond the photograph to the right. At one time, Water Street was considered a prime residential area, as these substantial homes attest.

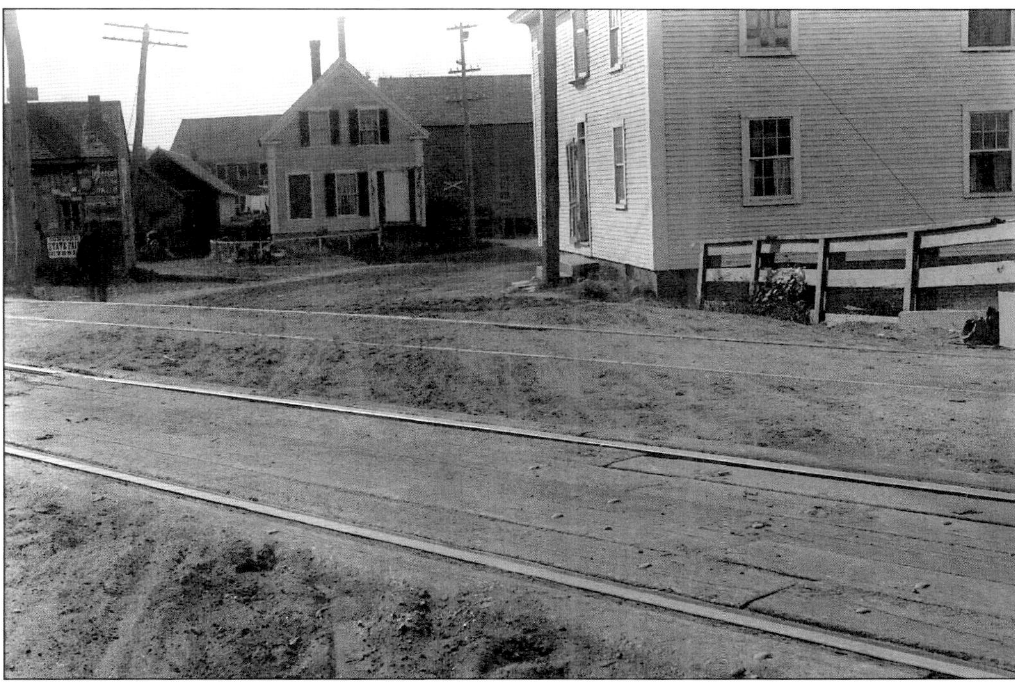

The Water Street railroad crossing, 1908. Today, The Citizen newspaper plant is located straight ahead, with a parking lot on the left and the Salta Tire Co. on the right.

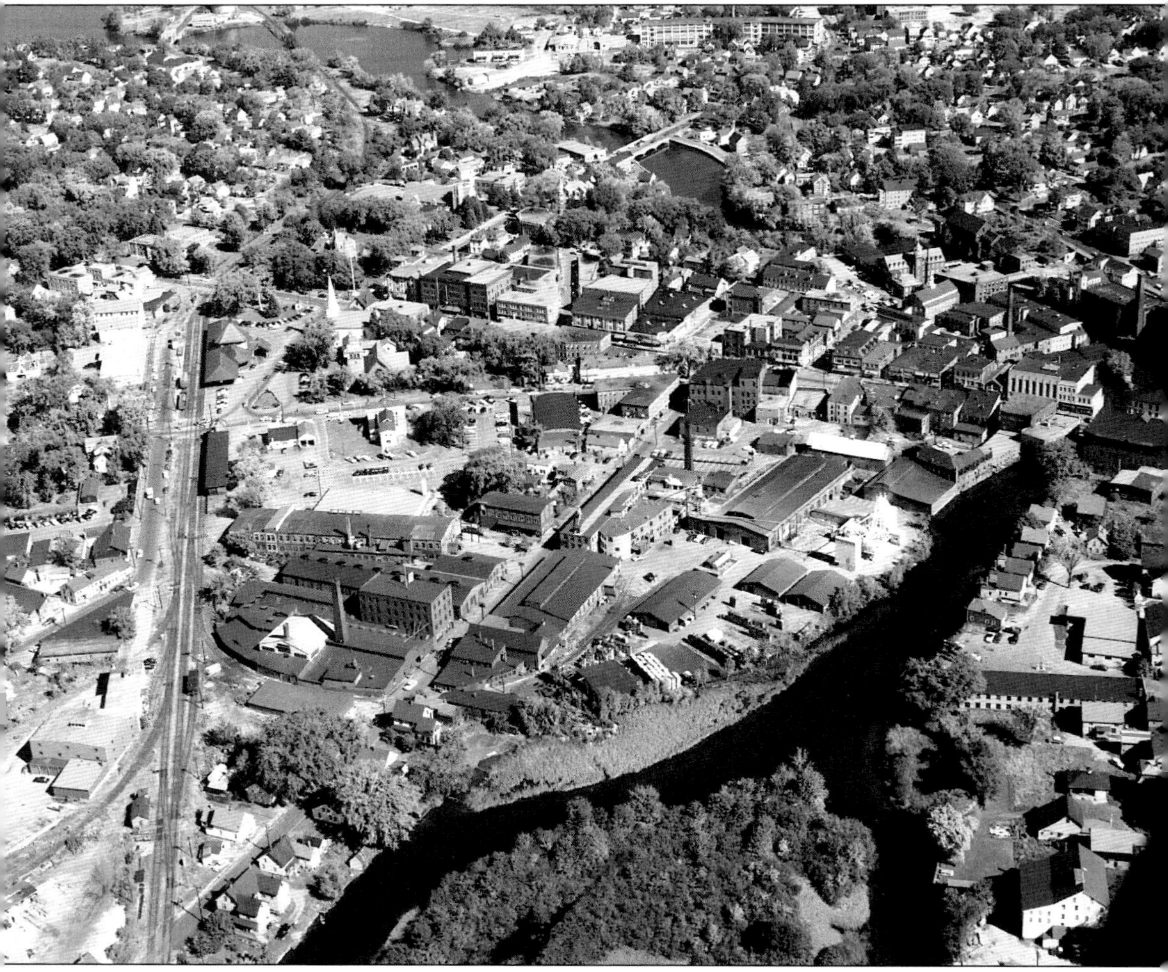

An aerial view of the Laconia Car Shops area (center foreground) and downtown Laconia, 1956. City hall (center left) is now the site of the Laconia Savings Bank. The buildings to the left of the old city hall include the Depot Square Auto Supply and the freight depot. (Located on the site of the original passenger station, it was moved to New Salem Street in 1892 when the new station was built). The old passenger station is now part of the J.J. Morin complex. The Scott & Williams plant (top center) at Normandin Square is also visible.

# *Six*

# Main Street to Depot Square

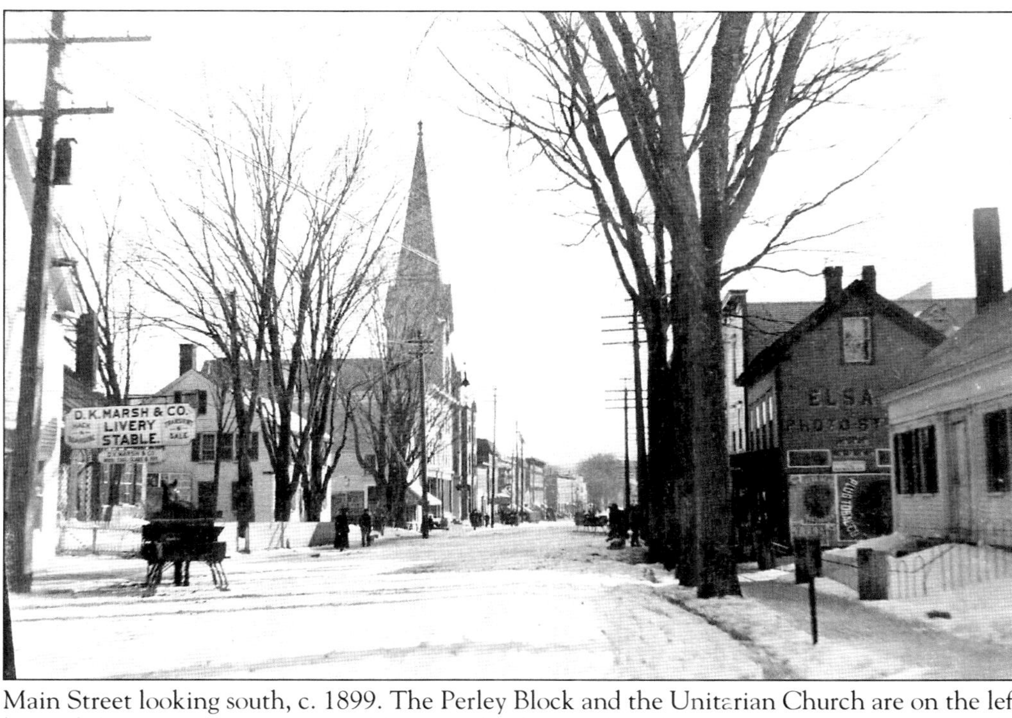


Main Street looking south, c. 1899. The Perley Block and the Unitarian Church are on the left beyond the Dr. Harriman House (the site of today's Colonial Theater). Today the area to the right is a parking lot. The Masonic Temple is located to the left off the photograph.

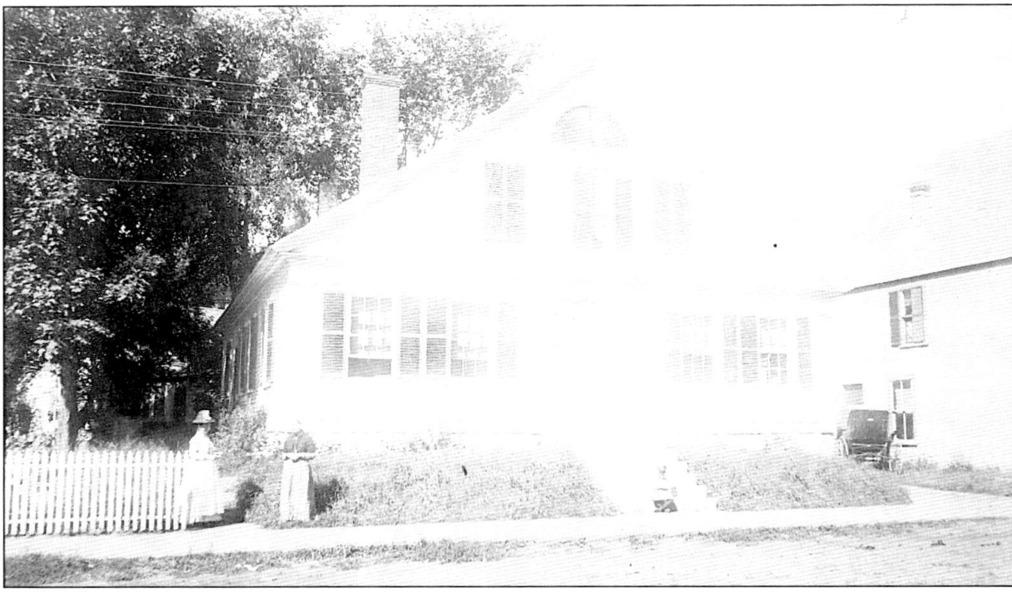

The Noyes House on Main Street, opposite today's Colonial Theater, c. 1890. This house was moved back in 1898 to permit construction of the Cook Block.

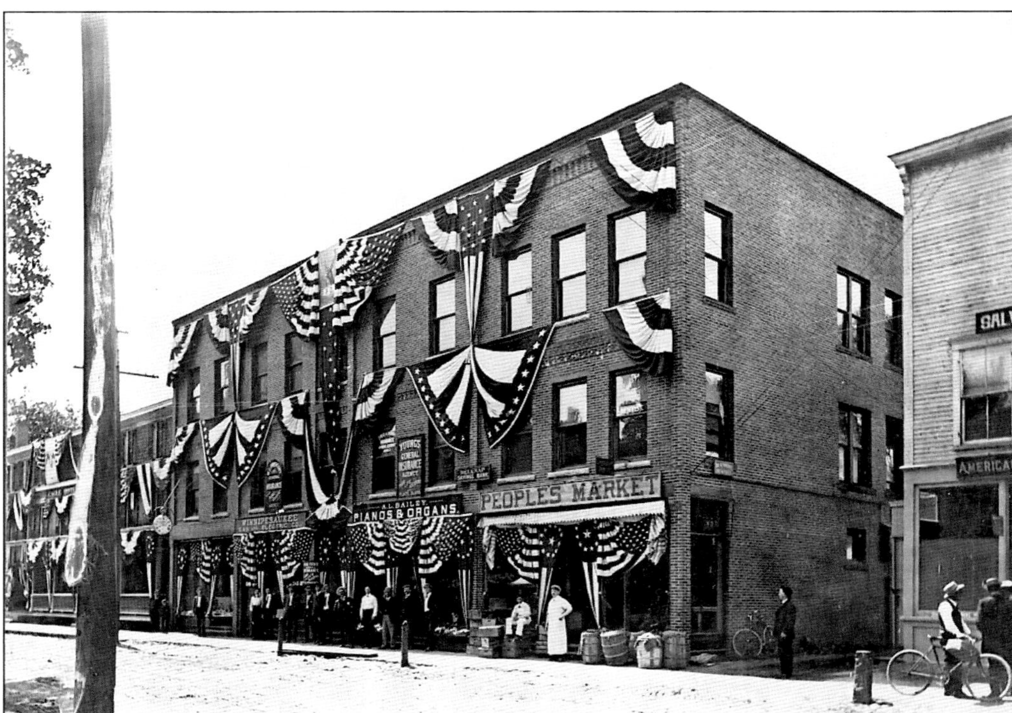


The Cook Block, c. 1908. The Eagle Hotel is on the left. The Pemaco building would later be built (in 1926) on the right; Pemaco stood for the Peoples Market Co. of the McIntyre family.

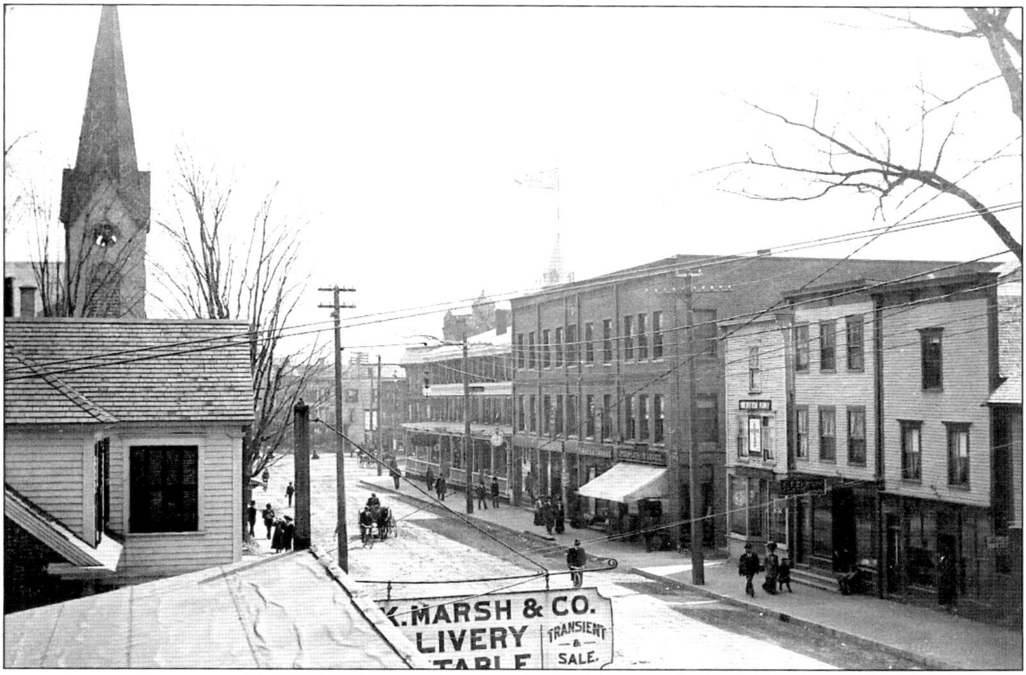


Main Street looking south from the Masonic Temple, c. 1900. The Unitarian Church is on the left, with the Eagle Hotel, Cook Block, and future site of the Pemaco building across the street.

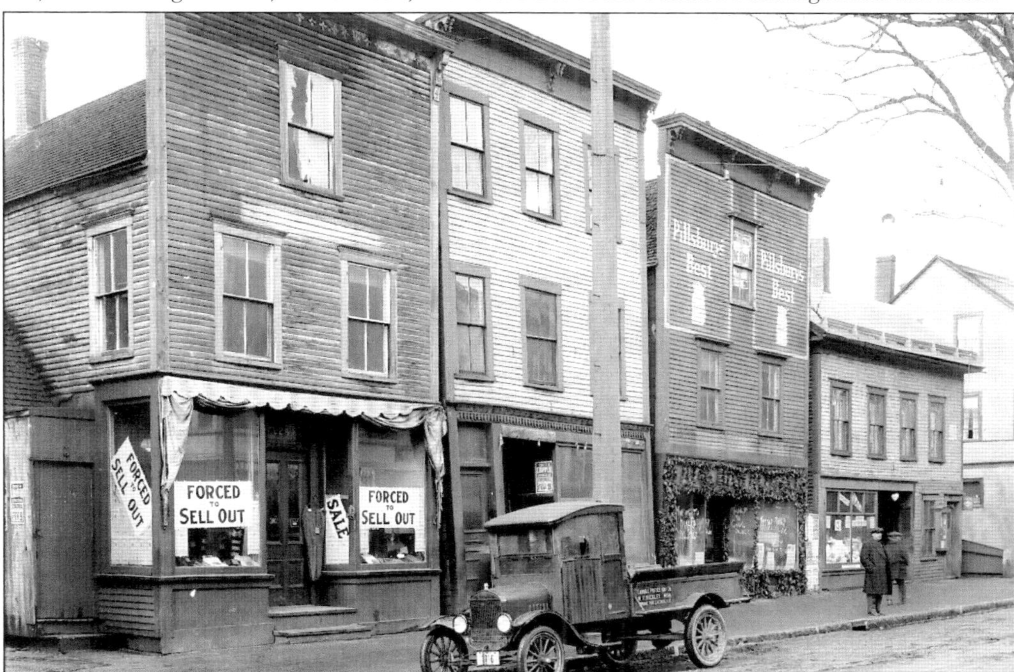


Main Street, c. 1920s. These old wooden buildings were razed in 1926 to make way for the construction of the Pemaco building. The building on the left was at one time occupied by the Salvation Army.

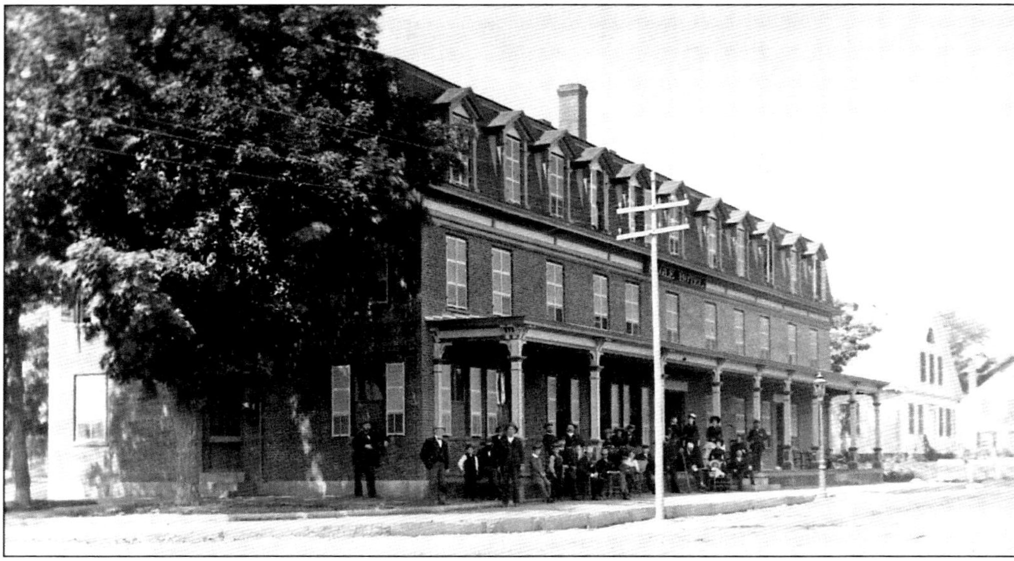

The Eagle Hotel, c. 1890. The Noyes House (right) was later moved back for construction of the Cook Block in 1898.

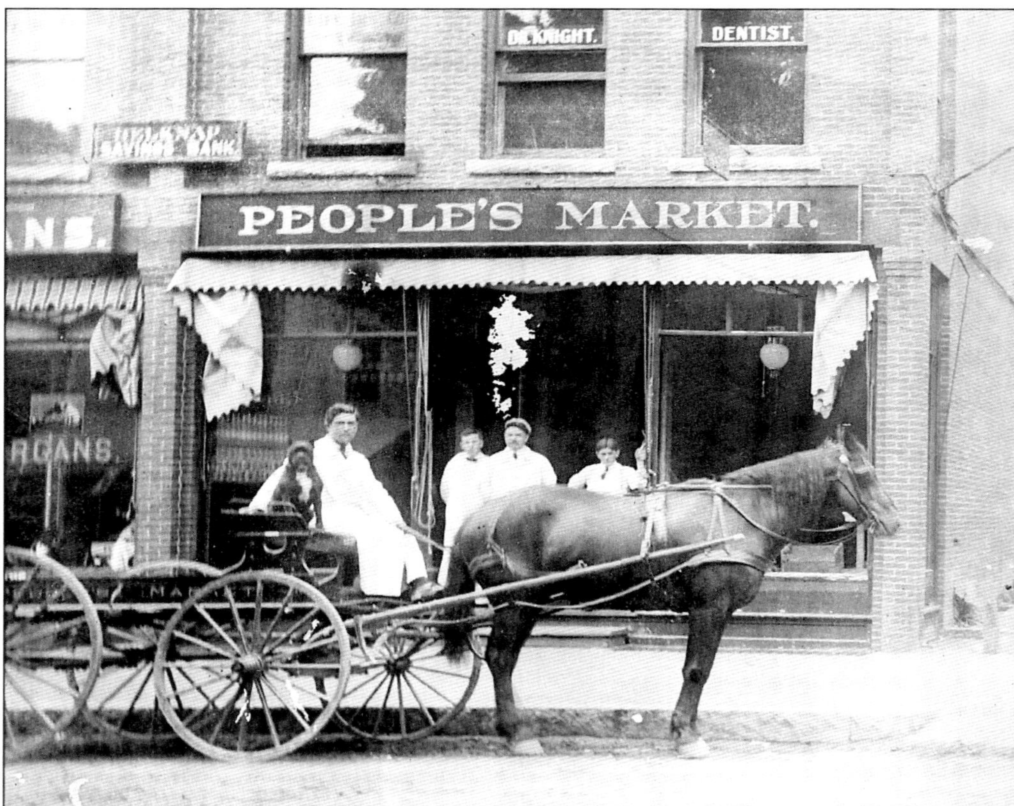


The People's Market, Cook Block, c. 1908. Walter Leavitt is in the wagon, while George Hughes, Martin Cunningham, and Tommy McGloughlin stand in the doorway.

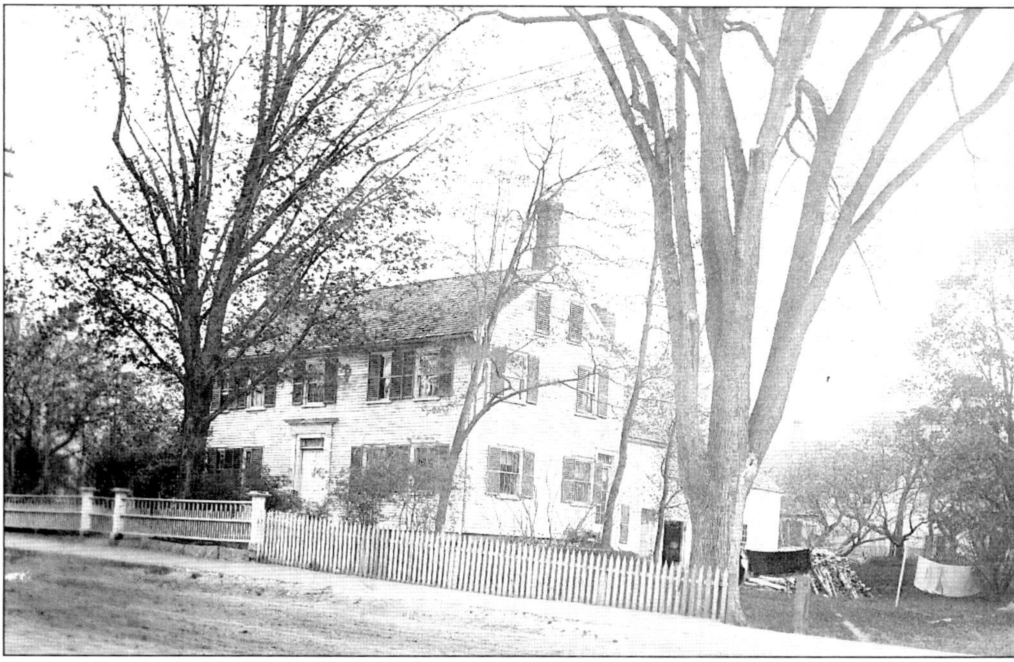

The Coffin House, c. 1890, the site of today's Masonic Temple building.

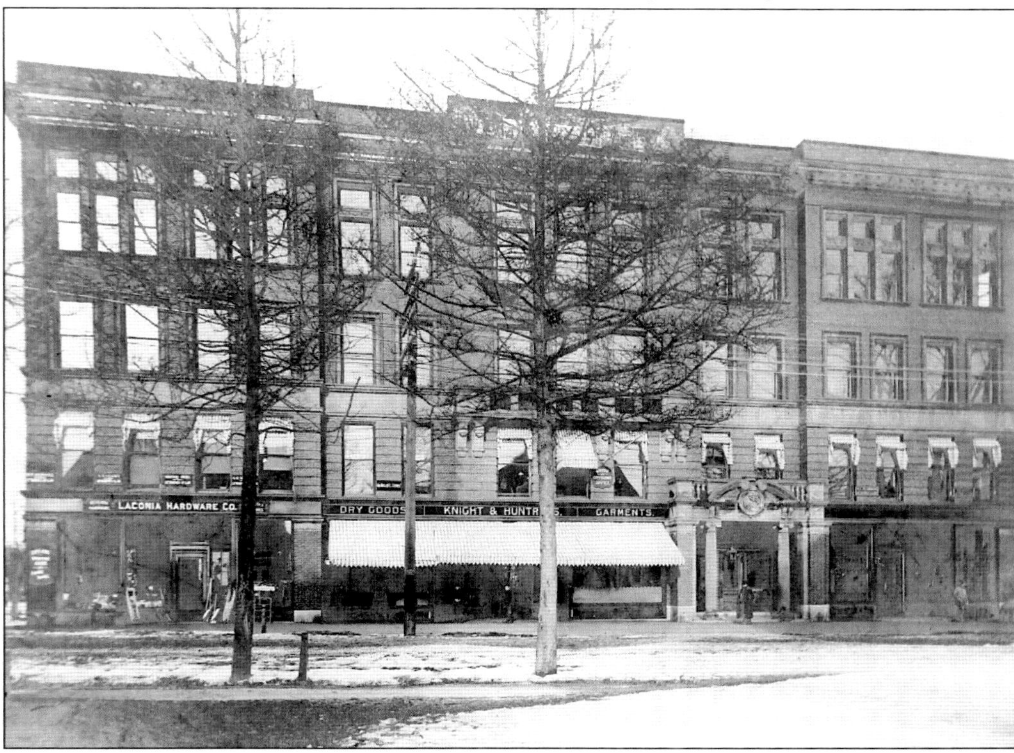


The Masonic Temple building, c. 1894. Tenants included the Laconia Hardware Co., Knight & Huntress, the post office, and city offices.

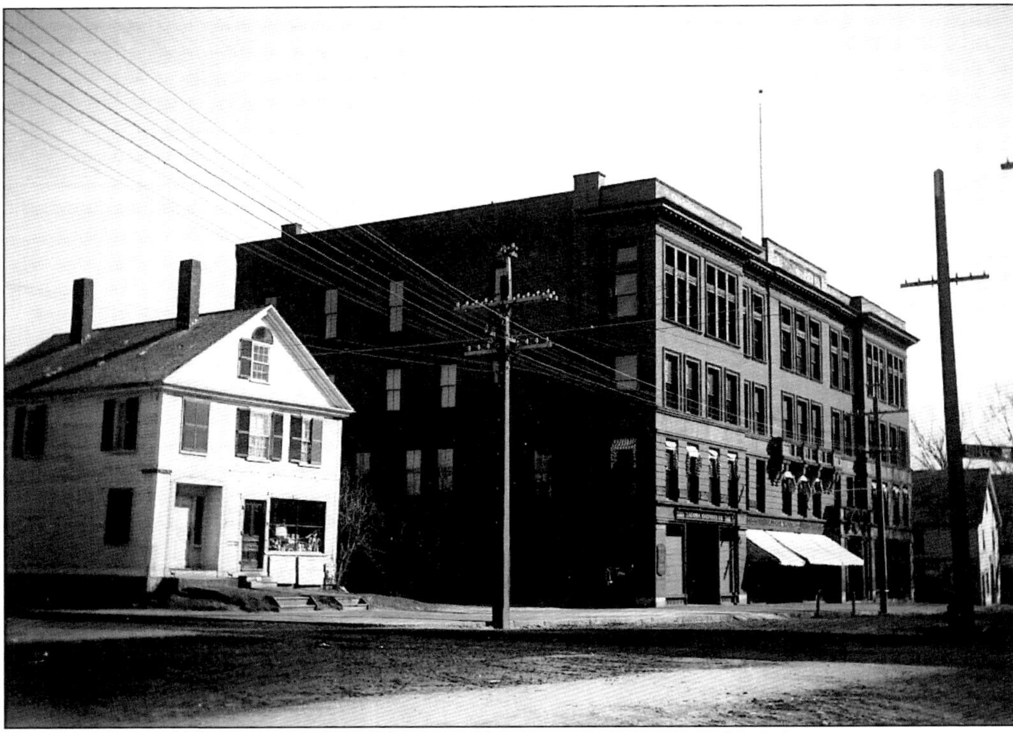

The Masonic Temple building, c. 1894, with a grocery store on the left and the D.K. Marsh livery stable on the right.

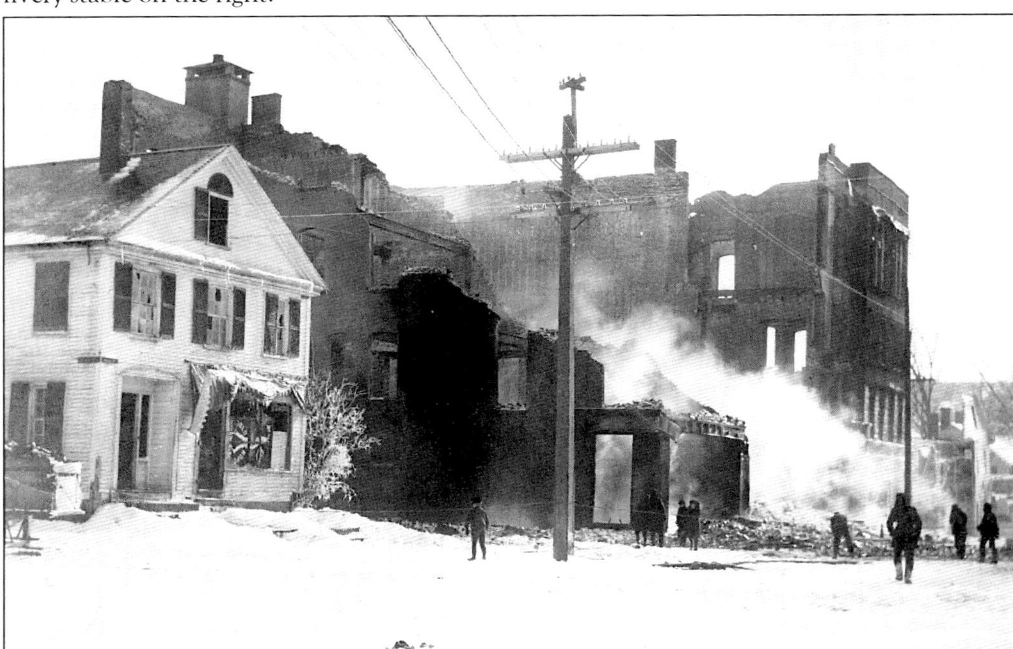

After the fire and massive explosion of December 6, 1902.

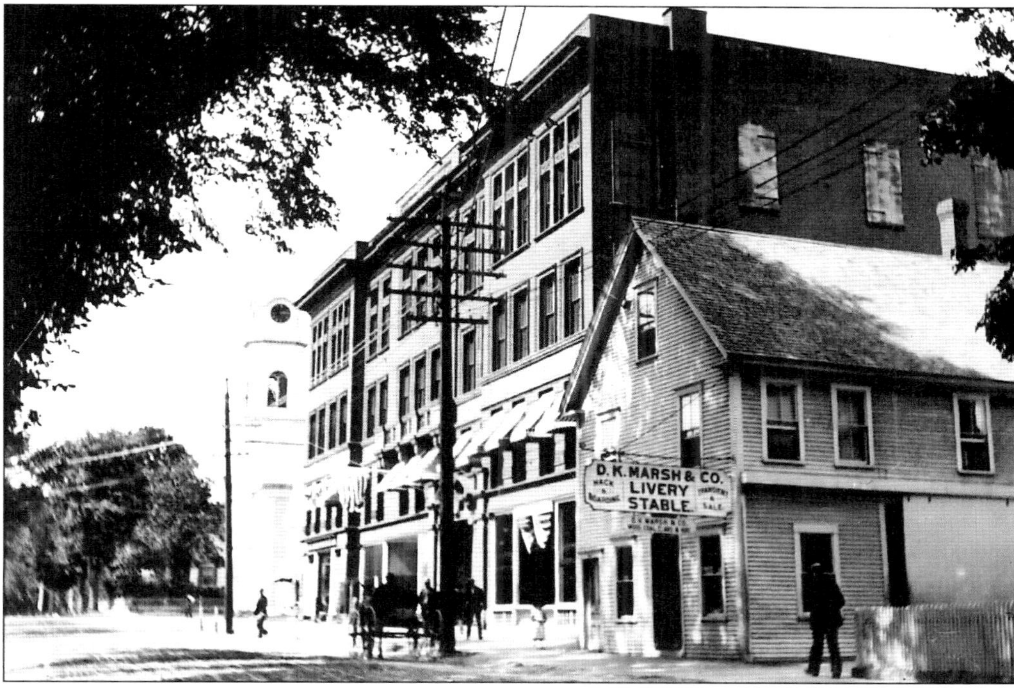


The Masonic Temple building seen from the south, c. 1900. The Old North Church (Congregational) is on the current site of the library's flagpole.

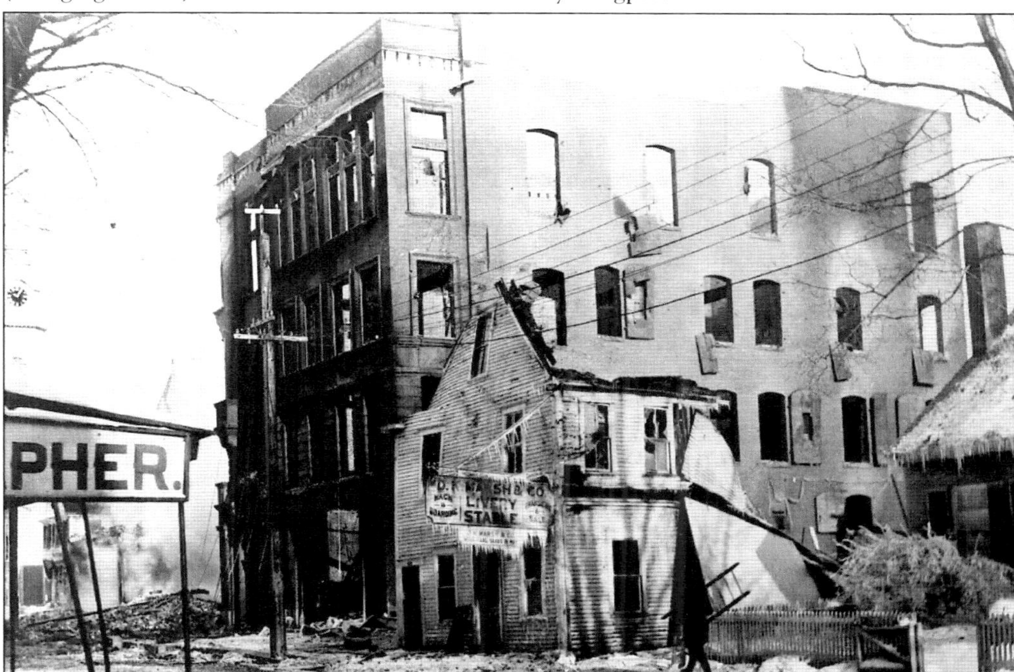


The ruins of the Masonic Temple building and the D.K. Marsh livery stable, the morning after the explosion.

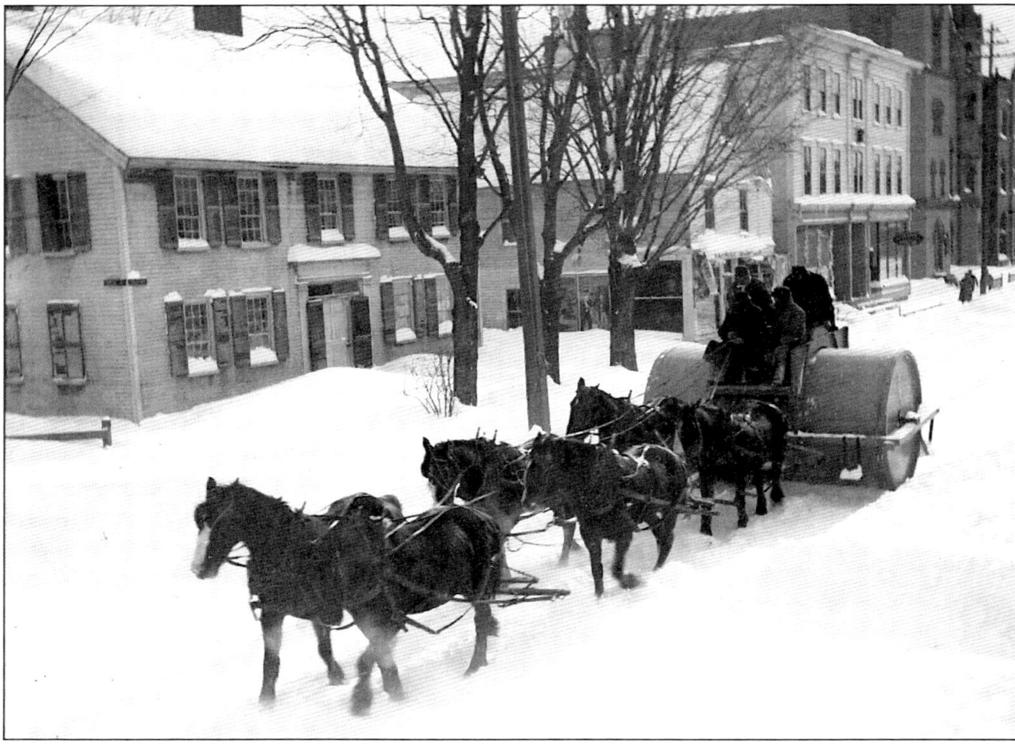

A snow roller on Main Street, c. 1899. The Russell House (later owned by Dr. Harriman) and the small commercial building to the right of it were removed for construction of the Colonial Theater, 1913–1914. The Perley Block can be seen next, followed by the Unitarian Church.

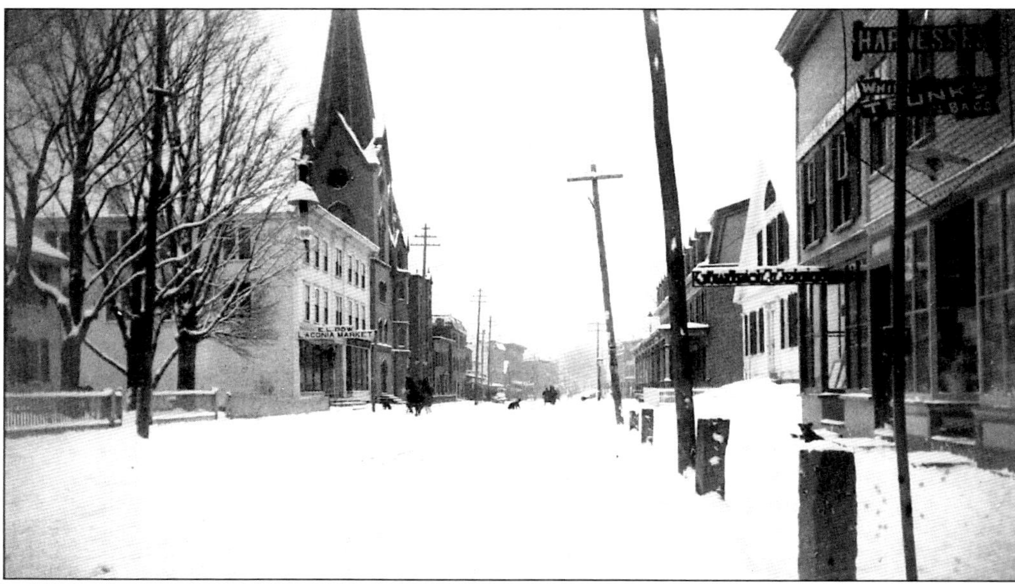


Main Street looking south, c. late 1890s. The Perley Block (center left) was built in 1885. E.L. Dow's Laconia Market (later Dow & Roberts) was the first tenant. The white-gabled Noyes House on the right was moved back for construction of the Cook Block in 1898.

# *Seven*

# Depot Square

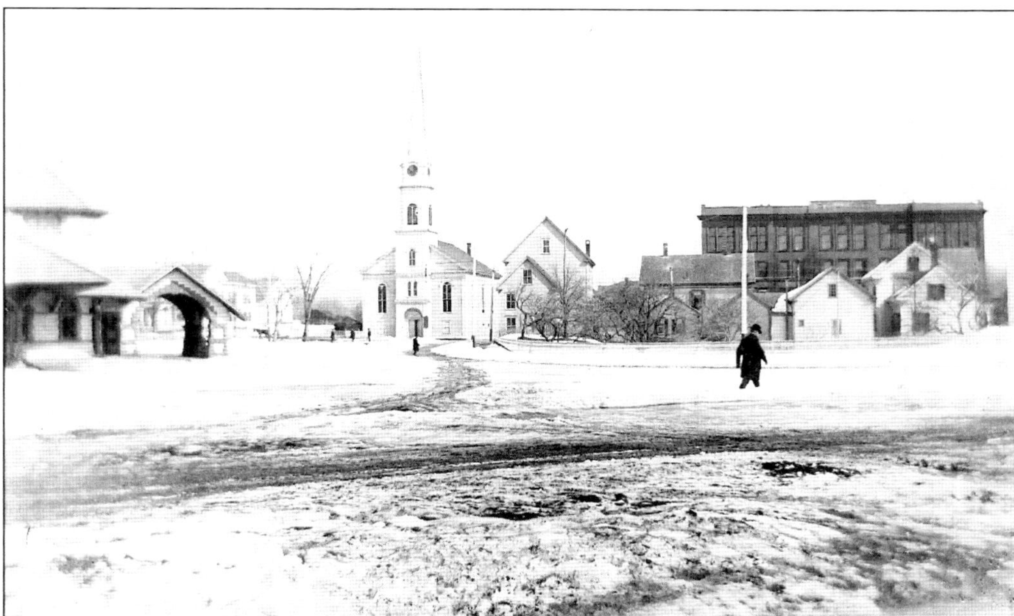

Depot Square (later Veterans Square), c. 1900. The railroad station (left) was dedicated in 1892. At the time of this photograph, the John C. Moulton House still occupied the site of today's Gale Memorial Library building and the Old North Church was in its original location. The first Masonic Temple building is visible on the right in the distance. The broad square replaced the earlier crowded area (see pp. 90–91).

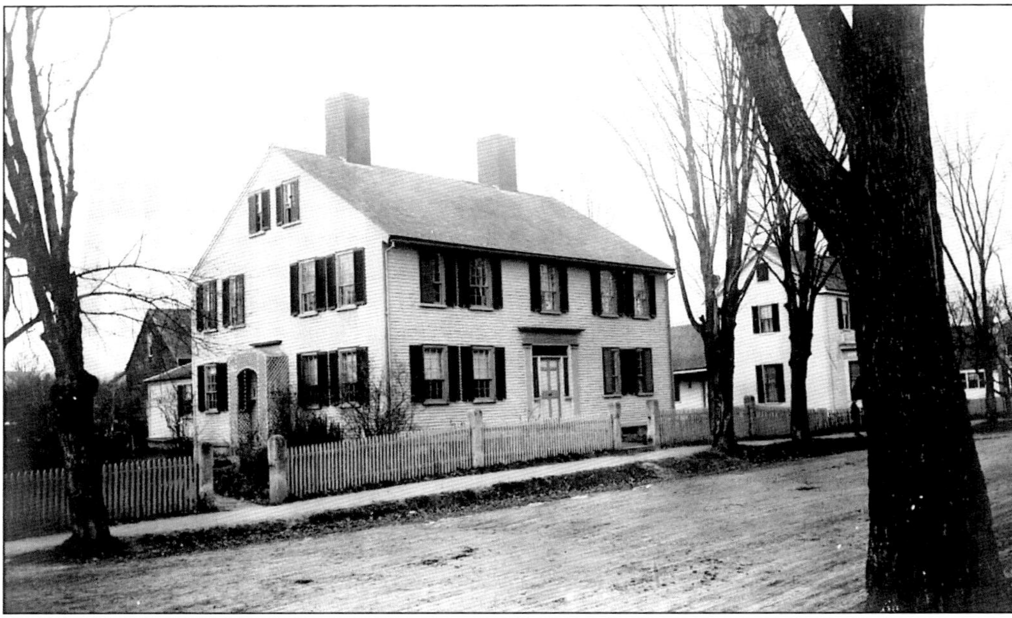

The Charles W. Parker House (later the Orsino A.J. Vaughan House) on North Main Street, c. 1890. When the Concord & Montreal Railroad built the new passenger station behind these buildings, the Vaughan House was moved to Wentworth Avenue. The Lane House (right) was moved further up North Main Street to a site adjacent to today's Central Fire Station. The area in this photograph is now a park containing the veterans' memorials.

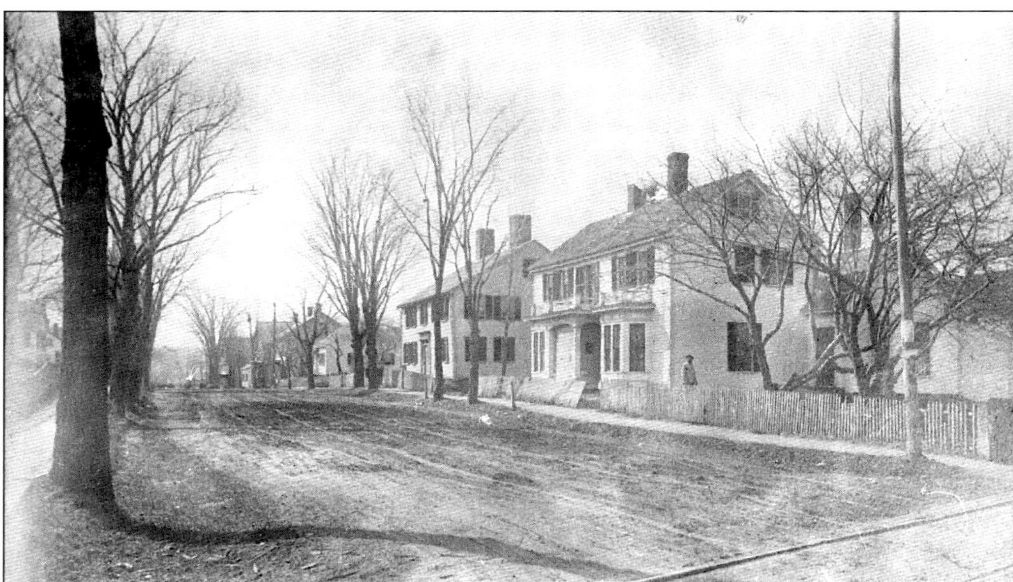

The Lane and Vaughan Houses on North Main Street, c. 1890. This is the same location, viewed from the opposite direction.

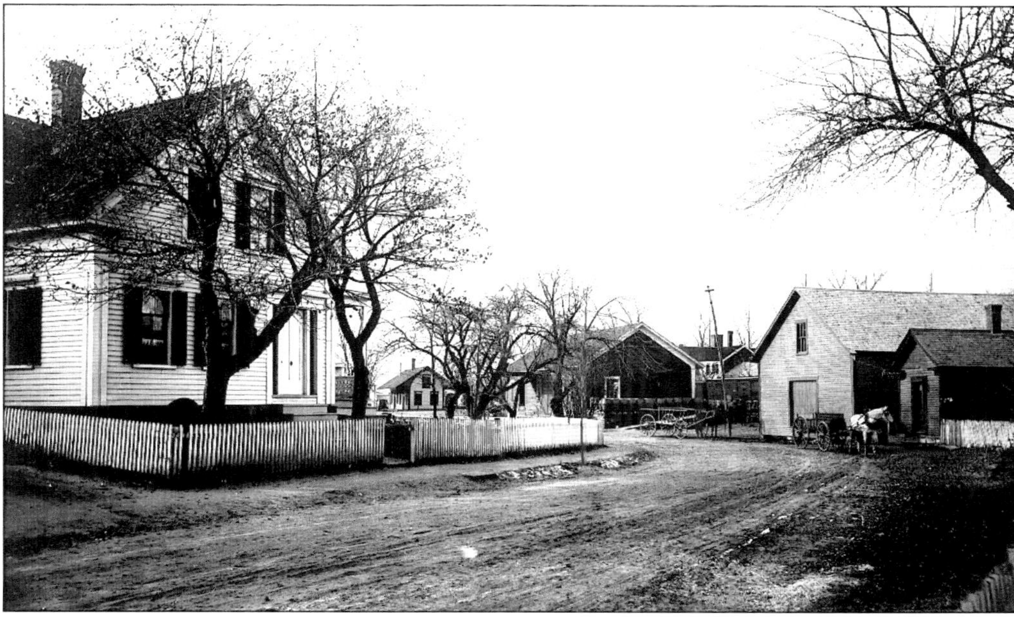

The intersection of North Main and Church Streets looking west, c. 1890. The freight depot (the large building at center right) and the barn and shed of the Vaughan House were removed to allow the construction of the new passenger depot in 1892. The horse and wagon (center right) stand approximately where the porte cochere of the current railroad station is located. The former passenger station (center left) is visible in distance.

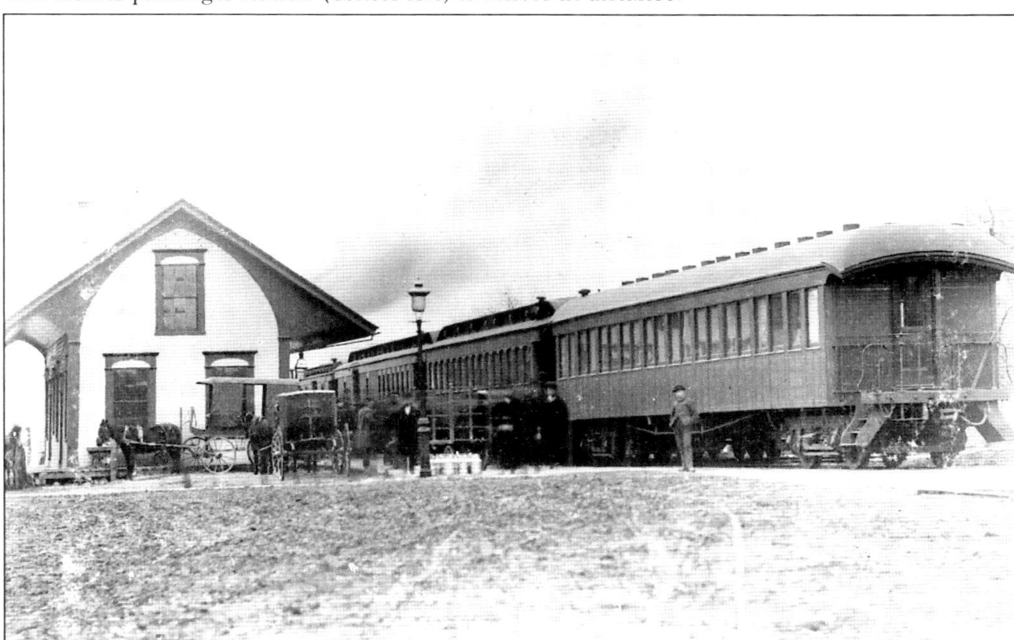

The Laconia passenger depot, c. 1886. The observation car (right) partly blocks the Pleasant Street crossing. Today, Beacon Street West runs through the site of the old depot (later occupied by the brick freight depot). See next page.

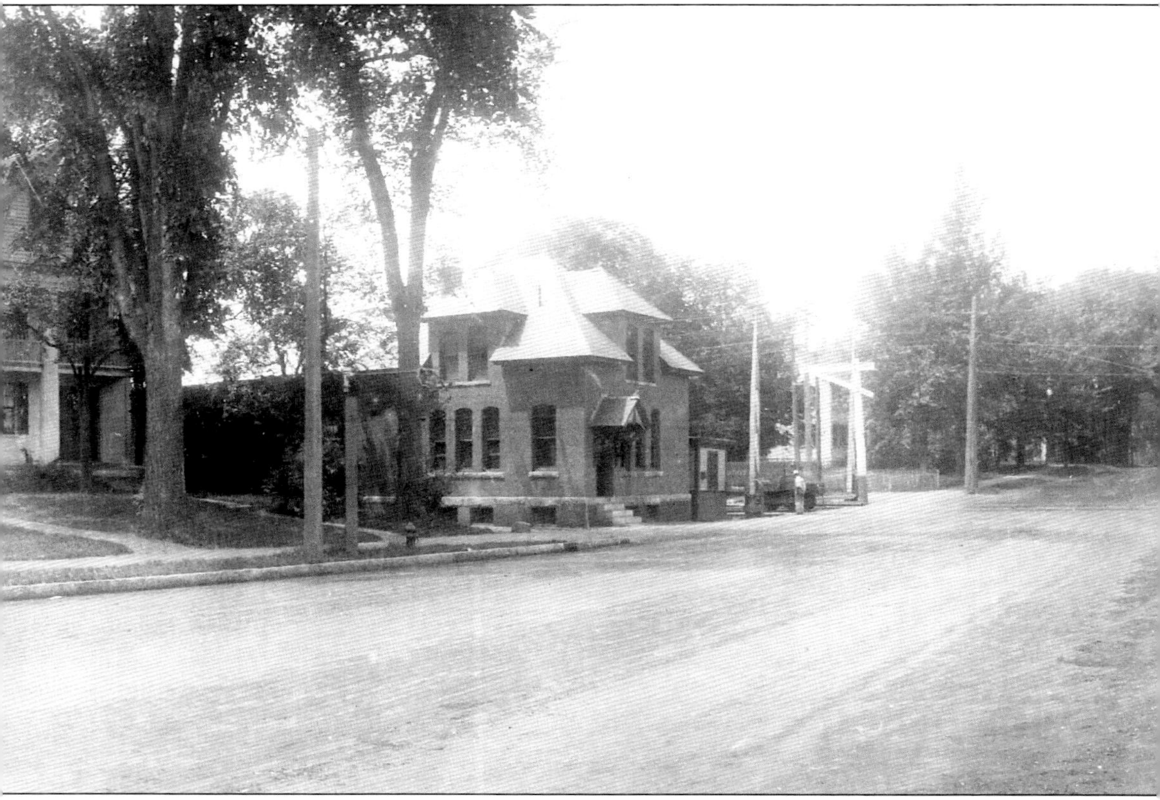

Pleasant Street at Depot Square, c. 1900. The brick freight depot (left) was built on the site of the first passenger station (see preceding page). The Beaman House (extreme left) was torn

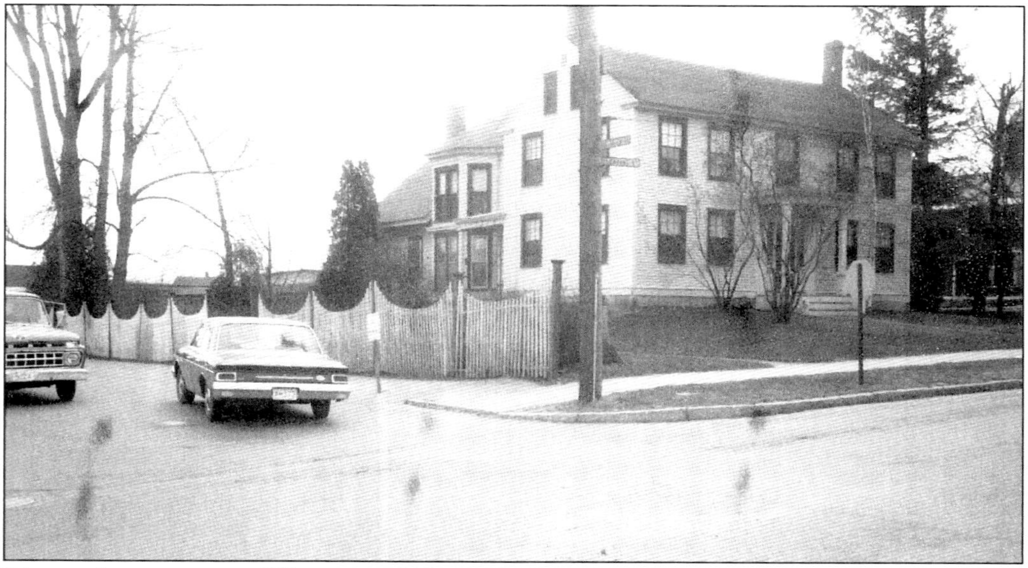

The northwest corner of Pleasant and New Salem Streets, c. 1970. The site is now a vacant lot, with the J.J. Morin complex located beyond the photograph to the left.

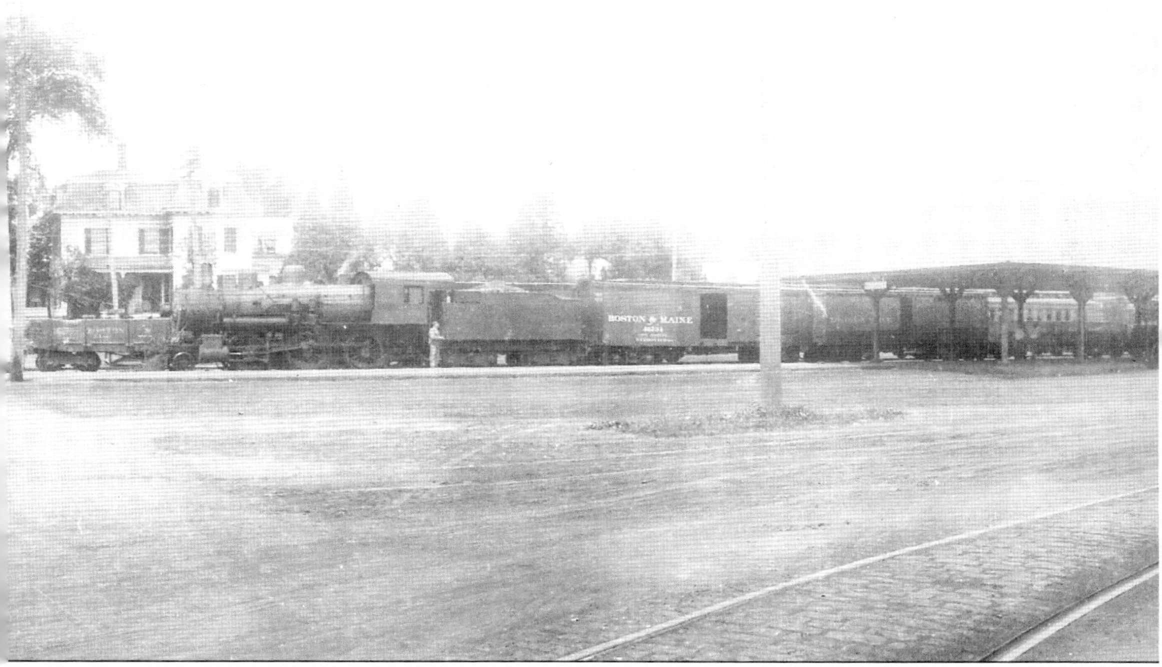

down in 1951. The tracks of the Laconia Street Railway curve gracefully toward the 1892 depot and Church Street.

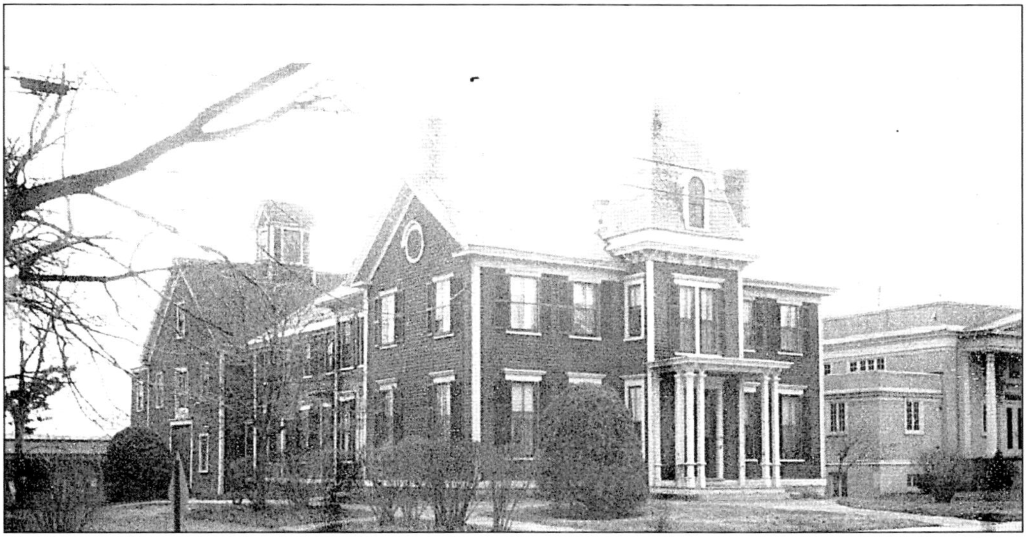

The Lewis F. Busiel House on Pleasant Street, c. 1970. Brother of J.W. Busiel, Lewis owned the mill adjacent to the Belknap Mill on Mill Street, which he sold to William Esty in 1889. The Christian Science Church, built in 1923–1924, can be seen on the right.

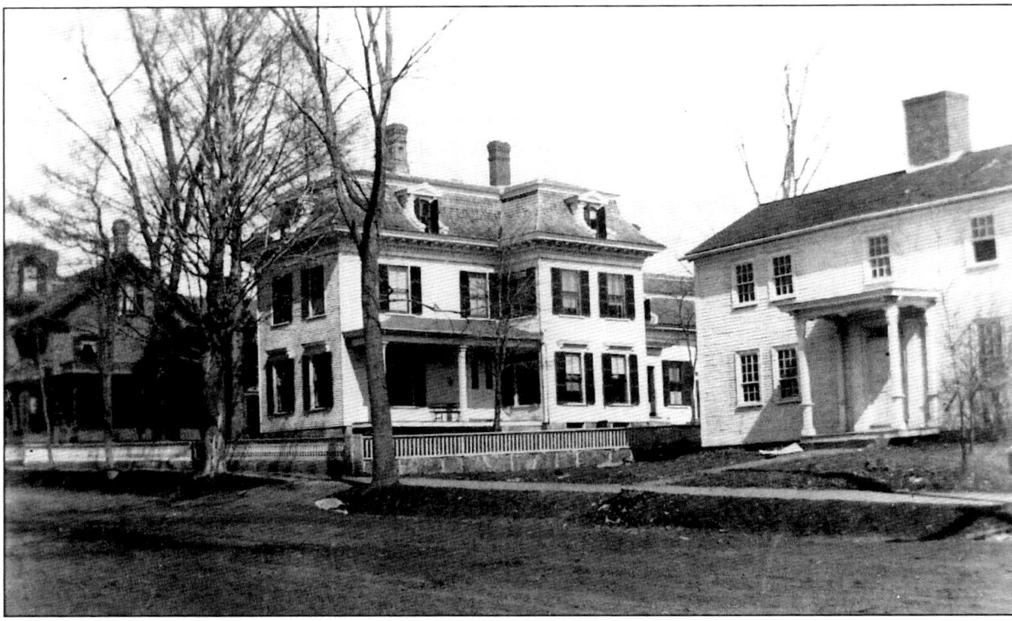

Pleasant Street before 1892. The Sanborn House (right) was removed when the railroad tracks were rerouted in 1892 in connection with construction of the new passenger station. The Leavitt House (middle) and the Frank E. Busiel House (left) can also be seen.

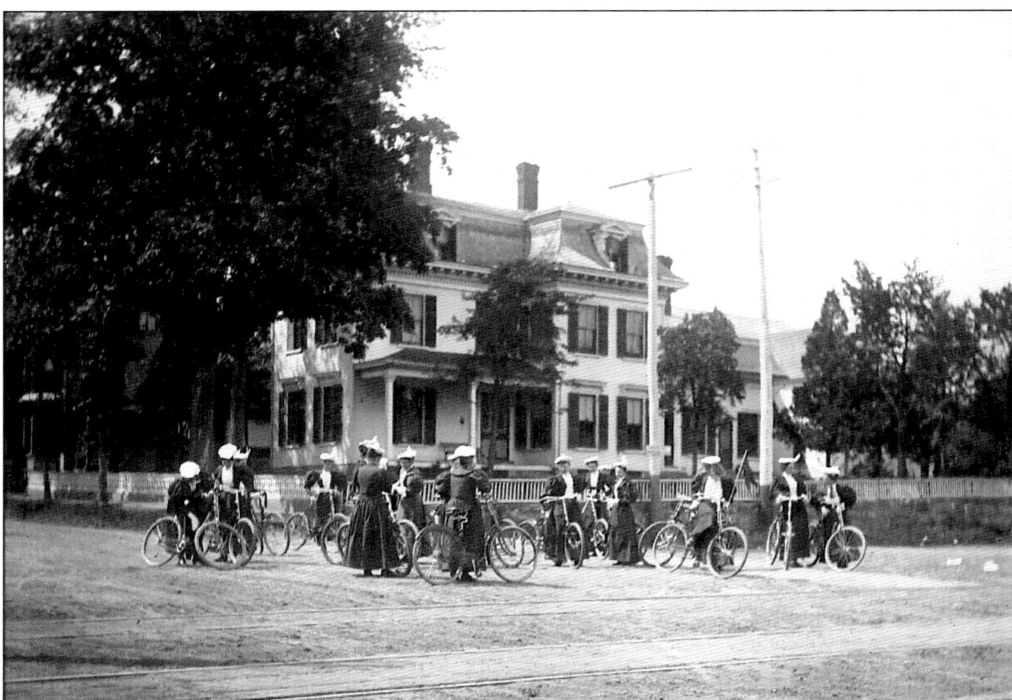

Bicyclists in the late 1890s at the intersection of Pleasant and New Salem Streets.

The Old North Church (Congregational) was built in 1836. This edifice, at the corner of North Main and Church Streets, replaced an earlier building (located on South Main Street somewhere between today's Promise You Gift Shop and Dunkin' Donuts) which burned earlier that year.

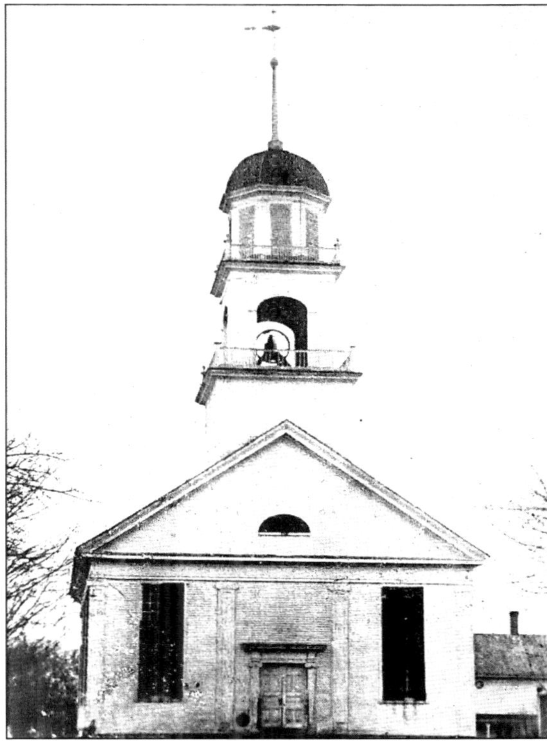

The Old North Church (Congregational) after the renovations of 1871–1872. This photograph was taken after 1903, when the library (left) was built. The second Masonic Temple building is under construction (extreme right). The frame structure, at the corner of Church and Main Streets, was later removed when the Laconia Tavern was built in 1913.

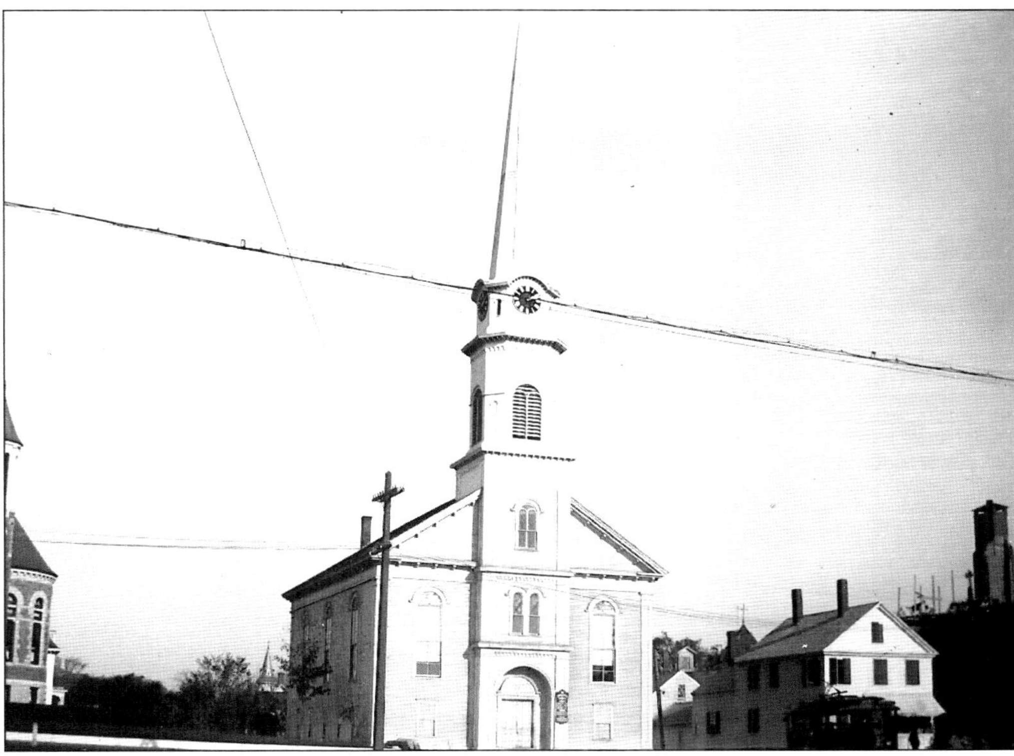

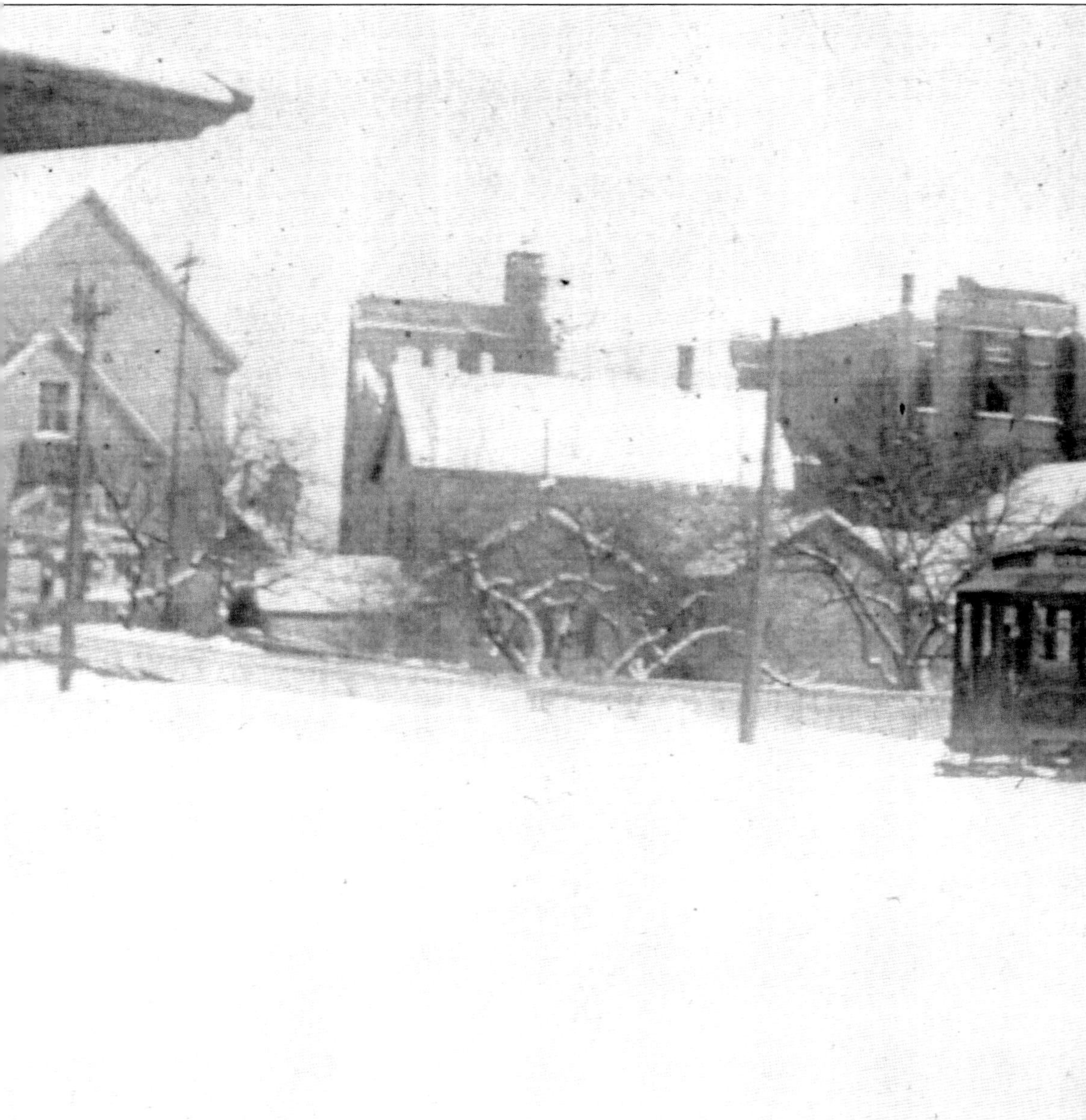

A trolley car heads east through Depot Square towards Church Street, c. 1902. The ruins of the Masonic Temple building, after the 1902 fire and explosion, are visible at the top and the overhang of the railroad station canopy is visible at the upper left.This view would change a

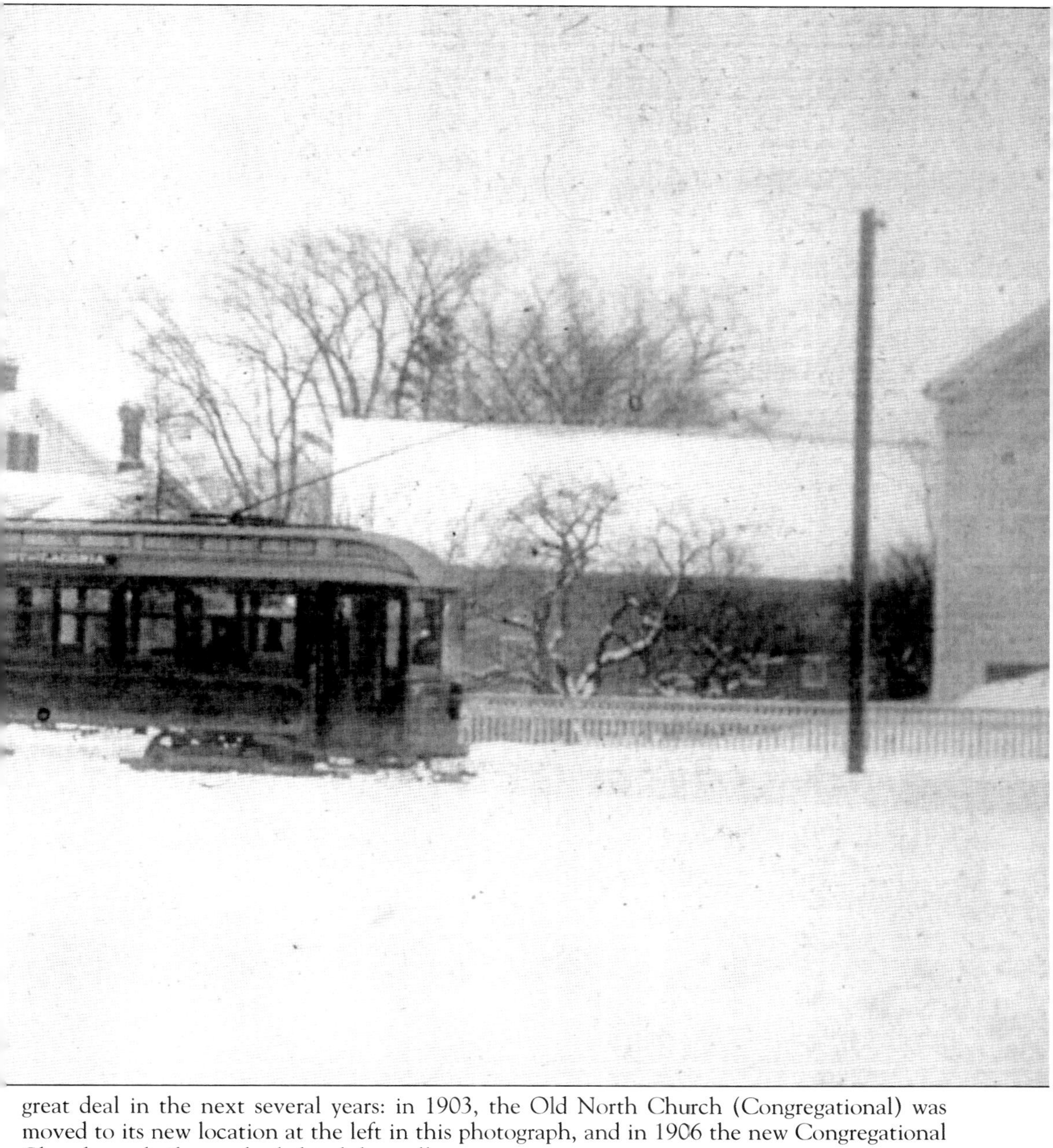

great deal in the next several years: in 1903, the Old North Church (Congregational) was moved to its new location at the left in this photograph, and in 1906 the new Congregational Church was built on a lot behind the trolley.

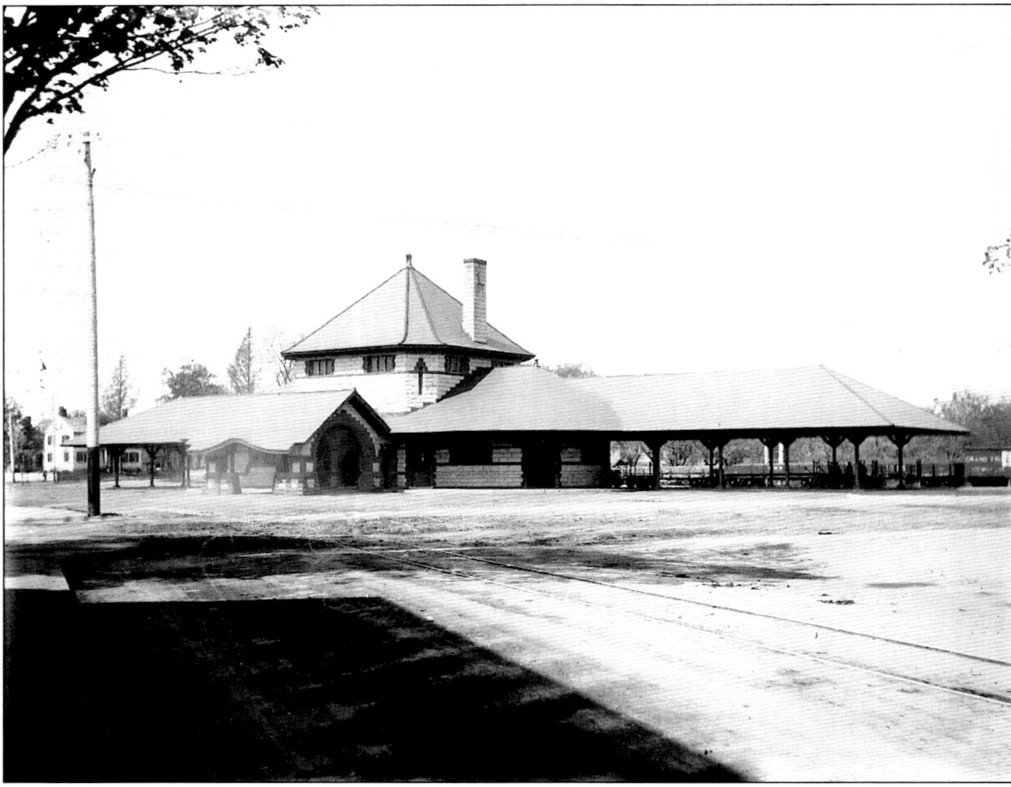

The passenger depot in the early 1900s.

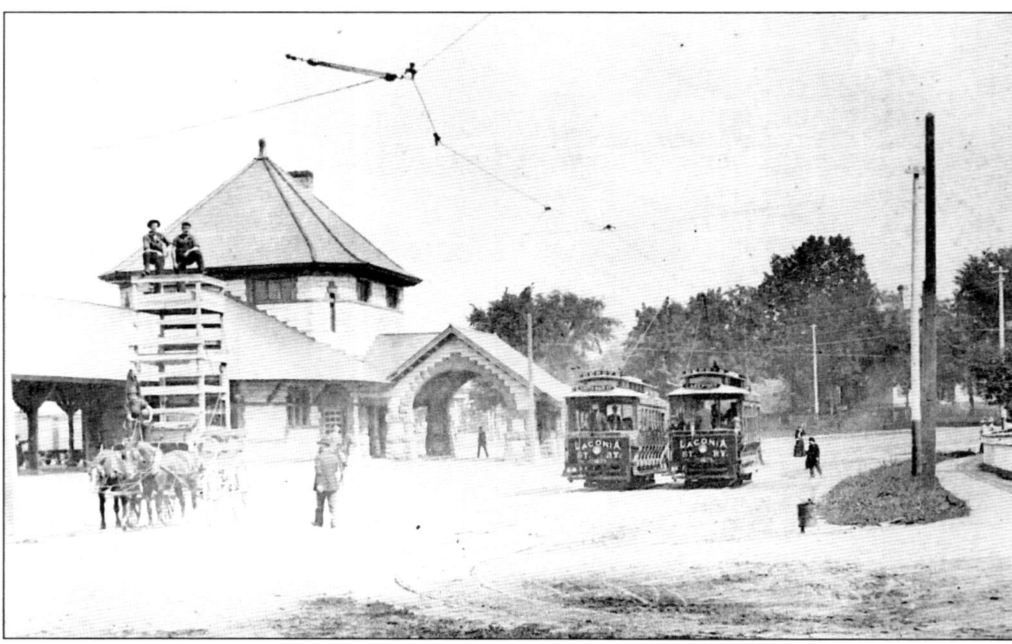

Depot Square, 1899.

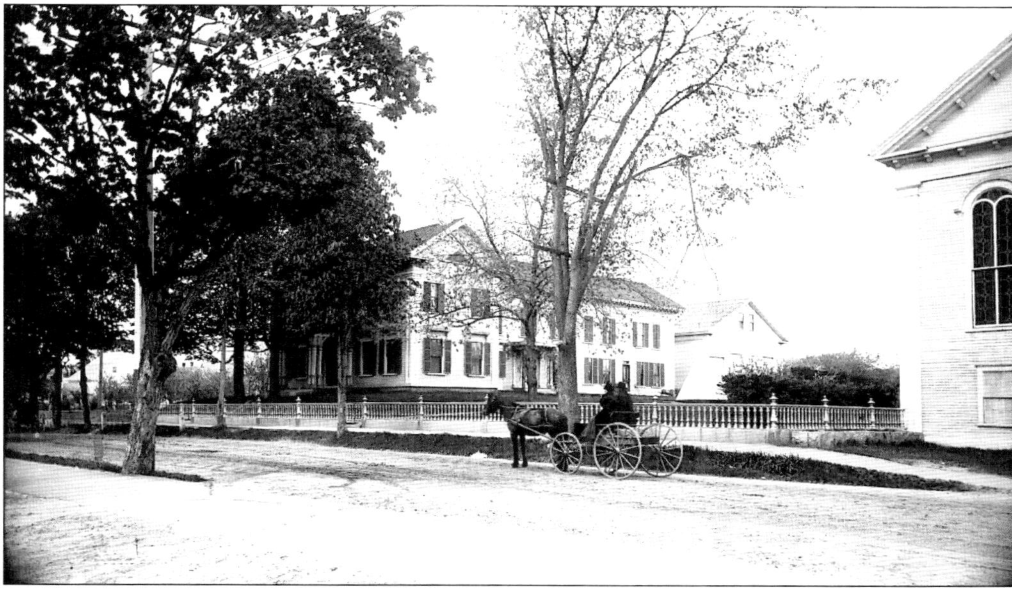

The John C. Moulton House on North Main Street, c. 1880. The Gale Memorial Library building was built on this site in 1903. The Old North Church (Congregational) is on the right.

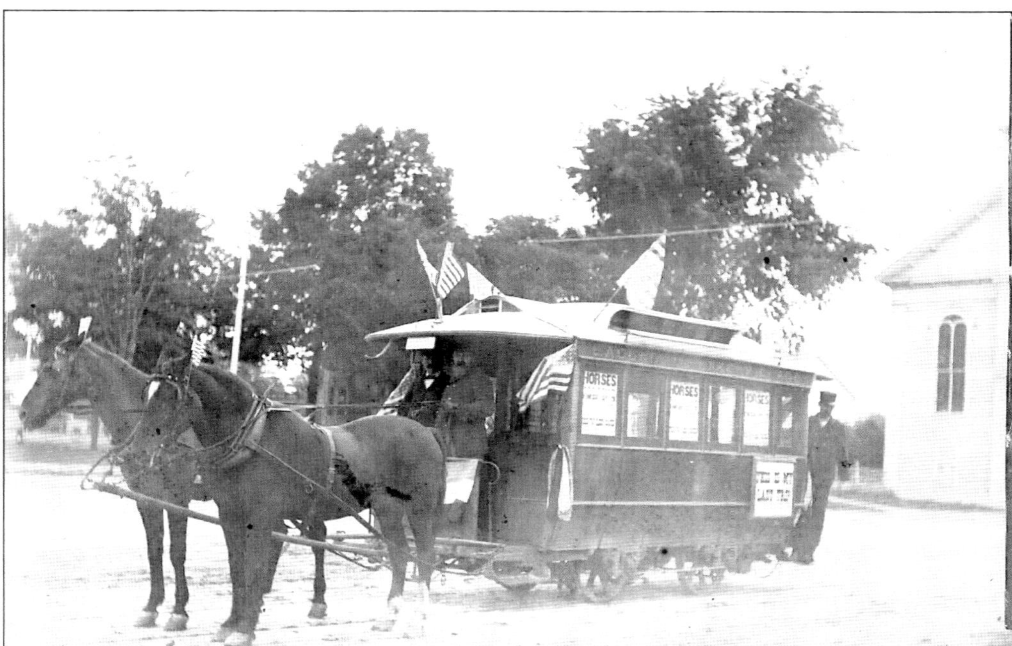


The last trip of the horse railway in 1898, after which the line shifted over to electric trolleys. According to the posters in the windows, horses David and Lil were for sale. The Old North Church (Congregational) can be seen on the right.

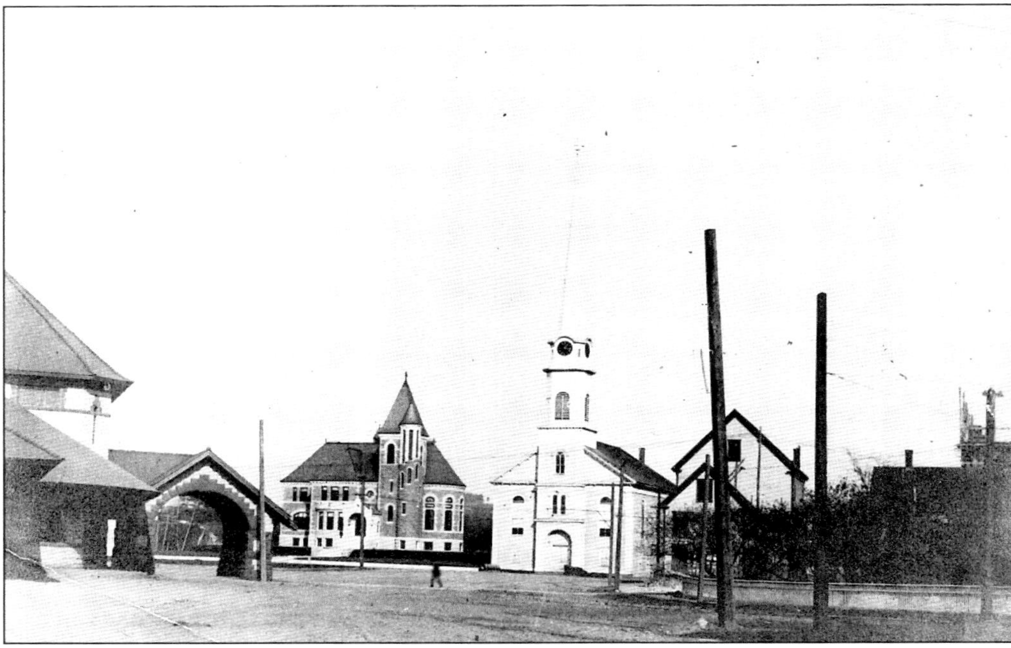

The Old North Church (Congregational) begins its move to a new location, 1903.

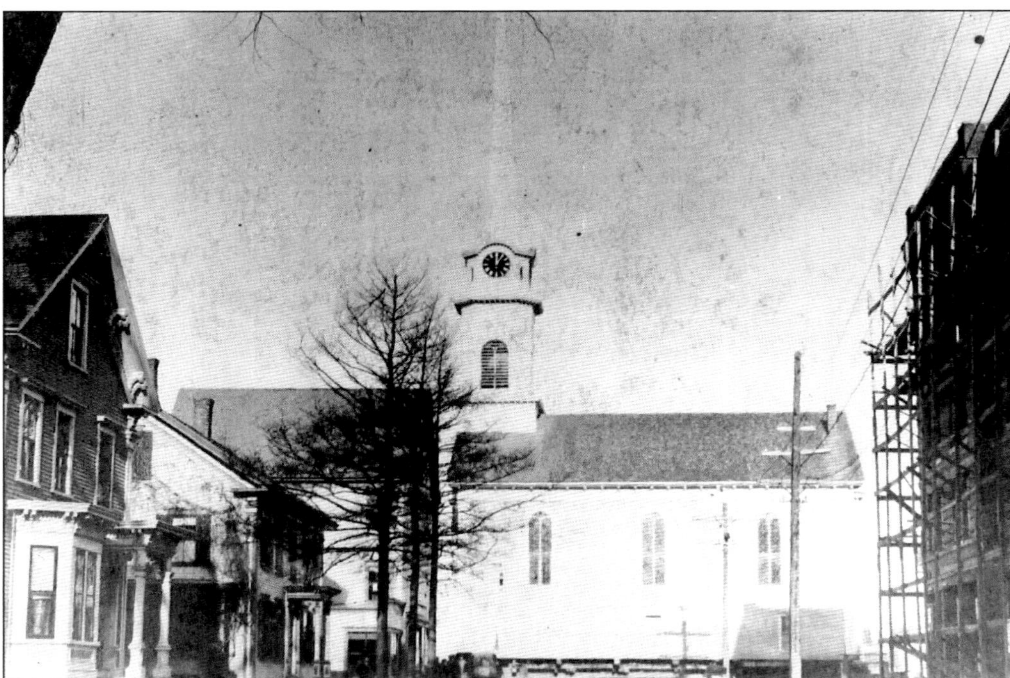

On the move, 1903. The construction of the new Masonic Temple building (right) is under way. The Baldi Block was later built on the site of the second house on the left.

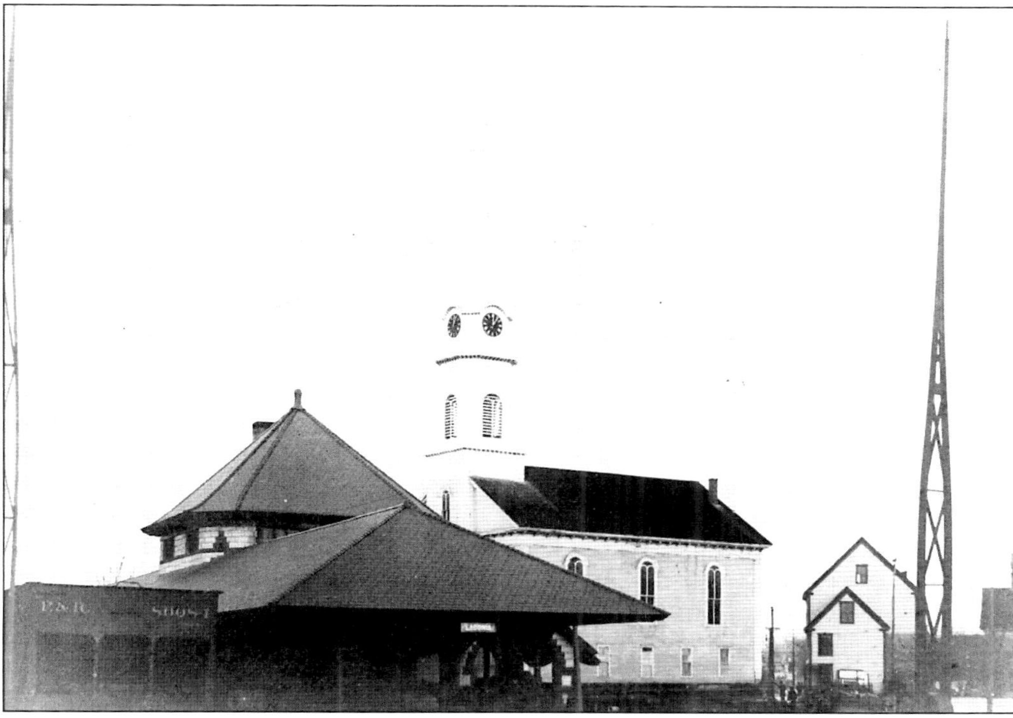

Halfway there, as the church was being turned to back into its new location. This photograph was taken in 1903 from between the Pleasant Street crossing gates.

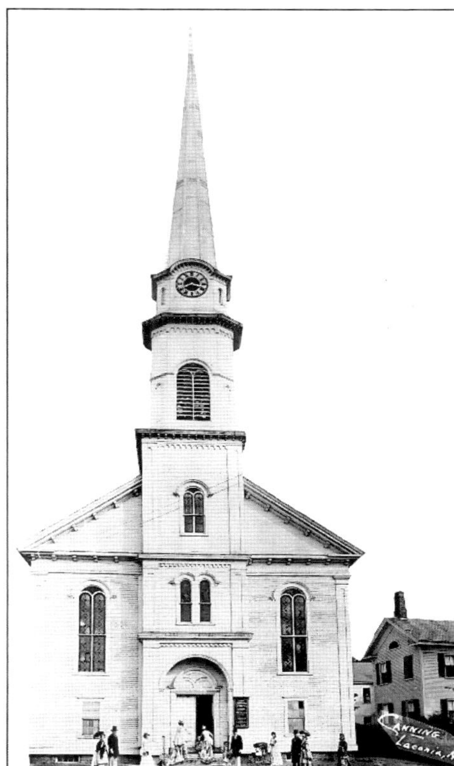

The new location. This 1936 photograph also shows the Harriet Gale House (right), relocated here to make way for construction of the 1906 stone Congregational Church. The town clock, in the steeple, served until the hurricane of 1938, when the steeple came crashing down.

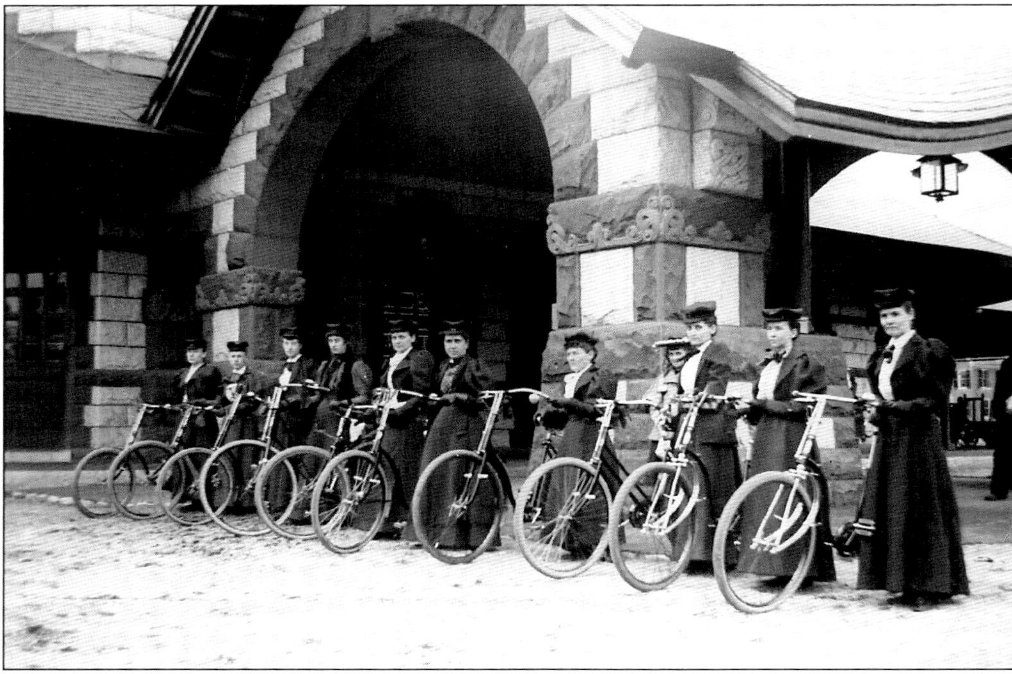

An early 1900s photograph of the Ladies' Bicycle Club, at the porte cochere of the Laconia passenger station.

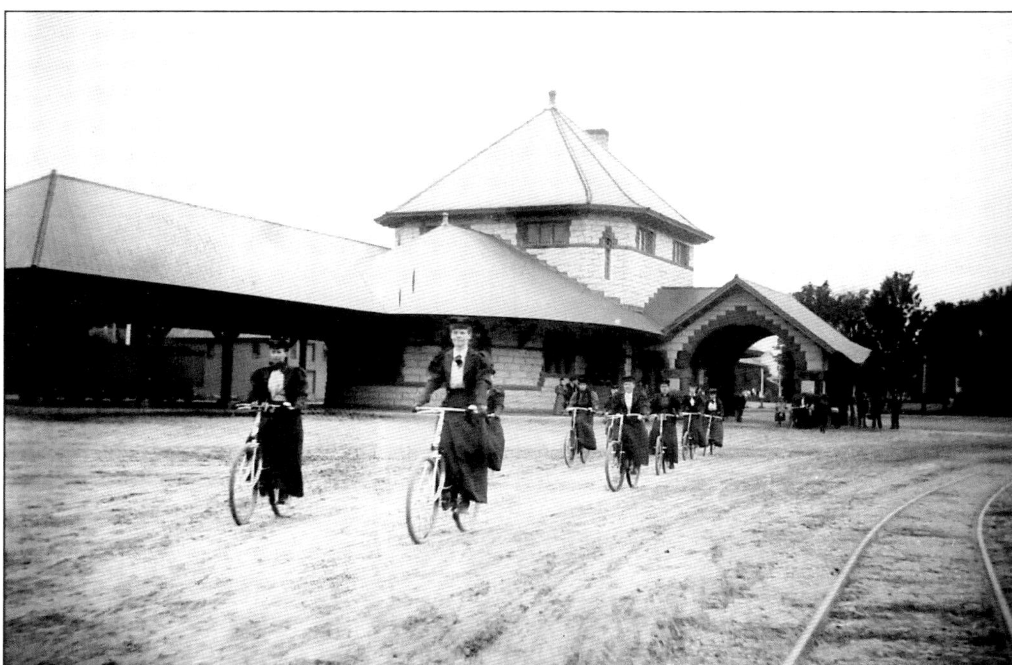

Heading west through Depot Square in the early 1900s. The tracks of the Laconia Street Railway appear on the right.

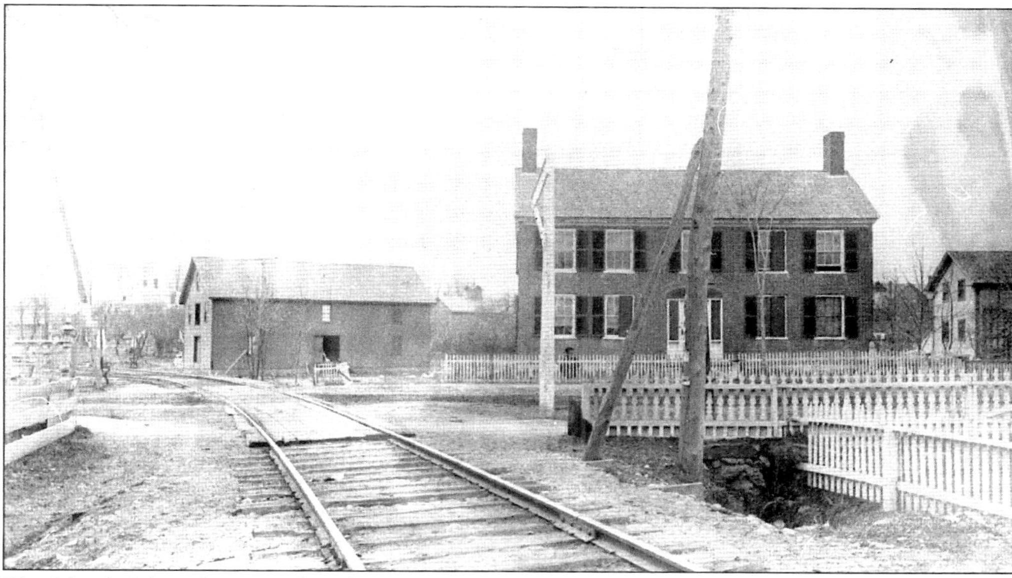

The North Main Street railroad crossing, c. 1890s. John Y. Mugridge, a Concord lawyer, was born and lived here. The house was later turned 90 degrees and moved slightly further west down New Salem Street. Later, the Merrimack Farmers Exchange was built on this site, now part of the entrance to the Laconia Clinic.

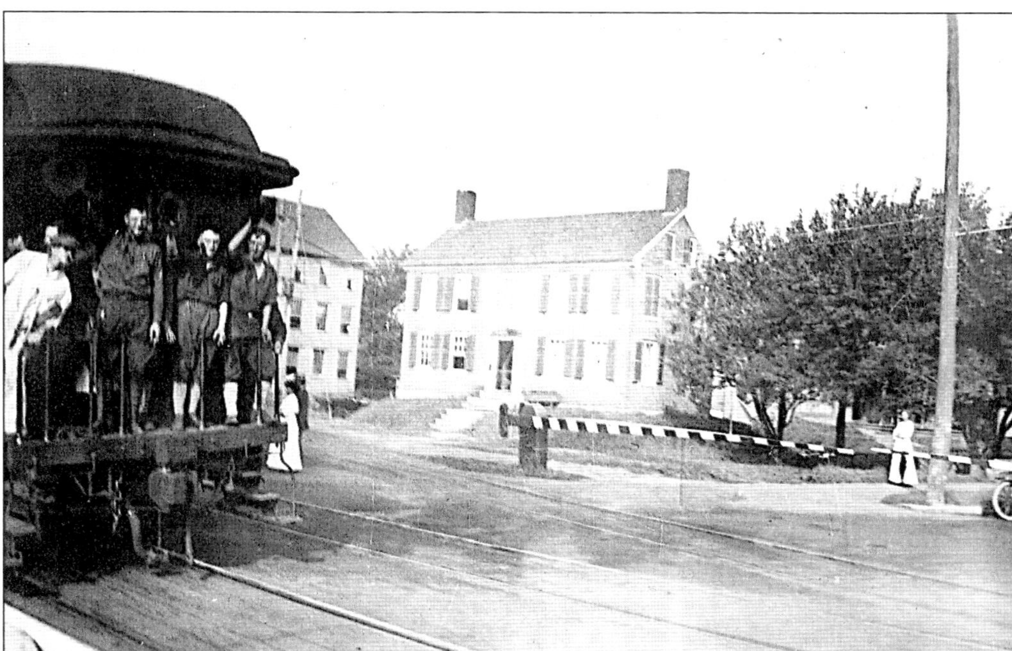

The North Main Street railroad crossing after the Mugridge House was relocated.

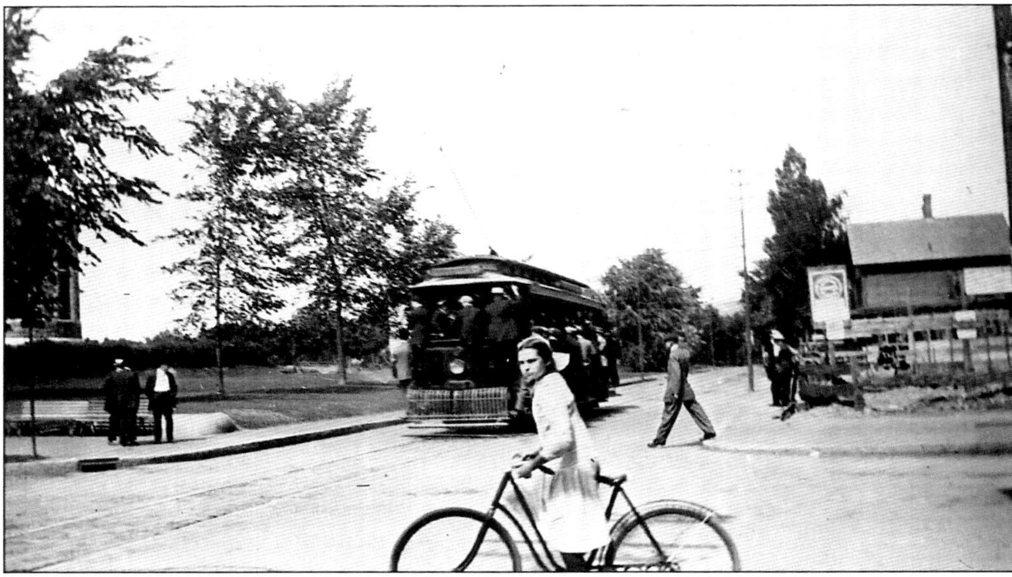

The intersection of Church and Main Streets, looking east, in the early 1900s. The open trolley car was probably headed for The Weirs. The library (1903) appears on the left; the Laconia Tavern (1913) has not yet been built on the lot at right (see p. 105-106).

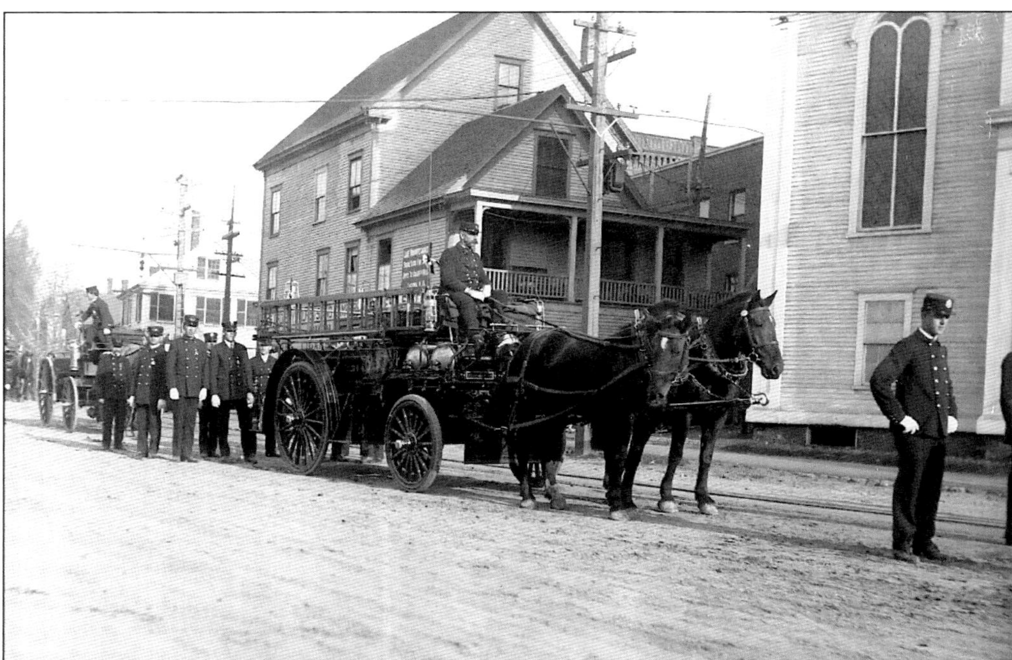

The ladder truck of the Laconia Fire Department in Depot Square in the early 1900s.

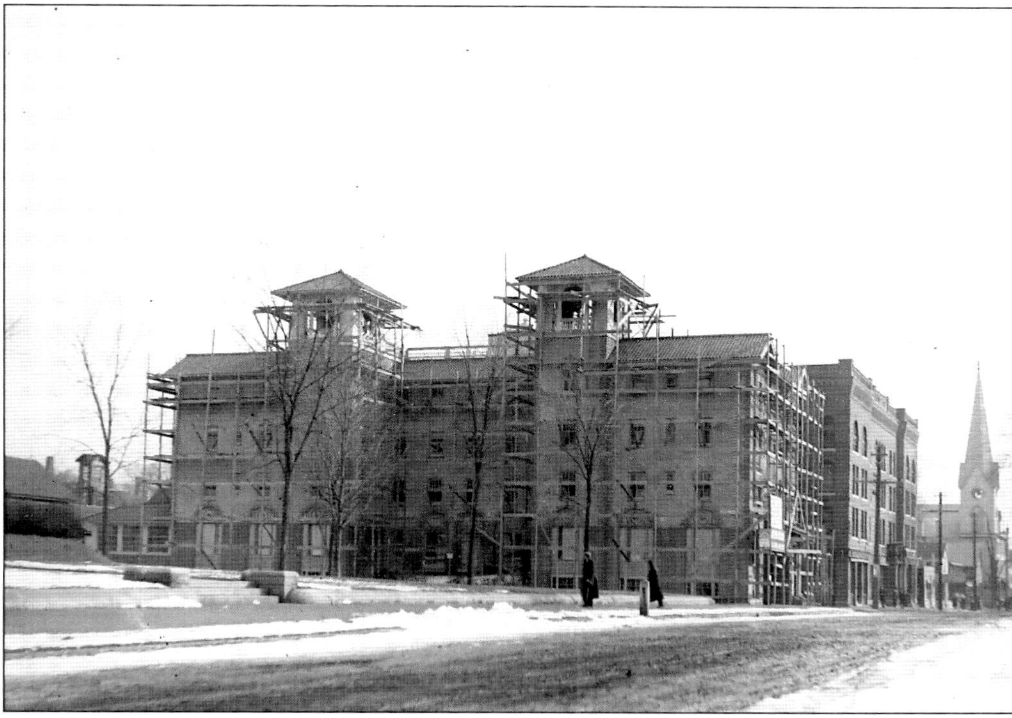

The Laconia Tavern under construction in 1913.

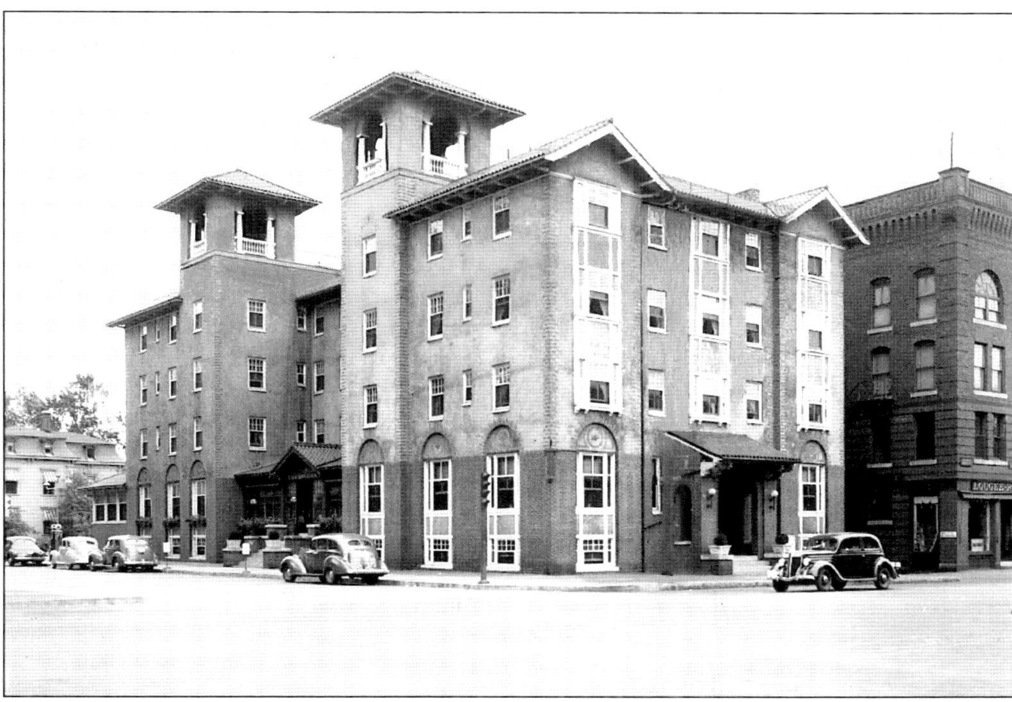

The Laconia Tavern in the 1930s. Part of the Governor Busiel House is visible at the extreme left.

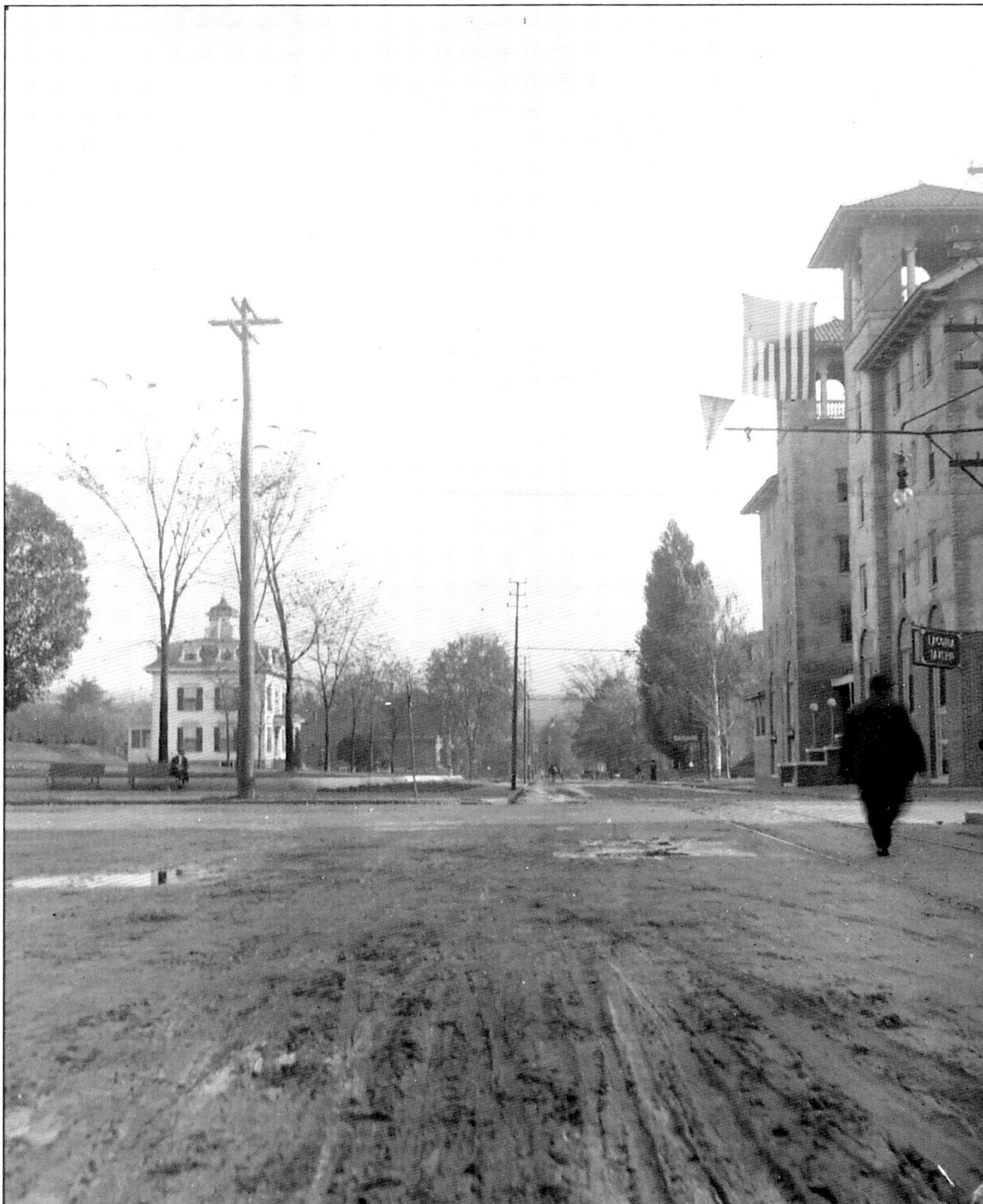

The Church and Main Street intersection in the early 1900s. The J.W. Busiel House (left) still sports a cupola. Trees and mud still give a rural aspect to the city.

# *Eight*

# Church Street

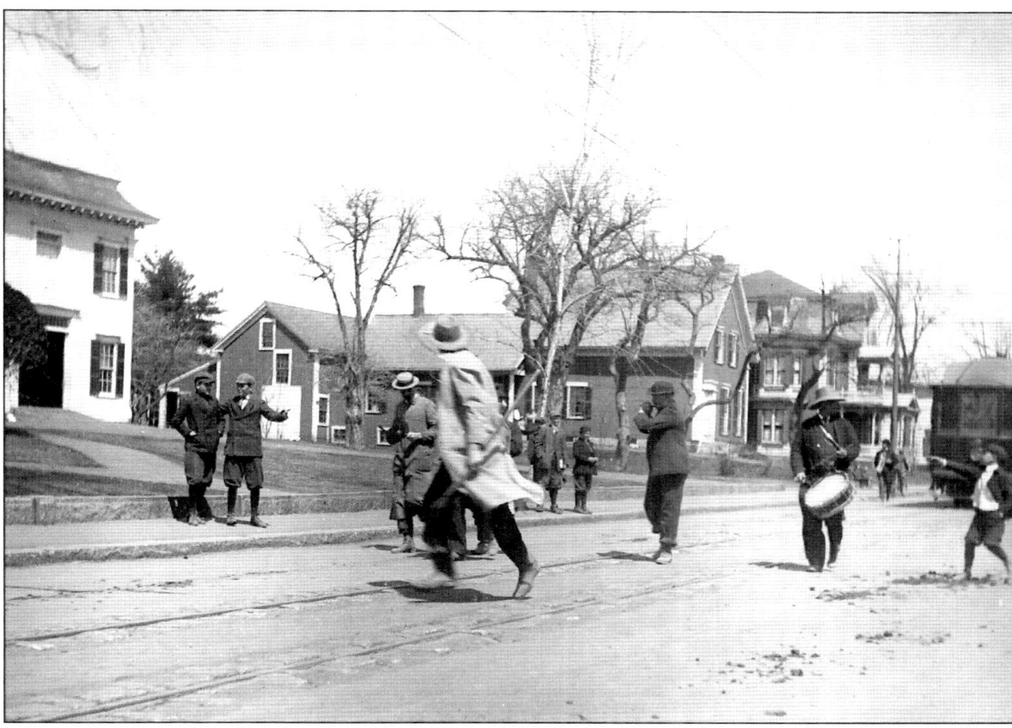

Church Street in the early 1900s. An impromptu parade leads a trolley car (right). The carriage house of the J.W. Busiel House is on the left, followed by the Sanborn House (torn down to allow the construction of the 1929 St. Joseph Church) and the Perley Putnam House at the corner of Messer Street (moved back for the St. John—now Holy Trinity—School in 1926).

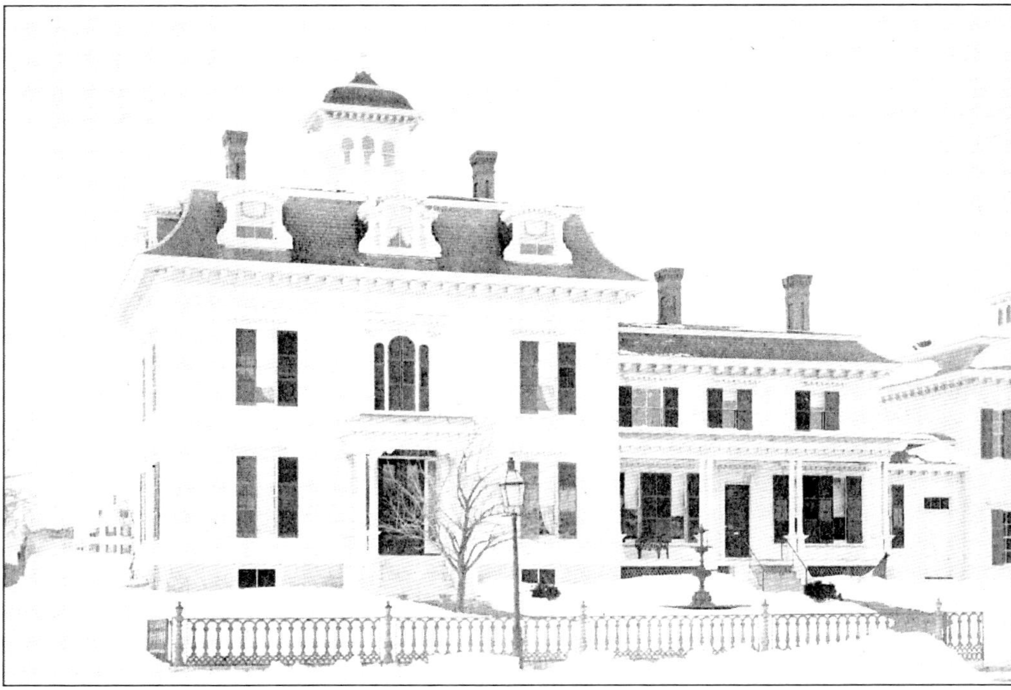

The John Weymouth Busiel House, Church Street, c. 1880s. One of the earliest designs of Laconia architect Arthur L. Davis, the stately "French Villa" was built in 1865 by the founder of the Busiel Mill. Today the house is the rectory of the St. Joseph Parish.

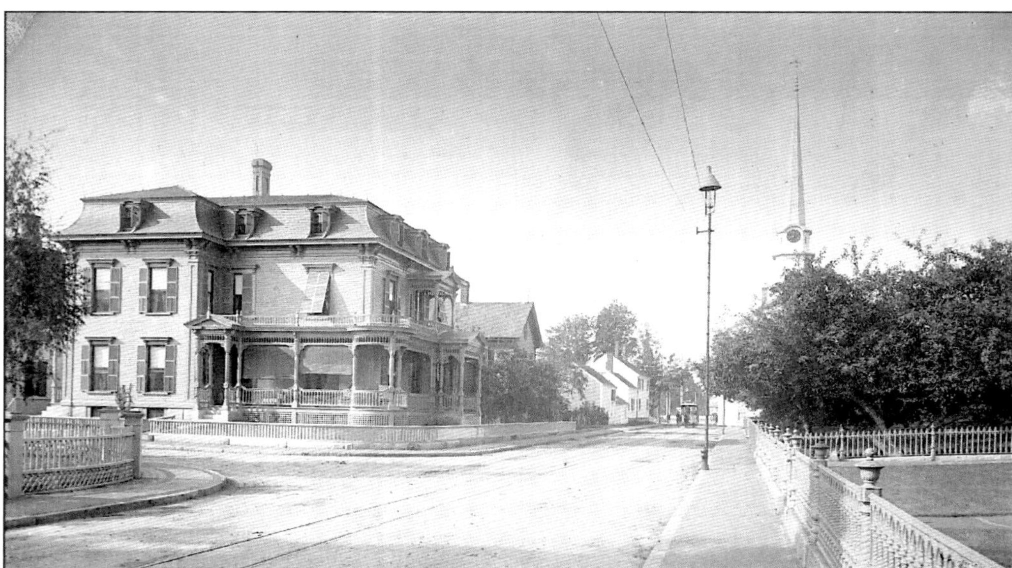

The Governor Charles A. Busiel House on Church Street, in the 1880s. Beacon Street is on the left, with the Old North Church (Congregational) in the distance on the right. The Russell Carter House (the modern site of the post office building) is off the photograph at the left; the front lawn of the J.W. Busiel House is behind the fence on the right.

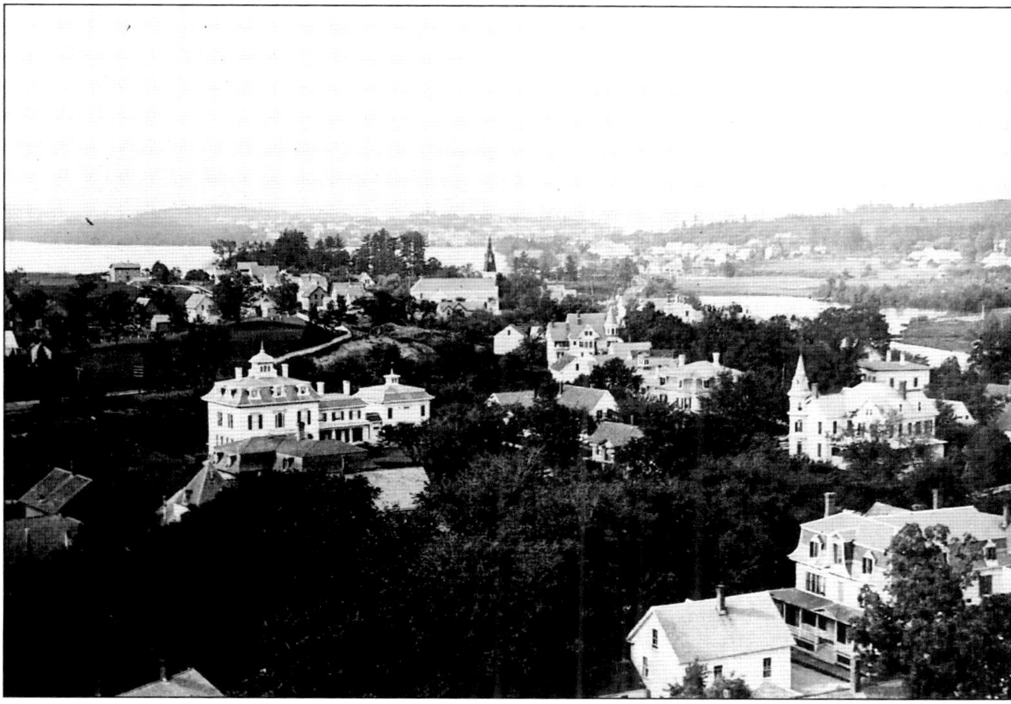

The Church and Messer Street area in the early 1900s. The J.W. Busiel House dominates the center left of the photograph. The turreted J.T. Busiel House appears at the center right. Below it, the Lewis Wilkinson House (later the Wilkinson Funeral Home) is located on the site of today's Beacon Street parking lot. Across the street is the site of today's First NH Bank drive-in facility. Lake Opechee is in the upper left and the 1877 St. Joseph Church, on the corner of Lyford and Messer Streets, is at the top center.

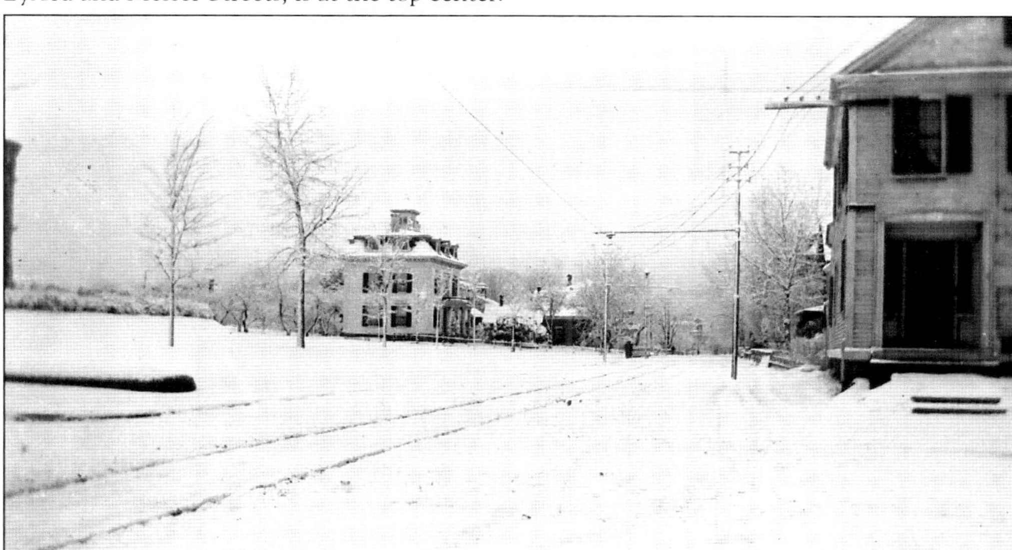

A grocery store (right), the library (left), and the J.W. Busiel House (center left) make up this winter view of Church Street, c. 1906–1907.

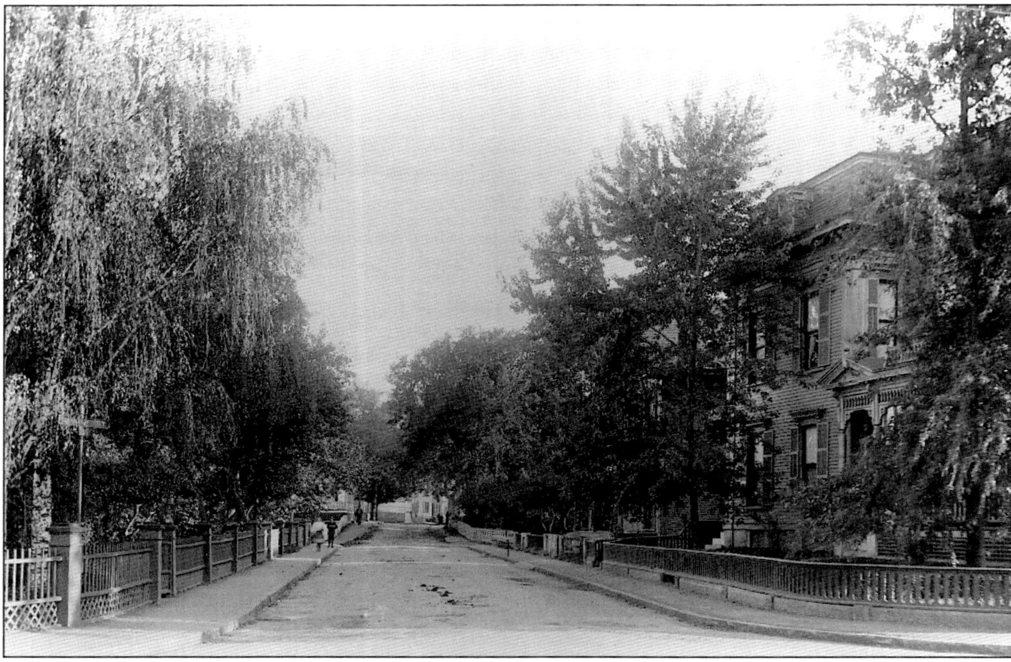

Beacon Street, c. 1917. The Russell Carter House lies beyond the photograph on the left; the Governor Busiel House is on the right. Obscured by trees, the Dr. Easton House adjoins the governor's mansion, with its yard fronting on Canal Street (see p. 112). The Tavern Exxon Station parking lot and the brick business block containing the Belknap Agency and other offices now occupy the site.

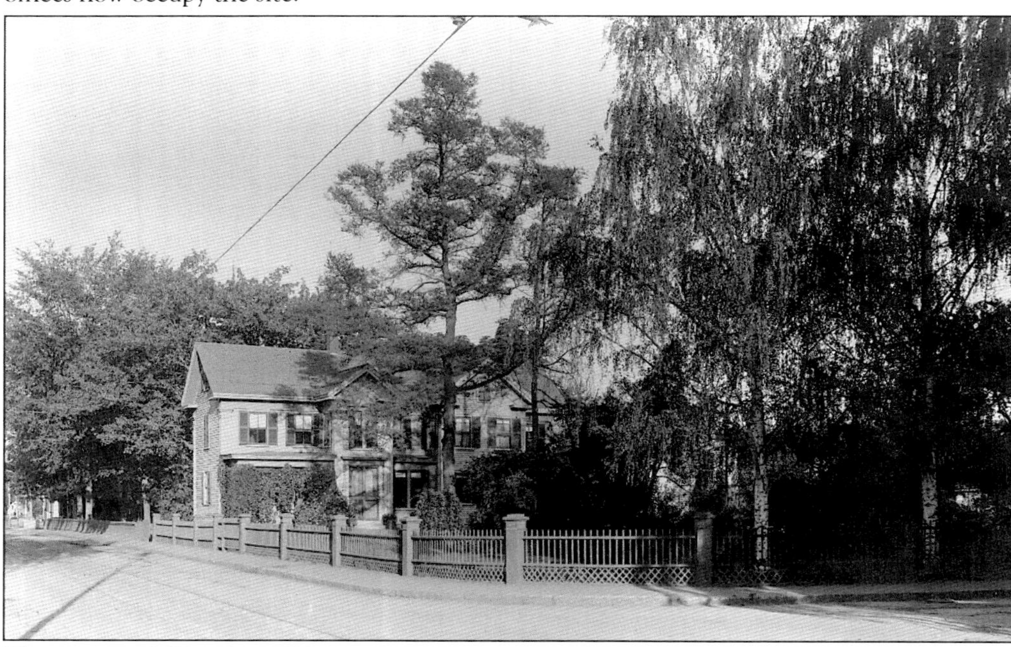

The corner of Church and Beacon Streets, c. 1917. The Russell Carter House was removed to make way for the construction of the Laconia Post Office, 1917–1919.

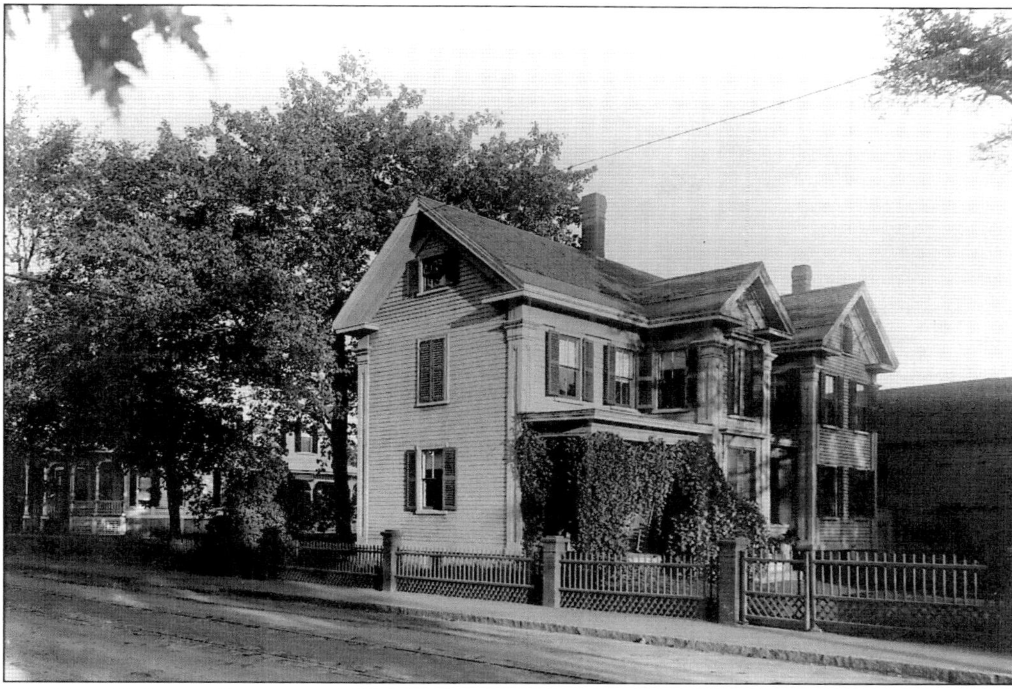

The Russell Carter House, c. 1917. The J.T. Busiel House can be seen beyond, partly obscured by the trees.

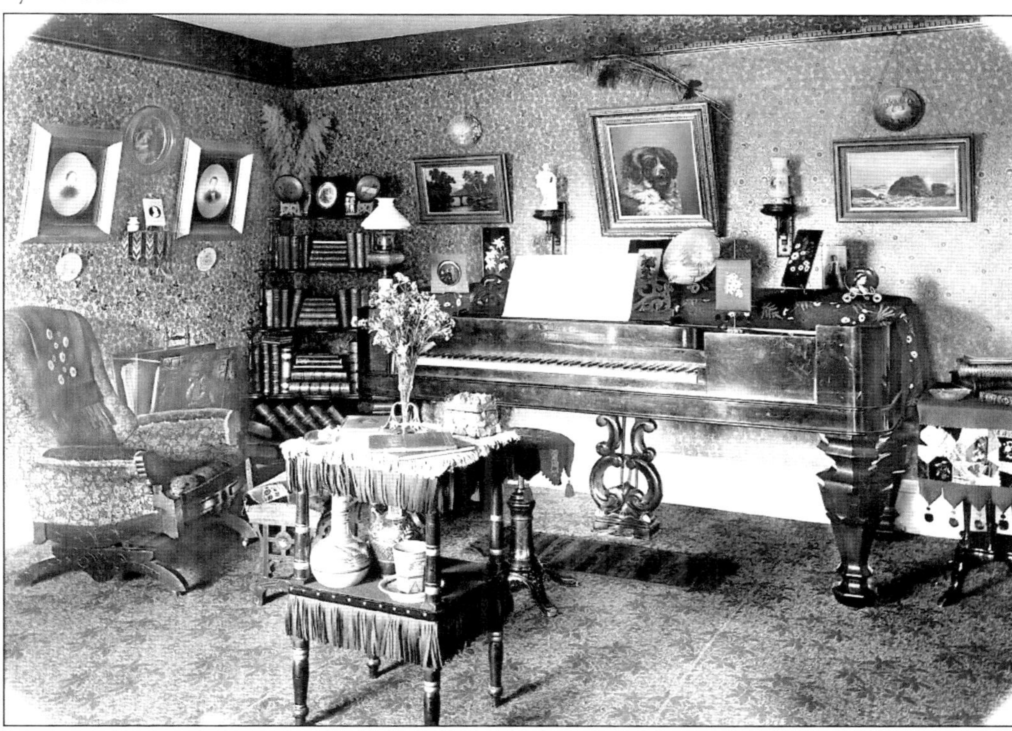

The parlor of the Russell Carter House.

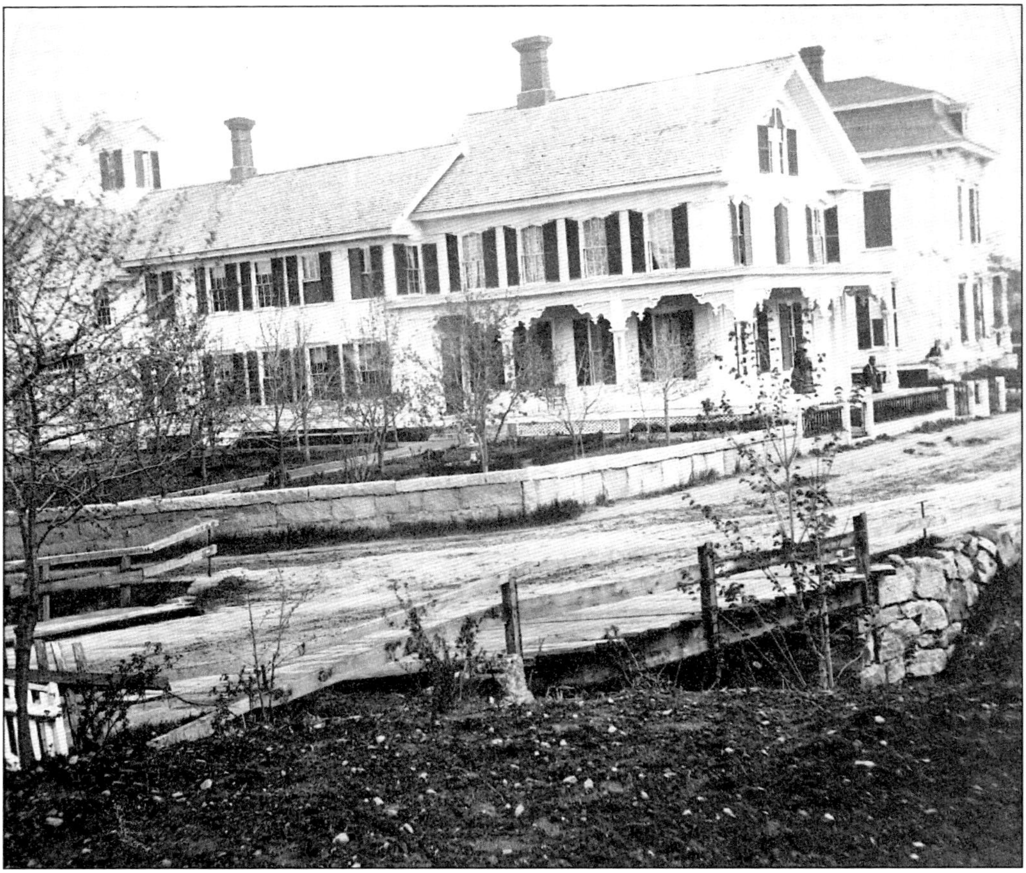

The Dr. Easton House, c. 1870s. With its walled yard located at the corner of Canal Street (left) and Beacon, the large structure was at one time used as a convent and school by the St. Joseph Parish. Later, the building was known as The Beacon (or Beacon Apartments). Beacon Street was earlier called Franklin Street. The Governor Busiel House is on the far right; the Perley Canal flows under bridge at the near right. The corner is now occupied by a brick office and retail shops building beginning with the Belknap Agency. The post office is today located beyond the photograph at the right.

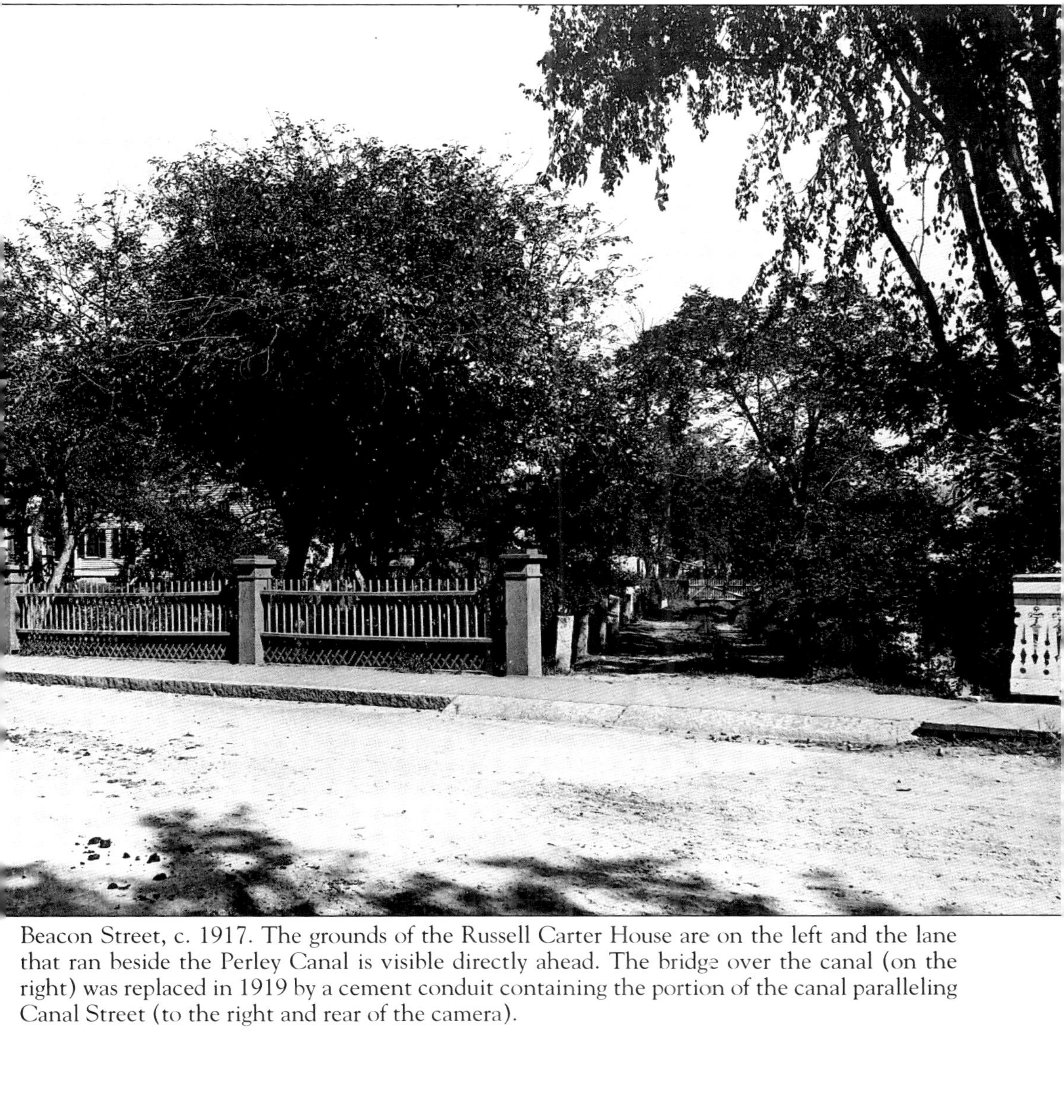

Beacon Street, c. 1917. The grounds of the Russell Carter House are on the left and the lane that ran beside the Perley Canal is visible directly ahead. The bridge over the canal (on the right) was replaced in 1919 by a cement conduit containing the portion of the canal paralleling Canal Street (to the right and rear of the camera).

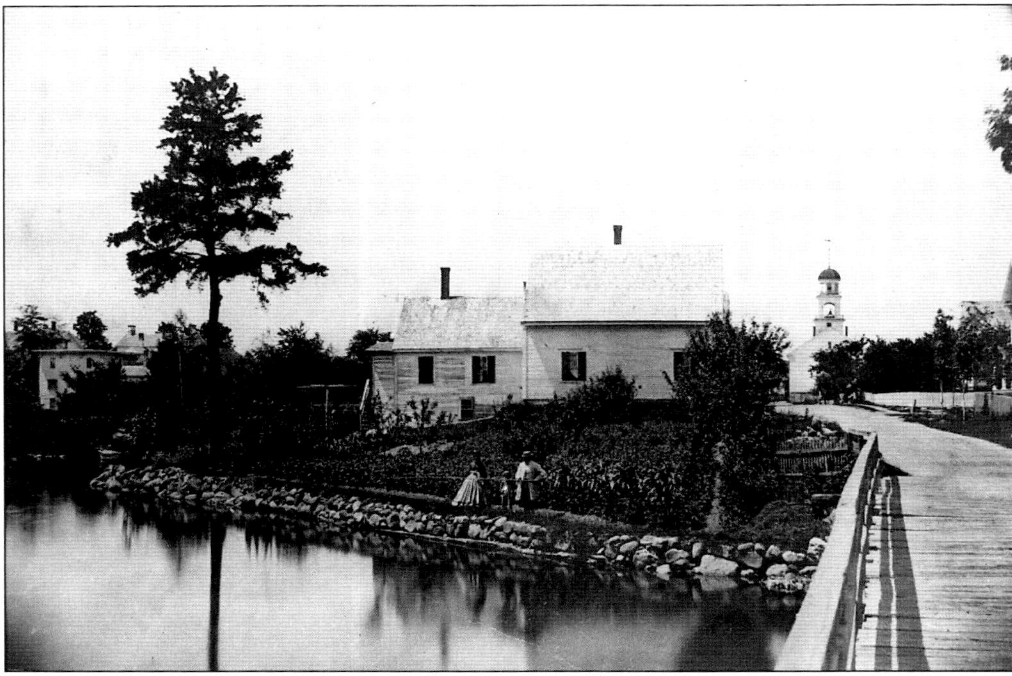

An 1860s view of Church Street from the bridge; the Old North Church (Congregational) appears in the distance on the site of today's library flagpole. The Laconia Spa now occupies the space between the frame buildings (center) and the river.

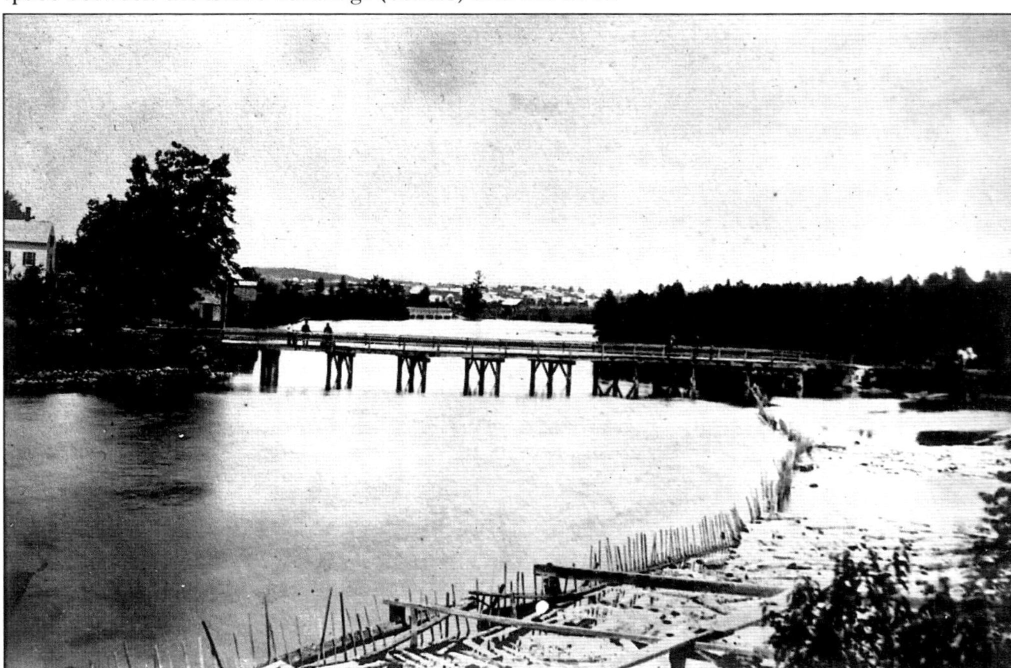

The Church Street Bridge, looking upstream. Here, construction of the east embankment and River Street is in progress, c. late 1880s–early 1890s.

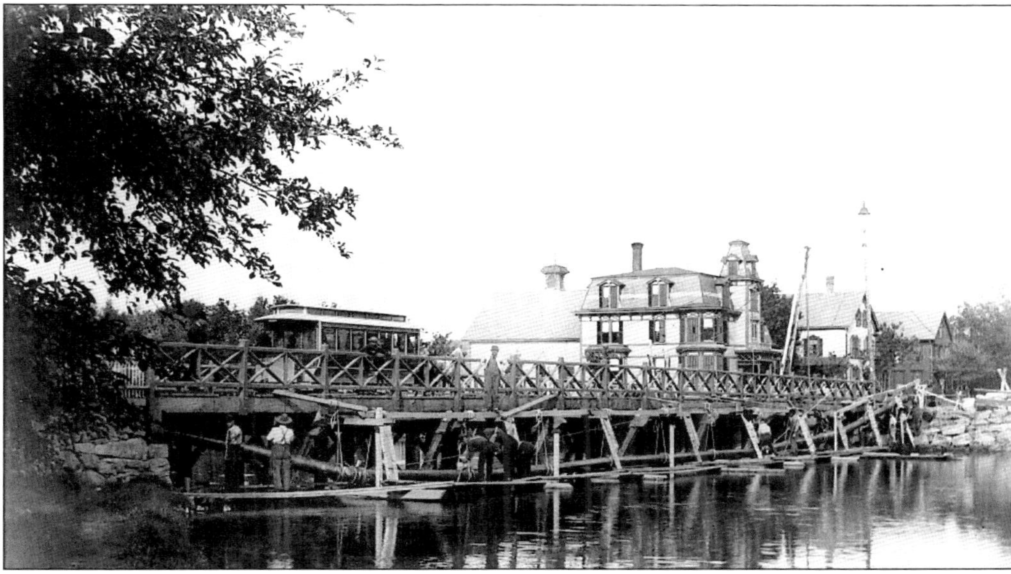

The Church Street Bridge, c. early 1890s. A horse car heads toward Casino Square (now Normandin Square). The George W. Riley residence, with mansard roof, is today's River Bank House. The staging beside the bridge was being used for the installation of the city sewer system. Today's Laconia Spa would be beyond the photograph, on the left.

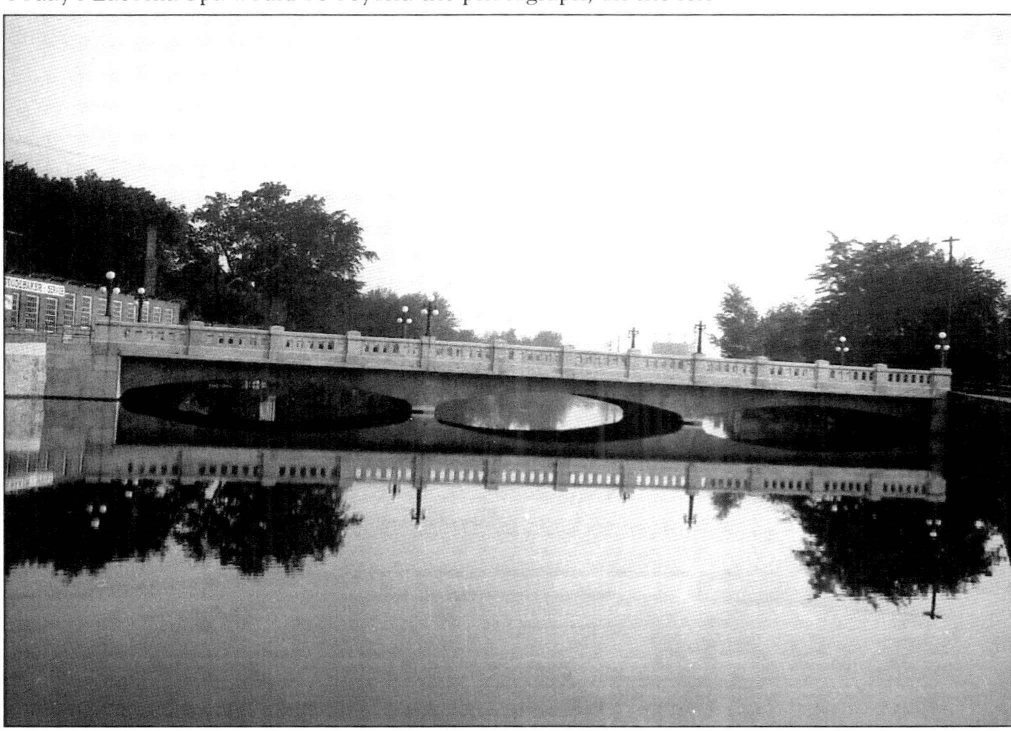

The Church Street Bridge, built 1928. The storage tank of the Laconia Gas Works, on Messer Street, is just visible in the distance. The Laconia Spa would be off the photograph to the left, and the Riley House, obscured by trees, would be to the right.

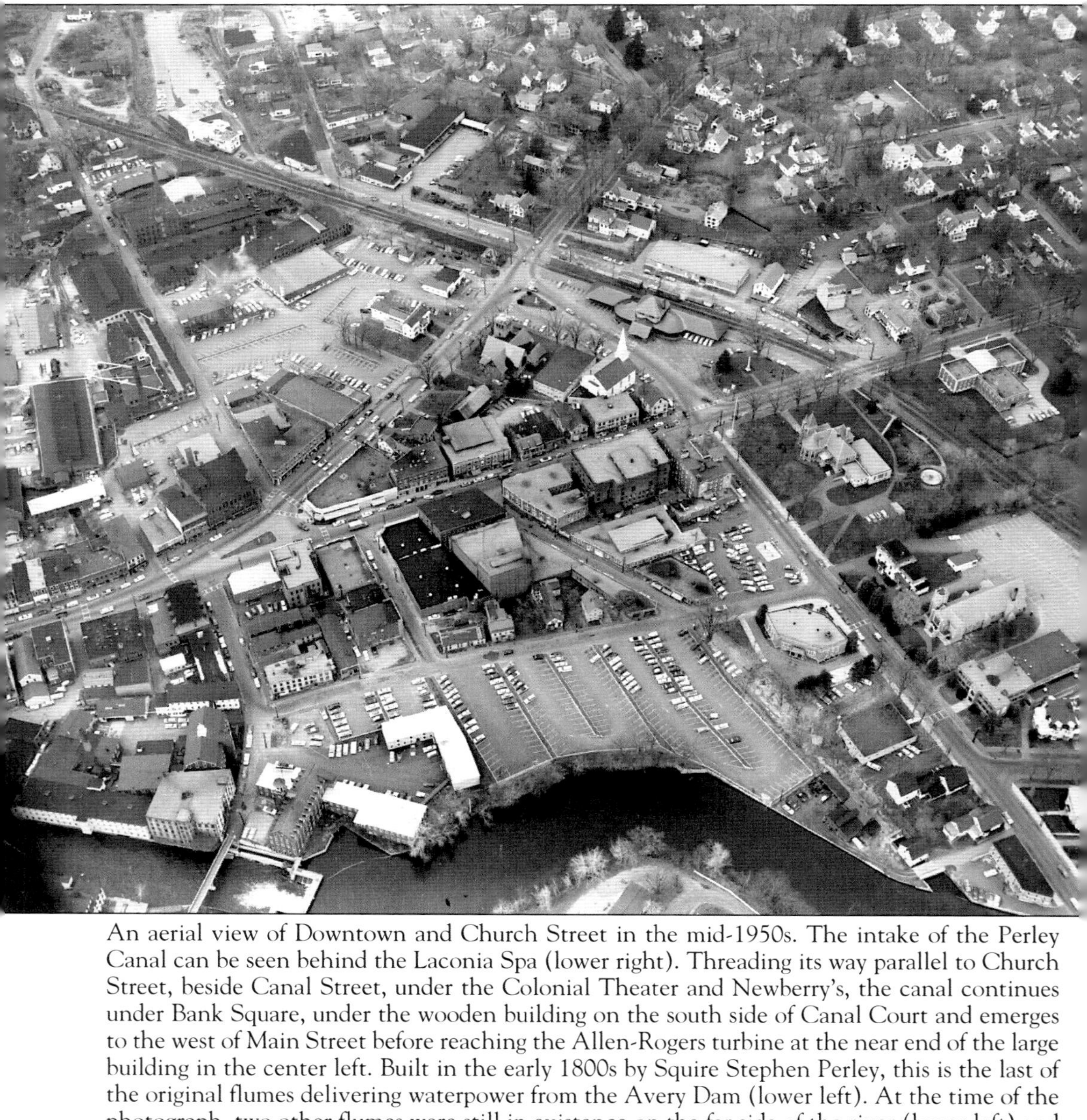

An aerial view of Downtown and Church Street in the mid-1950s. The intake of the Perley Canal can be seen behind the Laconia Spa (lower right). Threading its way parallel to Church Street, beside Canal Street, under the Colonial Theater and Newberry's, the canal continues under Bank Square, under the wooden building on the south side of Canal Court and emerges to the west of Main Street before reaching the Allen-Rogers turbine at the near end of the large building in the center left. Built in the early 1800s by Squire Stephen Perley, this is the last of the original flumes delivering waterpower from the Avery Dam (lower left). At the time of the photograph, two other flumes were still in existence on the far side of the river (lower left) and one on the near side.

# *Nine*

# Neighborhood Potpourri

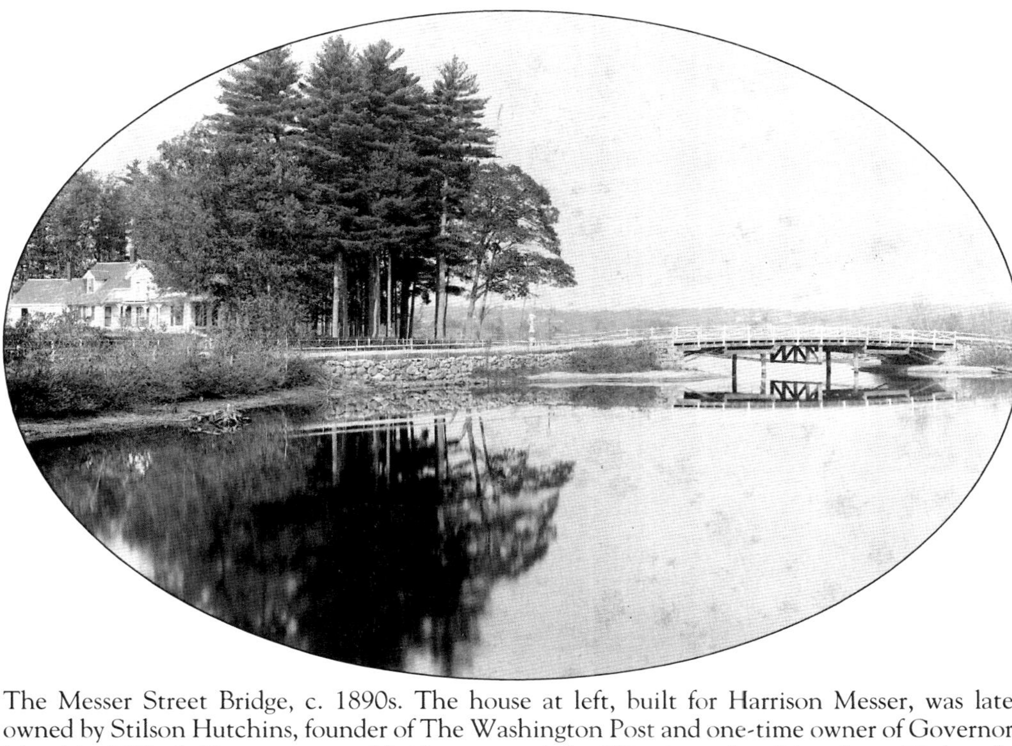

The Messer Street Bridge, c. 1890s. The house at left, built for Harrison Messer, was later owned by Stilson Hutchins, founder of The Washington Post and one-time owner of Governors Island in Gilford. Once, a covered bridge spanned the Winnipesaukee River here. Today, the Opechee Trading Post is located near the center of the photograph, beyond the bridge. The windmill—which inspired the name for Windmill Shores, a later residential subdivision on what was formerly Perley land—is in the background.

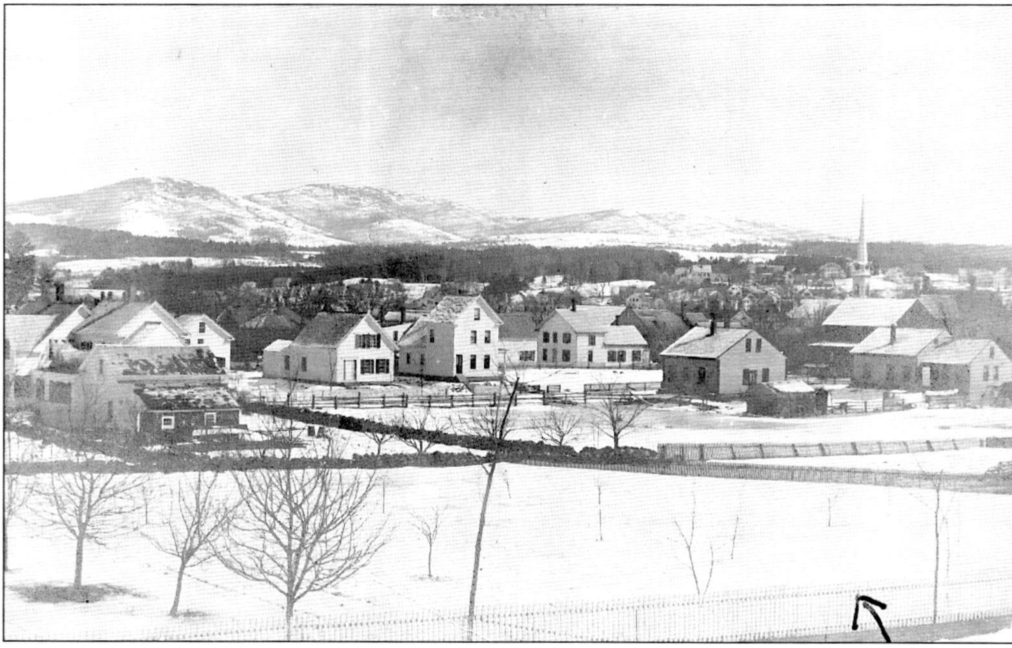

A view east from Pleasant Street, before the construction in 1903 of the Oscar Lougee residence (arrow) at 229 Pleasant Street. The homes in the center face Middle Street (now Dartmouth Street). The Old North Church (Congregational) is visible to the right. The Harvard Street School would be located off the photograph at the right.

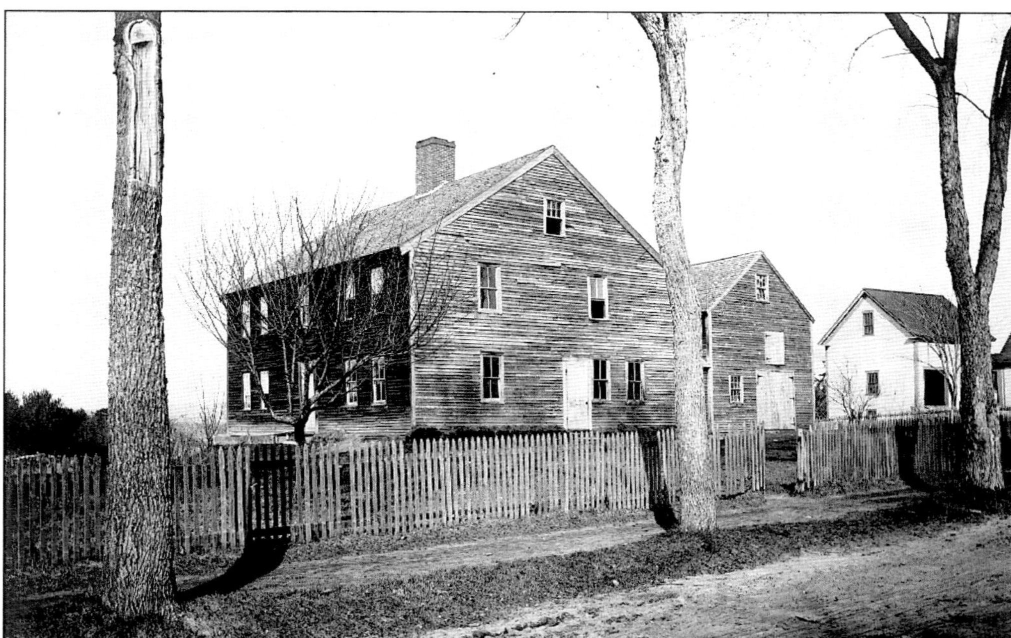

The Old Red House on Pleasant Street. This typical farmhouse of the early 1800s stood on the site of the house later built by Joseph W. Pitman at 208 Pleasant Street.

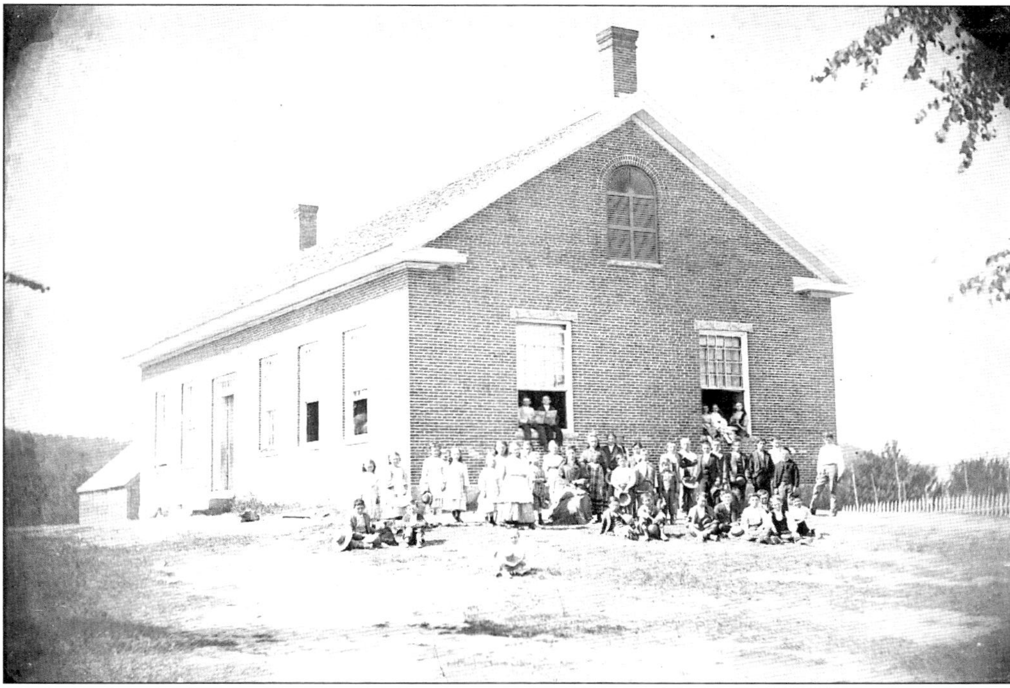

The Bowman Street School, c. 1860s. Built in 1854, the building was enlarged several times before being converted to the law offices of Wescott, Millham & Dyer.

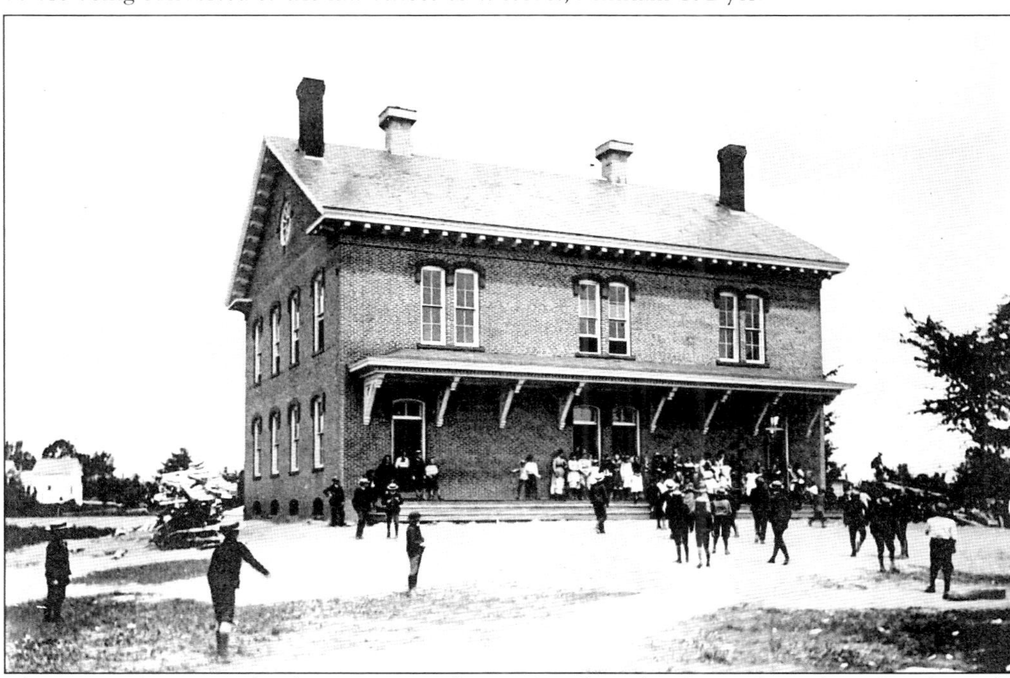

The Harvard Street School, c. 1870s. Built in 1870, this school was also enlarged and is today the offices of School Administrative Unit 30 (Gilford, Gilmanton, and Laconia). Harvard Street was earlier called School Street.

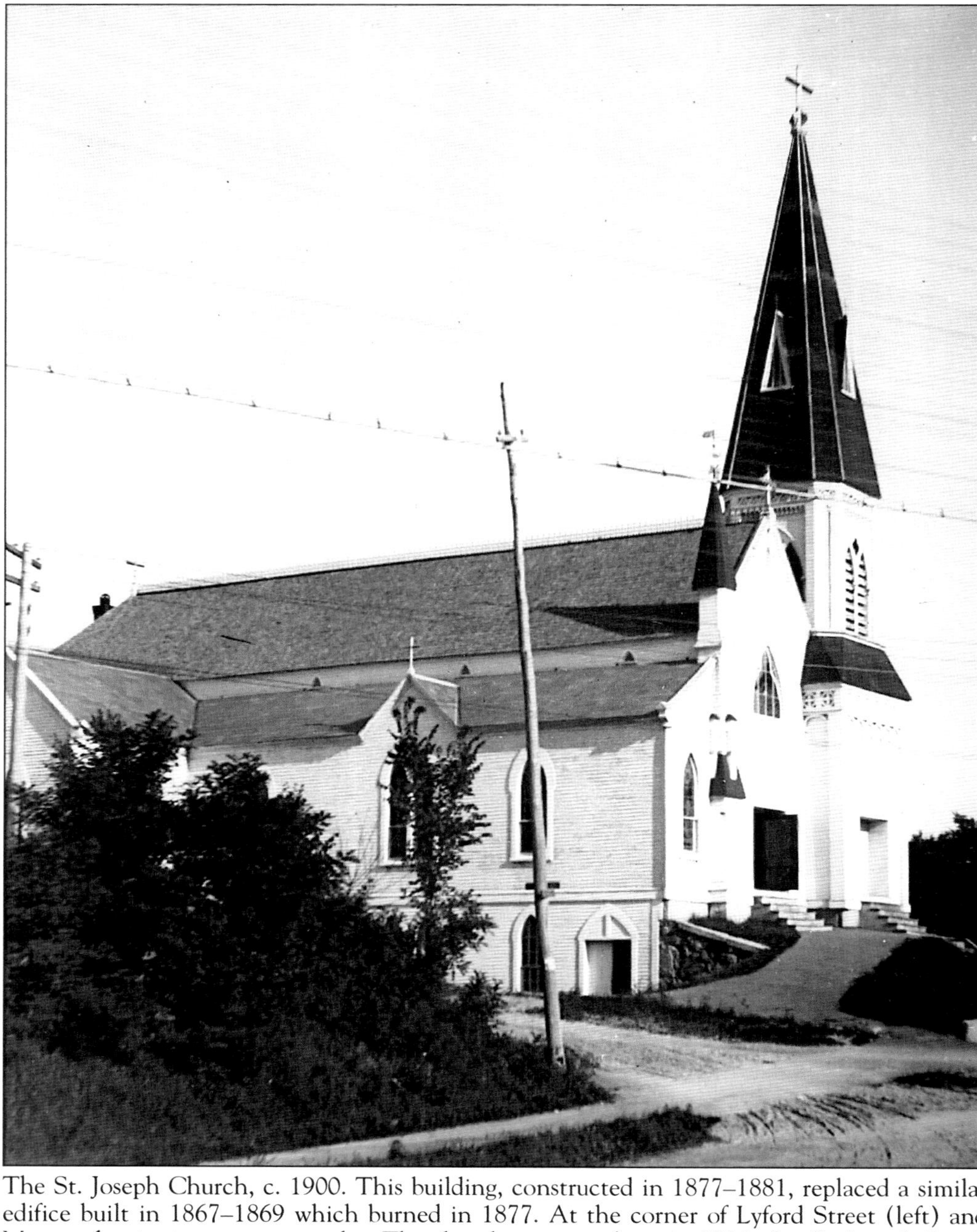

The St. Joseph Church, c. 1900. This building, constructed in 1877–1881, replaced a similar edifice built in 1867–1869 which burned in 1877. At the corner of Lyford Street (left) and Messer, the site is now a vacant lot. The church was torn down in 1934 after St. Joseph Parish dedicated its new church on Church Street on September 12, 1930.

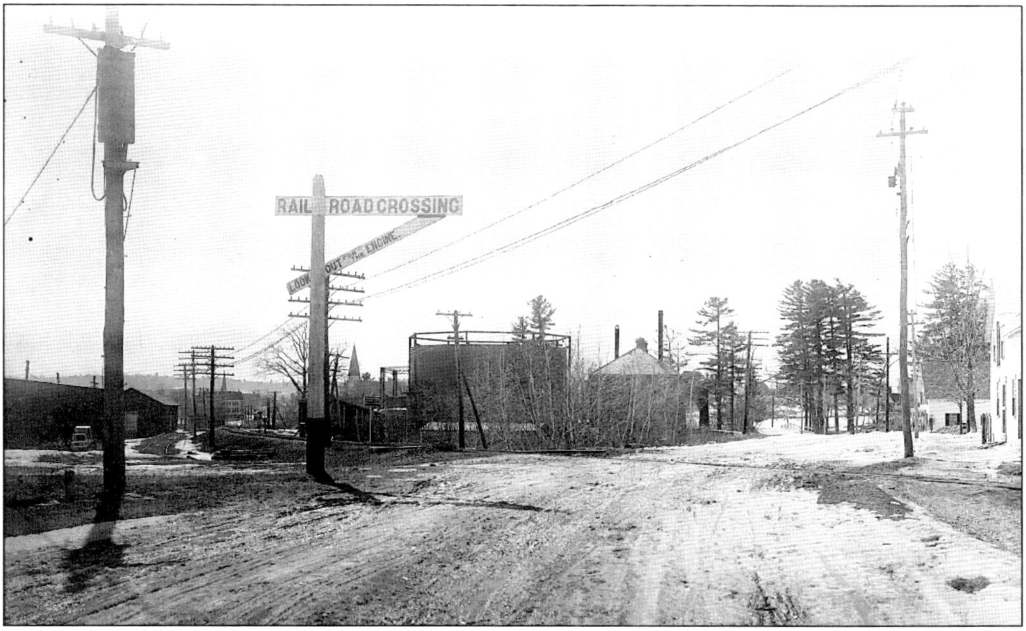


The Gas Works on Messer Street, 1910. Built in 1894, this plant replaced an earlier one, dating from the 1860s, just upriver of the Main Street Bridge. Today's Bisson Avenue would be visible at left, just before the railroad crossing. The steeple of St. Joseph Church (see p. 120) can be seen to the left of the large collecting tank.

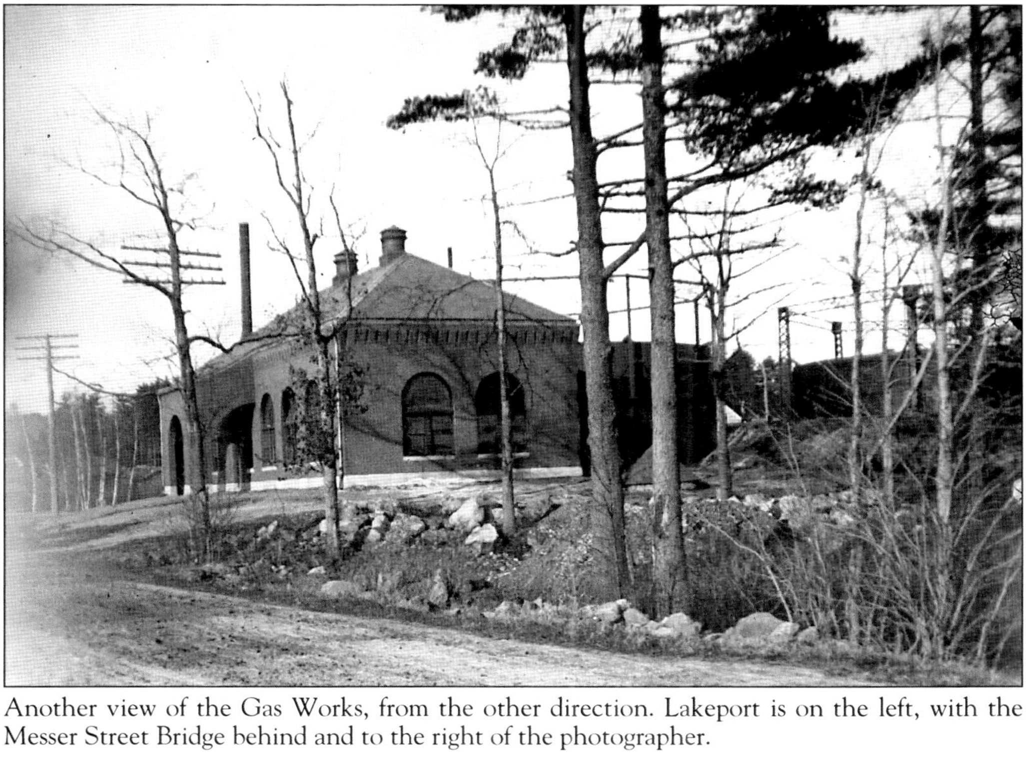

Another view of the Gas Works, from the other direction. Lakeport is on the left, with the Messer Street Bridge behind and to the right of the photographer.

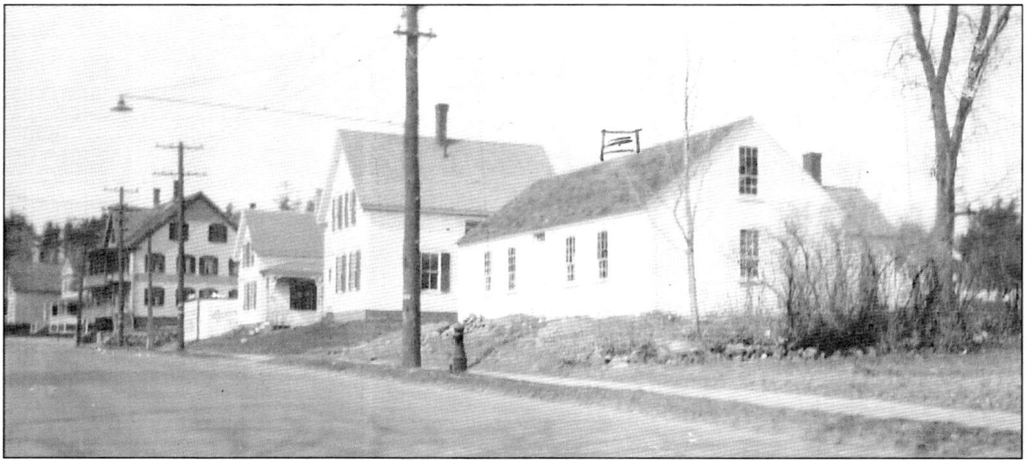

Union Avenue in the early 1920s. The houses in the center occupy the current site of the driveway to Laconia High School. The large frame structure (left) still exists, serving a number of businesses. Diagonally across the street was the carbarn for the Laconia Street Railway trolleys (today's Decorative Interiors).

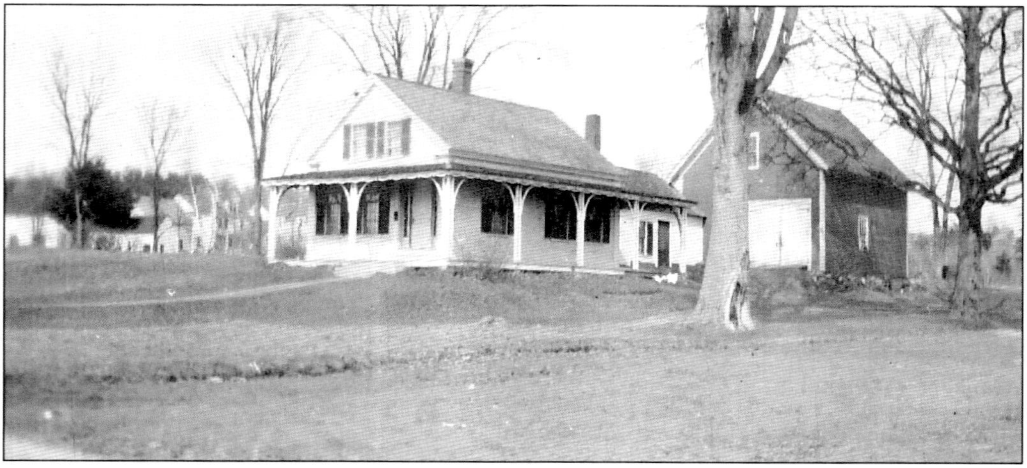

The "Chicken" Folsom House on Union Avenue in the early 1920s. This was another residence removed from what is now the lawn in front of Laconia High School, which was opened in 1923.

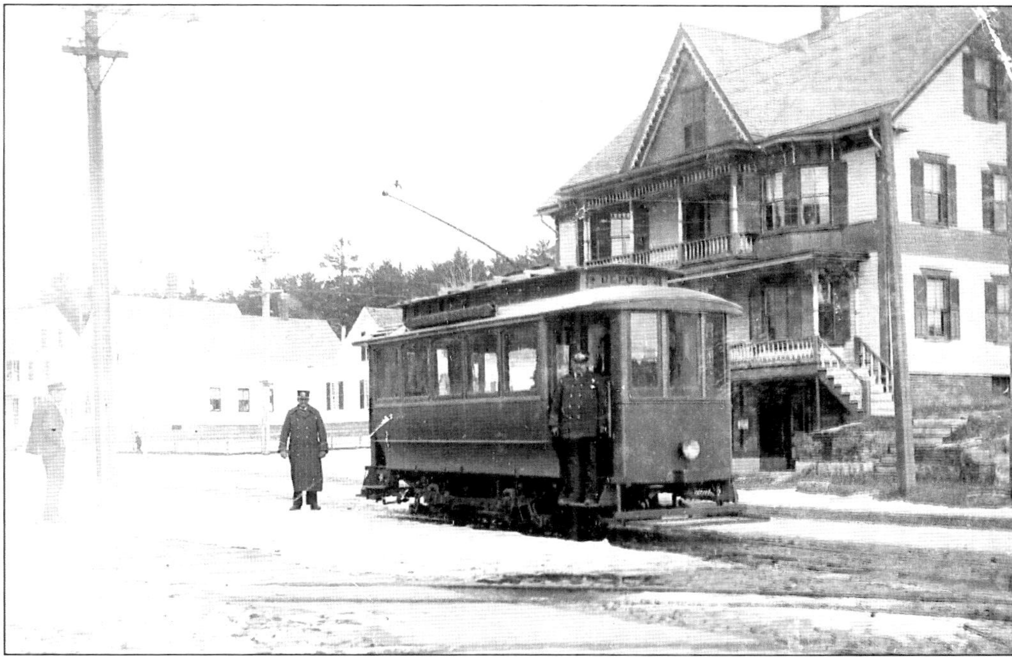

A trolley car headed for the South End in the early 1900s. The large frame building is at the corner of Lyman Street and Union Avenue.

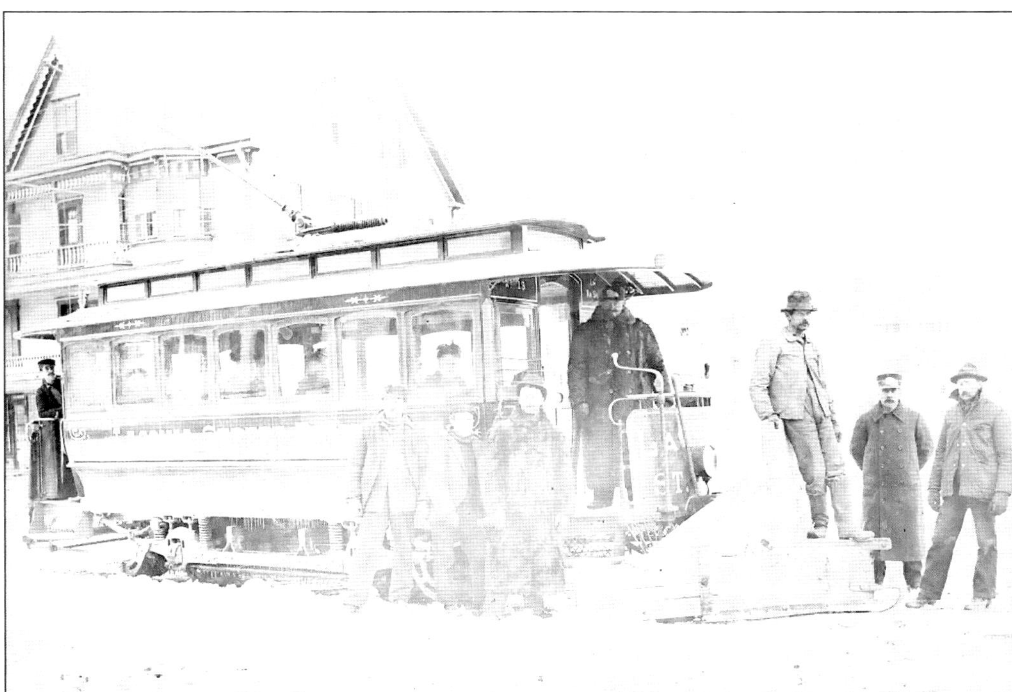

Car 13, with plow, headed south about 1897. This photograph was taken at about the same location as the one above.

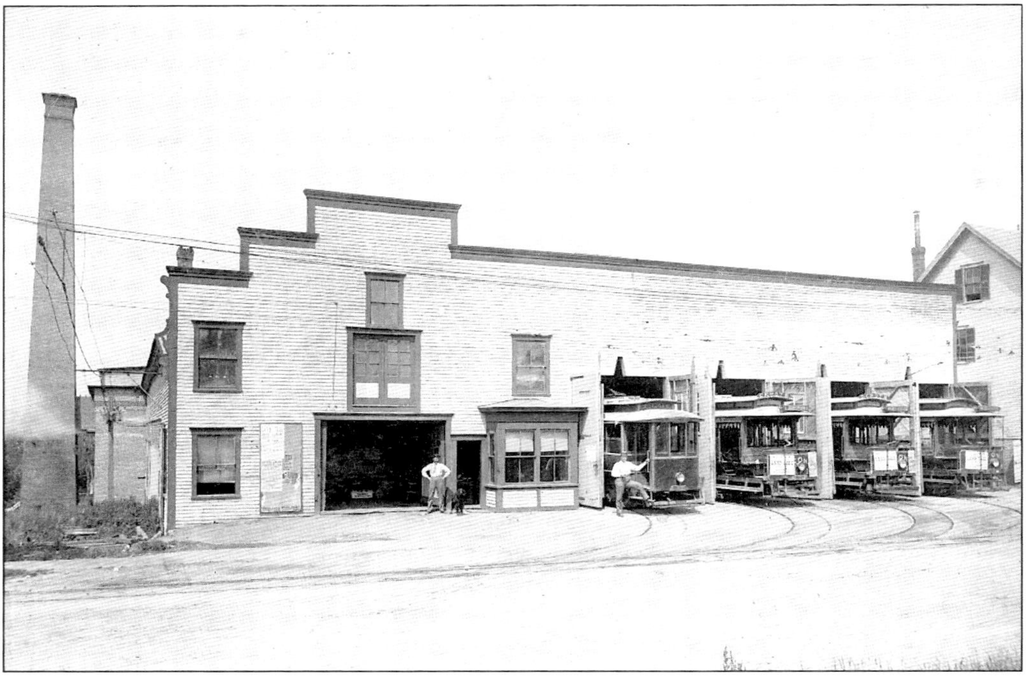

The carbarn on Union Avenue in the early 1900s. The smokestack on the left was for the power station operated by the Laconia Street Railway. This site was later occupied by Moody Motors, among others. Today, the location is that of Decorative Interiors. The building on the right is part of today's Union Square.

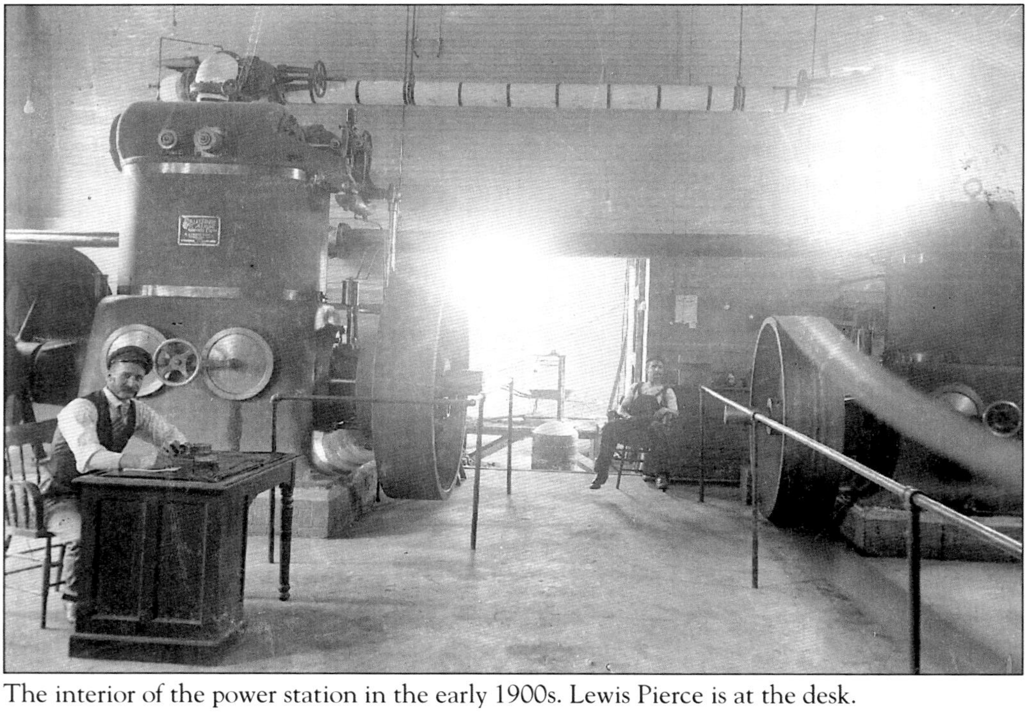

The interior of the power station in the early 1900s. Lewis Pierce is at the desk.

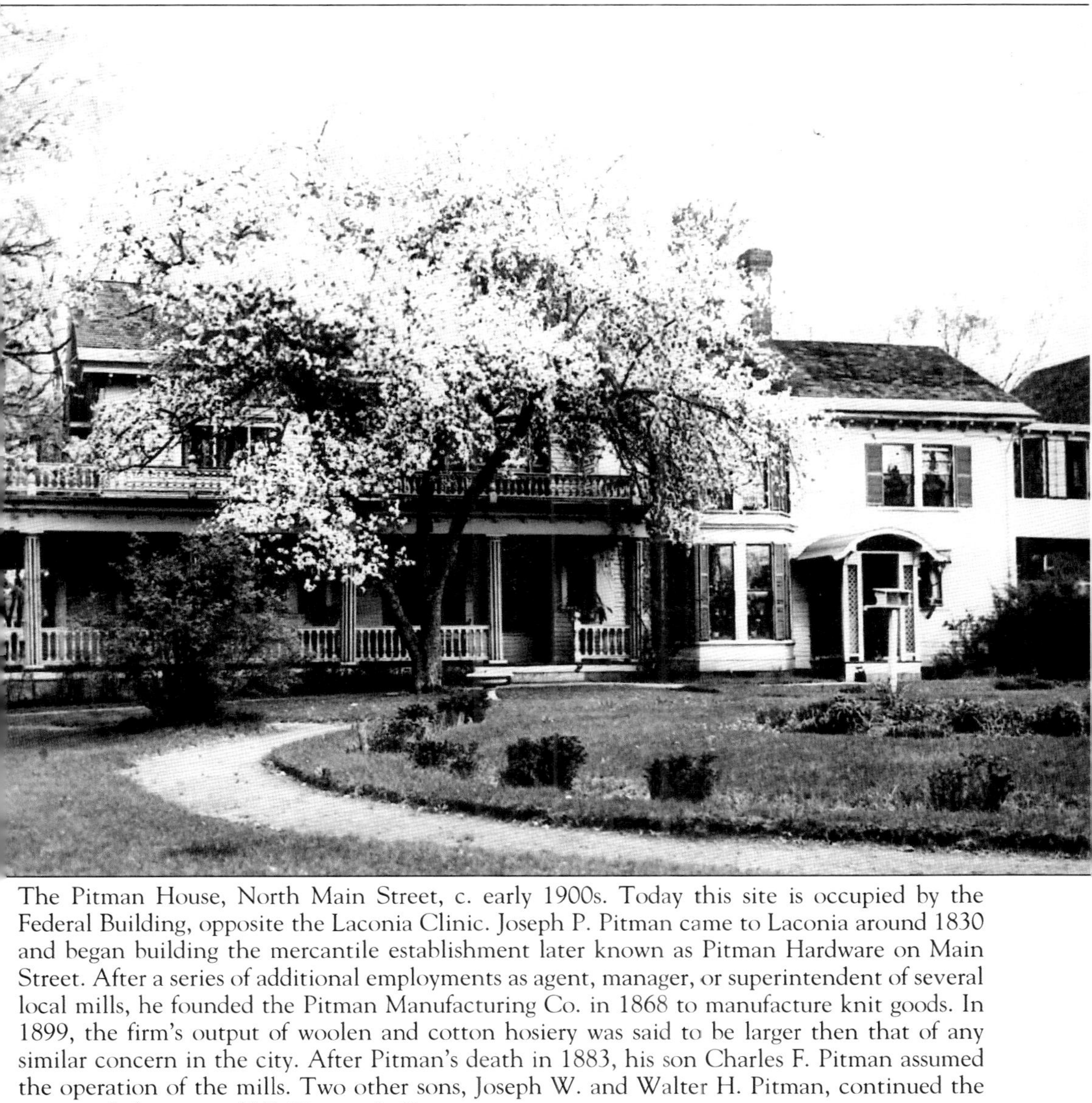

The Pitman House, North Main Street, c. early 1900s. Today this site is occupied by the Federal Building, opposite the Laconia Clinic. Joseph P. Pitman came to Laconia around 1830 and began building the mercantile establishment later known as Pitman Hardware on Main Street. After a series of additional employments as agent, manager, or superintendent of several local mills, he founded the Pitman Manufacturing Co. in 1868 to manufacture knit goods. In 1899, the firm's output of woolen and cotton hosiery was said to be larger then that of any similar concern in the city. After Pitman's death in 1883, his son Charles F. Pitman assumed the operation of the mills. Two other sons, Joseph W. and Walter H. Pitman, continued the mercantile business of J.P. Pitman & Co.

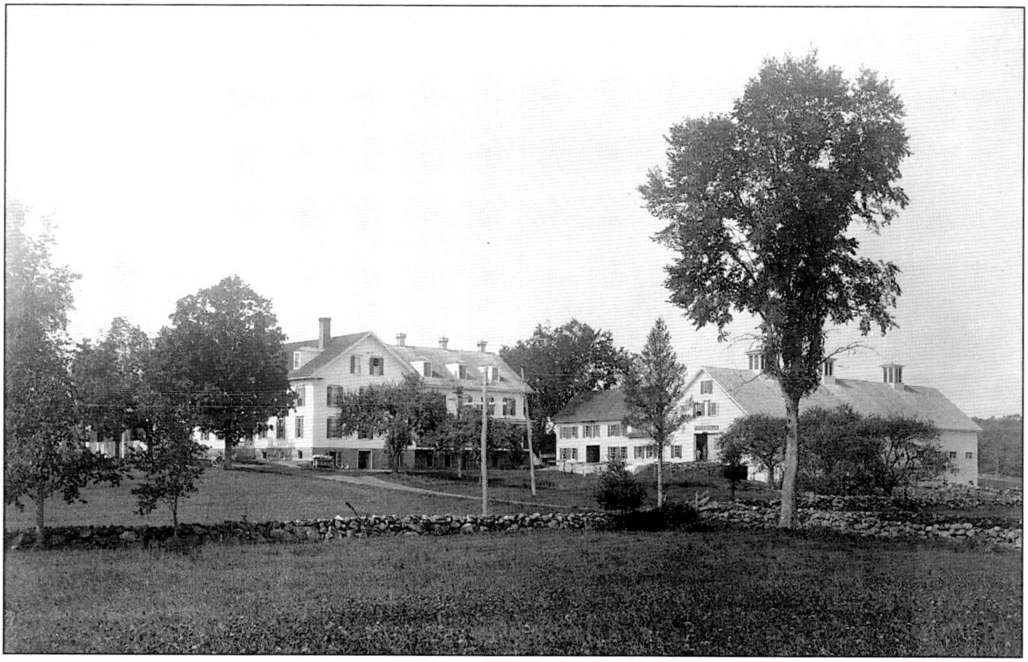

The Belknap County Farm, c. 1910. These buildings, off North Main Street, have been replaced by the modern county nursing home and jail.

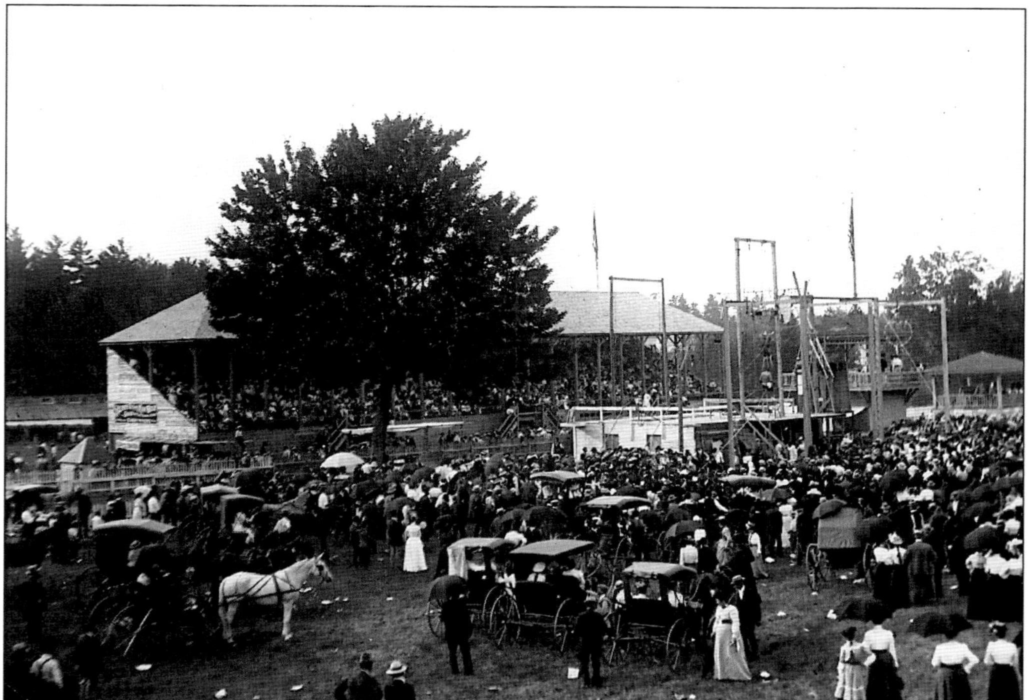

The Laconia Fair, 1902. For many years, an annual fair was held at the Fairgrounds, now Opechee Park.

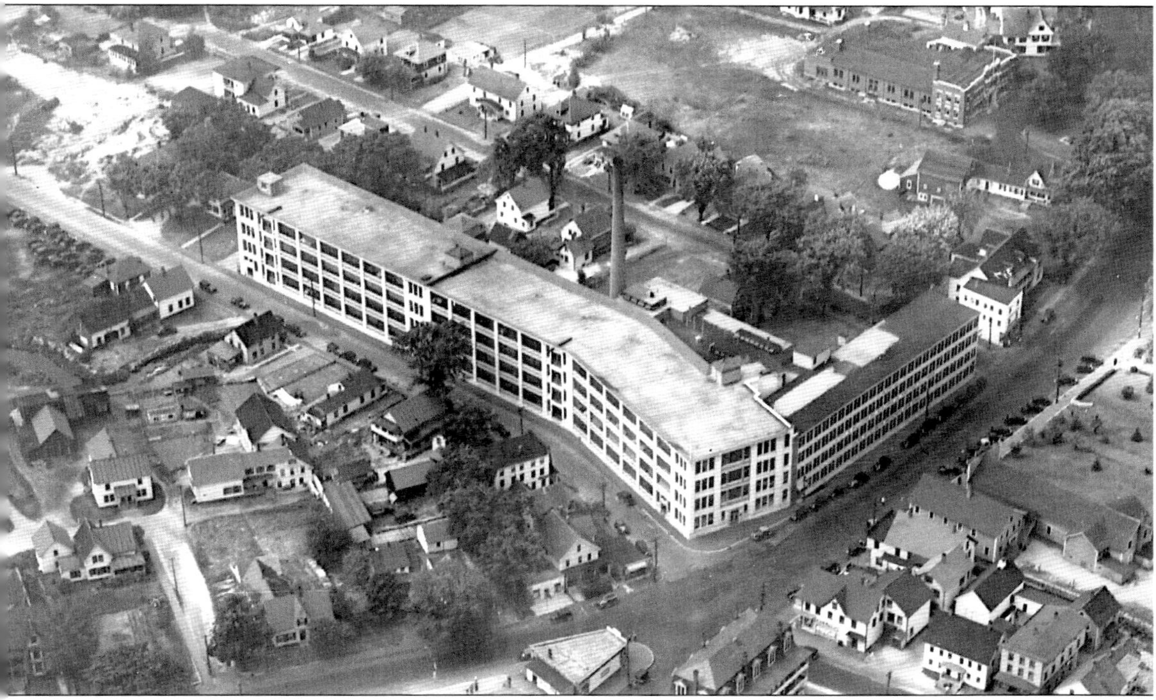

Casino Square (now Normandin Square), c. 1930s. In the days of the horse cars, a roller skating rink called "The Casino" was located on the site of the Scott & Williams plant (center). In 1896, the casino building was relocated down Davis Place and converted into apartments, and a factory building for the Waverly Shoe Co. was constructed in its place. Later, the George W. Mayo Co., manufacturers of knitting machinery, took over the Waverly plant; and in 1910, Scott & Williams moved here from Philadelphia. Eventually, the Casino building was torn down, but the name lasted until 1948, when the square was renamed in honor of Dr. Armand Normandin. The Scott & Williams plant manufactured and shipped knitting machinery worldwide. After the Car Shops went out of business, Scott & Williams was the city's largest employer. With defense contracts during World War II, the work force swelled to more than 2,000 people. The State Armory (today's Community Center) is in the upper right, and the long building at the lower right was the Casino Auditorium. Remodeled out of the former Kellogg Carriage Shop, it was operated by Sacred Heart Parish, and had the largest seating capacity (780) of any Laconia hall until the Colonial Theater opened in 1914 with 1,200 seats. The Busy Corner Store is at the bottom center.

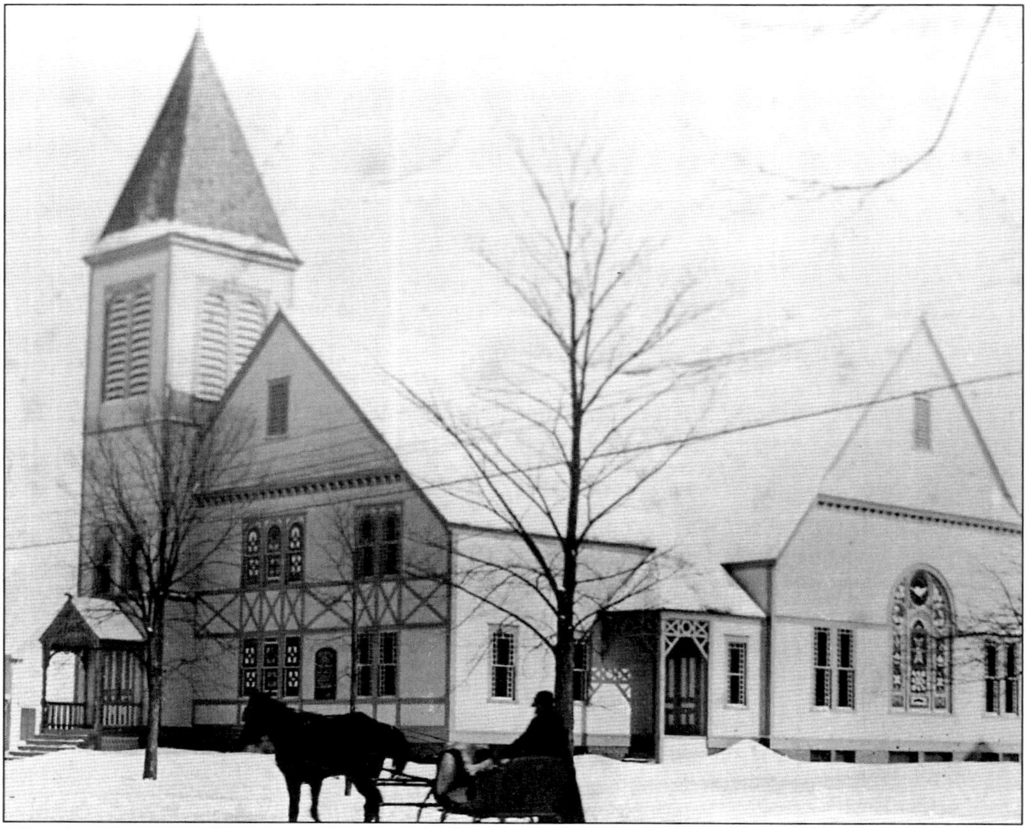

The First Baptist Church, at the corner of Spring Street and Union Avenue, was dedicated in 1895. After the church merged with First Freewill Baptist Church on Court Street to form the South Baptist Church in 1918, the Pitman Hosiery Mill used the building from 1919–1921 as a day-care center for children of its employees. From 1922–1936, it became home to the Knights of Columbus; during this period it also housed the Palace movie theater and a roller skating rink. Finally, from 1936–1941 it was used by the Church of the Nazarene. In the mid-1940s, the building was demolished. The St. Jean de Baptiste Society built on the site in 1950, and since 1981 their building has been occupied by the Salvation Army.

# Acknowledgments

While most of these photographs appear here for the first time in book form, about fifteen of them were included in Slates, Shingles and Shakes, published by the city of Laconia in 1978. Julie Upham made available the postcard of the Vue De l'Eau, p. 10; the South Baptist Church, the small photograph on p. 16; Gilbert S. Center, the engraving of the Gove Block, p. 26; Douglas B. McGowan, the photographs on pp. 37 and 68; and Nancy Weeks Paquette, the two small pictures on pp. 92 and 93.